THE PSYCHOLOGY OF MOTIVATION

Denis Waitley

Nightingale Conant

Nightingale-Conant Corporation, Niles, Illinois

ISBN: 1-55525-458-6

Published in conjunction with Nightingale-Conant Corp.

Printed in the United States of America

10 9 8 7 6 5 4 3 2 1

Editor/Designer: David Buscher
Editor: Karen Stelmach
Illustrations: Jennifer Hagerman

Introduction

I've logged nearly 700,000 airline miles each year for over twenty years in my journeys of teaching principles of high achievement and successful living to corporate and public audiences all over the world. Throughout this incredible journey, I've learned much more than I've taught; but for every question I've answered, I've discovered many more that still need to be answered. Some of the most fascinating questions of all concern human motivation and the many misconceptions surrounding that subject.

Think about it. We read motivational books, listen to motivational audiotapes, and watch a variety of motivational videotapes and TV programs. Yet do we really understand what motivates us, at the deep-down core level of our being, to do the things we do, day in and day out, throughout our entire lives?

If we're not really sure about the sources and rationale

of our own motivations, how are we going to understand the motivations of others in our professional and personal relationships?

We're in the midst of a new age of human growth and development. We need to reexamine, reevaluate, and maybe even completely redefine the way we think and the way we choose our actions and responses to life's daily challenges in this era of unprecedented change.

We need a fresh, new, enduring strategy for mapping out our goals. That way, we can ensure that our goals are really worthwhile, believable, and achievable, and that they will benefit others as well as ourselves when we attain them. What will make this happen? We must be properly motivating ourselves and others to do what needs to be done.

This is especially critical in today's global neighborhood, where the game of life is unbelievably complex, where the players are more knowledgeable and sophisticated, where the pace is much faster, where the stakes are higher, and the playing field is anything but level.

If you're successful in your business and personal life, and you would like to stay motivated and on-track and gain even more fulfillment than you are presently enjoying, this book is designed with you in mind.

If you have had success before and are facing challenges today in renewing and recapturing that success, this book is also designed for you.

And if you are highly motivated much of the time but sometimes find it difficult to stay "up," stay focused, and keep driving forward, this book can make a real difference in the way you view yourself and your world.

My mission in this book is to give you the most up-to-date scientific research available, as well as the practical tools and applications necessary for you to build solid, enduring success in everything you do.

—Denis Waitley

Contents

Motivation: Bridging Need and Achievement

Section One: What is Motivation?

Intrinsic vs. Extrinsic Motivation 23
Six Types of Achievement Motivation 25
A Motivation Self-Evaluation 29
A Concern for Excellence 32
Creating Your Own Motivation 36
The Support Beams of Motivation 39
Your Magnificent Obsession 45
Finding a Compelling 'Why' 51

Section Two: Achieving with Others

Stimulating Children's Motivation 55
The Power of High Expectations 57
Motivation from Mentors 60
Finding Support in Coaches and Mentors 63
The Process of Selecting a Mentor 66
Being a Good Role Model 70
The Best Sources of Feedback 72
The True Nature of Competition 74
Avoiding Futile Competition 77
Leading with Relationship Power 79

Section Three: Mapping Your Strategy

The Power of Imagination 85
Developing Your Imagination 90
Getting Your Imagination to Work for You 94
Feedback from Cognitive Maps 96
Creating Positive Mental Images 99
Programming Your Inner Computer 102
Creating a Cognitive Map from One Idea 105
Expected Probability of Success 107
Cognitive Maps vs. Check-Off Lists 110
Visualization and Simulation 112

Section Four: Setting Your Goals

Focusing Your Energy	117
Following Your Dreams and Goals	120
Gathering Information for Goals	122
Creating Effective Sub-Goals	126
Goals and Intrinsic Motivation	130
Goal Setting and Job Satisfaction	132
Mistakes in Goal Setting	134
Three Profound Truths	136
Evaluating Your Goals	139
Creating Focused Goals	143
Resource Allocation	148
Putting Your Goals in Writing	150
Setting Goals so Everyone Wins	154
A Life of Creative Goal Setting	156

Section Five: Motivational Skills

Twenty Ways to Live in Prime Time	161
Creating Focus by Planning Your Time	166
The Rules of Decision Making	169
Crisis Decision Making	174
Framing for Decision Making	179
Becoming an Innovator	183
Taking Smart Risks	186
Steps for Smart Risk Taking	189

Section Six: Motivational Attitudes

The Power of Belief	195
Money vs. Personal Satisfaction	199
Self-Esteem: The Four-Legged Chair	201
Self-Confidence and Self-Efficacy	206
Developing Self-Efficacy	210
Four Factors in Increasing Self-Efficacy	215
Six Behaviors that Increase Self-Esteem	219
Living Life Hopefully	222
Making Your Hard Work Enjoyable	225

Section Seven: Sustaining Motivation

Cognitive Dissonance 237
Defensiveness in Times of Low Motivation 240
Failing to Justify Your Actions 242
Avoiding the Blame-the-Victim Syndrome 245
Staying Motivated during Tough Times 248
Finding the Right Search Image 251
Are You Chasing the Right Goals? 254
Doing What You Love 258
Helping Yourself by Helping Others 262
No One Is an Island 269

Section Eight: Overcoming Failure

Accepting Failure 273
Dealing with Failure Creatively 275
Overcoming Learned Helplessness 277
The Fear of Failure 284
High Achievers vs. Failure Avoiders 289
Risking Failure 294
Using Failure as a Teacher 298
Attributional Analysis 302
Paradigms of Attribution 305
Preparing to Combat Fear 311
Facing the Truth 315
Turning Failure and Hardship into Success 318
Allowing Setbacks to Spur You On 322
Keeping Problems in Perspective 325

Section Nine: Living in the Now

Making the Most of Today 331
Focusing on Now 333
Happiness Now, Not Later 335
Maintaining Your Energy and Motivation 337
Your Energy Bank Account 339
Consistency: Staying True to Your Values 341
Believing in Yourself and the World 343
Keeping Yourself Healthy 345
Focusing on Positive Results 349

SECTION TEN: FORGING YOUR DESTINY

Keeping a Goal Journal 357
Examining Your Childhood Dreams 361
Finding a Destiny Worthy of Yourself 364
The Virtue of Patience 368
Following through on Ideas 371
Breaking Out of the Jug 373
Your Ninety-Day Season of Success 375
Overcoming Self-Imposed Limitations 378
Getting Rid of Emotional Baggage 381
Becoming a Master of Change 384
The True Nature of Success 388

SECTION ELEVEN: A LIFE IN BALANCE

Juggling Your Priorities 395
The Assets of Time and Health 398
Controlling Your Lifestyle 402
The Importance of Being Flexible 405
Separating Personal from Professional 407
A Commitment to Excellence 409
Evaluating Your Life Balance 413
Developing Hope 416
Living Positively 419
Focusing on Positive Motivations 423

SECTION TWELVE: QUALITIES OF SUCCESS

What Is Success? 427
What Makes a Person Successful? 429
Having High Aspirations 432
Becoming Worthy of Your Own Approval 437
Successful Self-Expectation 439
What is Courage? 441
Cultivating Courage 444
Practicing Courage 448
Persistence: The Essence of Motivation 453
Becoming a Persistent Person 456

Motivation: Bridging Need and Achievement

For over 100 years, visitors to New York City have marveled at the wonder and design of the Brooklyn Bridge, which spans the river between Manhattan and Brooklyn. At the time it was built, it had the longest and highest span of any bridge in the world. Its roadway stretches 1,595 feet between the bridge's two towers. These towers, which are 278 feet high, were the tallest structures in all of New York City when the bridge was built, making it not only the city's greatest bridge, but also its first skyscraper.

Why am I offering you all these facts about the Brooklyn Bridge? If you're a real skeptic, you might think it's because I'm going to try to sell it to you. For years, we've heard stories of hundreds of people who thought they bought the Brooklyn Bridge but were actually ripped off by scam artists.

I'm not going to try to sell the Brooklyn Bridge to you, but I do want to tell you about it. It's one of the human-made miracles of our civilized world, and its story contains one of the greatest illustrations of human motivation that I have ever heard.

My interest in the Brooklyn Bridge was sparked many years ago during a visit to New York City. Captivated by its stark beauty, I decided to take a leisurely stroll across the bridge and experience the awesome scope of the Manhattan skyline, the people, the traffic, and the river itself. When I noticed a plaque on the bridge, I expected to read a tribute to a corps of engineers who made the bridge a reality.

Instead, the plaque reads:

"Dedicated to the Memory of Emily Warren Roebling, 1843–1903, whose faith and courage helped her stricken husband, Colonel Washington Roebling, C.E., complete the construction of the bridge from the plans of his father."

That simple and eloquent message intrigued me. Could one family have been so instrumental in the completion of the bridge? The answer is yes, and I think you'll be as inspired by this family's dedication and motivation as I am.

During the mid-nineteenth century, some the world's worst bridge builders were at work. Many lives were lost due to poor-quality engineering and construction. However, a young engineer named John Roebling built some impressive suspension bridges. When Roebling heard about the problems of the winter ice clogging up New York's East River, preventing ferryboats from operating for weeks at a time, he conceived the idea of building a magnificent bridge spanning the river and tying together Manhattan and Brooklyn. It was considered the ultimate, impossible dream at that moment in history. Bridge-building engineers throughout the world said it couldn't be done. The news media called it the bizarre fantasy of an eccentric.

How did John Roebling prove his critics wrong by making his impossible dream a reality? He nurtured and relied upon his high achievement motivation.

With the techniques you'll be learning in this book, you can put that same power to work in your life. Once you have the kind of motivation John Roebling had, any goal is within your reach.

It took nine years for Roebling to convince the New York politicians that he had a workable plan. Finally, in 1866, Roebling was appointed chief engineer for the Brooklyn Bridge.

Roebling was a man with a mission. He believed in the bridge and in his own ability to design and build it. He'd already built several high-quality suspension bridges, and he believed he would be successful with this one, although nobody had ever built one this long or tall.

But neither the general public nor the other engineers shared Roebling's optimism. They thought the whole idea was preposterous. A suspension bridge with an unheard-of span of nearly 1600 feet was beyond the imagination of Roebling's critics. And Roebling himself didn't claim to have all the answers, but he kept moving forward on his journey, one step at a time.

Up to that time, suspension bridges were hung with rope made out of hemp. With a bridge of this magnitude, Roebling conceived the idea of using wire rope, thus beginning the manufacturing process by which we make steel and wire cables today.

Even with this new innovation, it took two more years

to convince everyone involved that the bridge could be built.

Clinging to his strong belief and his abilities, Roebling continued working to develop the engineering systems that would make the bridge possible. Finally, after eleven years of red tape and incredible obstacles, Congress passed the enabling act that allowed John Roebling to begin construction of the Brooklyn Bridge. His persistence had paid off. His dream would become a reality.

Unfortunately, ironically, a week after Roebling received approval of his plans, he was fatally injured by one of the ferry boats his bridge would make obsolete.

Talk about roadblocks and setbacks! The future of the bridge looked bleak.

But there's an interesting characteristic about highly motivated achievers: Their enthusiasm is contagious.

Someone very close to John Roebling had been watching him closely for many years: his son, Washington Roebling. Washington learned from his father that when you have something difficult to accomplish that you greatly desire, it will be easiest to maintain motivation through setbacks if you recognize what your destination is, know it's there, and imagine the route you'll take—and the alternative routes if something gets in your way.

Washington knew that trial and error may build character, but they don't necessarily build 1600-foot suspension bridges. As the result of numerous discussions with his father about the design considerations for the Brooklyn Bridge, the young man had an unusually detailed cognitive map in his mind for the construction of the impossible bridge. He knew his desired destination, and he planned a number of viable routes for getting there.

* * *

Washington Roebling had worked previously with an engineer named Eads and decided to go to St. Louis to inspect the tile caissons Eads was building for his bridge. Roebling knew that these cassions would be critical engineering elements for the Brooklyn Bridge, and he knew that Eads had developed a special experience in that area.

Although the two had freely exchanged ideas in the past, Eads became overly competitive with Roebling . . . perhaps jealous of his work on the Brooklyn Bridge project. Eads refused to cooperate with his former friend, saying that Washington had "borrowed" too many ideas already. Constructing the cassions soon became the younger Roebling's greatest obstacle.

Cassions are enormous, box-like structures that are sunk deep into the riverbed and filled with concrete to support the bridge towers. As you may well imagine, it was very difficult to work in the underwater environment of these cassions. Electric lights were not in common use at the time, and candles posed a safety issue: In the compressed air of the chambers, fires were prevalent. In one particular instance, after Washington fought one serious fire for six hours, he lost consciousness and had to be rescued from one of the caissons.

Washington suspected that the major fire had not been extinguished, but had merely retreated deep into the timbers of the caisson. Another detour in his plan required flooding the chambers to put the fire out, then filling them with cement. The process of handling this setback may have cost extra time and money, but the cement had the unexpected benefit of making the cassion even stronger.

When the going gets tough, we should check our plans for a way around the roadblock to a new, and perhaps better, highway.

Until this point, there were many more problems than successes encountered in the building of the Brooklyn Bridge. I hope you can empathize with John and Washington Roebling and imagine the powerful motivation they must have had to continue in pursuit of their dream. Unfortunately, the setbacks only increased in intensity. Three years into the construction of the bridge, Washington Roebling developed caisson disease—commonly called "the bends"—from too rapid a decompression after working in the highly compressed atmosphere of the chambers. He suffered permanent brain damage and was unable to walk or talk. In constant pain, with diminished eyesight and muscular paralysis, it was impossible for Washington to go to the work site or communicate with his workers.

Everyone in America thought the bridge project should be abandoned since Washington Roebling was the only one who knew how the bridge could be built. They underestimated the power of his achievement motivation. After all, he was the son of John Roebling, and for fourteen years they had developed an awesome plan toward a passionate, all-consuming goal. With numerous obstacles already behind him, and with a lifetime of intrinsic motivation to spur him on, he refused to give up.

Lying in his hospital bed, Washington developed a plan. He could still move one finger, and his thinking faculties were as sharp as ever. He devised a form of Morse code to communicate with his wife, Emily Roebling.

Emily Roebling took on the full load of Washington's monumental project, proving her own worth as a highly motivated achiever. She learned mathematics and engineering, as well as every other facet of the bridge-building business. Each day, she visited the work site, communicated her husband's instructions to the workers, dealt with suppliers, kept records, and answered all calls and mail. Each night, she reported the progress to Washington and wrote down his "tapped" coded instructions for the following day.

People were still very skeptical about the strength of the bridge, let alone the capability of a man who scarcely had the strength to lift one finger. A number of bridges around the world had collapsed with disastrous losses of life, property, and money. What if this feeble young man was wrong? What if his wife misinterpreted his coded instructions? Nearly everyone thought it was a horrendous risk and a colossal waste of money.

But Washington Roebling never faltered. He continued tapping out the instructions that led to the construction of the strongest suspension bridge ever built. Instead of using iron cables, he decided to use steel cables, the pattern and strength of which had never before been attempted. To add even more strength, he designed steel trusses and high towers to support the bridge. All of these complex instructions were tapped out each day and relayed by Emily to the work crew.

It's an incredible story, isn't it? But lest you think it was finished in a mere few months, I want you to know that Emily and Washington worked on that bridge for thirteen more years before its completion. It took a total of twenty-seven years to build the Brooklyn Bridge.

The miracle of the Roebling family is one of the forgotten stories of triumph in American history. To me, *they* are the heroes and the role models for us and our children to emulate, not the entertainment and sports idols we clamor to see and touch.

For the grand opening of the bridge in May of 1883, Emily Roebling led a glittering parade across the magnificent, gleaming span from Brooklyn to Manhattan. Washington Roebling sat alone in his apartment across the East River with his wheelchair up against the window, watching the procession with his field glasses and no doubt tapping a personal salute with his one good finger: "Congratulations, Dad, we did it! We won!"

Like the Roeblings, we are building a bridge to the future for ourselves and generations to come. We may not have an actual plaque dedicated in our memory like Emily Roebling, but our contribution will be recognized all the same. It will be etched in the minds of all those with whom we've shared our goals and whose lives have been touched by our achievements.

The triumphant story of the building of the Brooklyn Bridge illustrates the awesome power of one family's achievement motivation. You, too, can use motivation to bridge the gap between need and achievement.

WHAT IS MOTIVATION?

Intrinsic vs. Extrinsic Motivation • Six Types of Achievement Motivation • A Motivation Self-Evaluation • A Concern for Excellence • Creating Your Own Motivation • The Support Beams of Motivation • Your Magnificent Obsession • Finding a Compelling 'Why'

"Having intrinsic motivation means doing something for its own sake, like playing a game just for the joy of playing. On the other hand, extrinsic motivation pulls you by the power of some external benefit or tangible reward you'll attain by taking action, like in the case of a professional athlete who plays primarily for money rather than for the fun or challenge of the sport."

"All of the top achievers I know are life-long learners. They are constantly looking for new skills, insights, and ideas. They recognize that if they are not learning, they are not growing, and if they aren't growing, they are not moving toward excellence."

"Far too many people have disconnected their person from their profession. It is crucial to your long-term motivation to feel the power of purpose and to recognize the difference that you make in your work, your company, or in the lives of those you serve."

"I think it all comes down to why. I firmly believe that if the why *is big enough, the* how *is usually not a problem."*

Intrinsic vs. Extrinsic Motivation

Psychologists make a basic distinction between *intrinsic* and *extrinsic* motivation.

Having intrinsic motivation means doing something for its own sake, like playing a game just for the joy of playing.

On the other hand, extrinsic motivation pulls you by the power of some external benefit or tangible reward you'll attain by taking action, like in the case of a professional athlete who plays primarily for money rather than for the fun or challenge of the sport. It also, for example, influences business and sales executives who are driven fundamentally by the income the receive rather than by the love of the service they provide.

Of course, extrinsic motivation can be very powerful. Many people go to a job they neither enjoy nor care about just to receive a paycheck. You can bet these people would not go to their job every day if they knew no one was going to pay them for their work. Some of these people actively hate their jobs, but the extrinsic motivation is strong enough to keep them going faithfully every day.

But how powerful is extrinsic motivation in a larger sense? How does the power of extrinsic compare to intrinsic motivation when the topic is doing one's best, peak performance, or human greatness?

For instance, you may recall from history that the exquisitely beautiful armless statue of Venus de Milo was carved by an unknown sculptor.

When a farmer dug up the soon-to-be world-famous work of art while plowing his field, a renowned museum official sadly reflected what a great pity it was that the sculptor would never be recognized by thousands of admirers, nor would he ever know how valuable the statue became hundreds of years later.

The farmer retorted that it must have been a labor of love for someone to be able to have envisioned such perfection and bring it forth with just a chisel and a shapeless piece of stone. "Just creating something of such quality," said the farmer, "would have been payment in full for me."

You can't commission a masterpiece. Human greatness can't be extrinsically motivated. It must be compelled from within.

Do you see what that means for you? If you want to be the best—whether it's the best manager, the best salesperson, the best parent, or the best pitcher on your softball team—you have to light that fire within yourself.

Real motivation is that drive from within. You know where you're going because you have a compelling image inside, not a travel poster on the wall.

Six Types of Achievement Motivation

One of the classic studies of motivation that leads to achievement was done by a team of scientists under the leadership of Dr. D.N. Jackson. They identified six types of "achievement motivation."

As we review each of the six motivations, ask yourself the following questions: Is this an intrinsic or extrinsic form of motivation? How strongly motivated am I by this particular type of motivation? How well does this type of motivation help me achieve my goals?

The first type of achievement motivation is *Status with the Experts*—in other words, gaining recognition as a leader in your field. In my case, this could be a desire to be thought of in the same league as Earl Nightingale. In your case, it could mean being treated with deference and respect by your immediate boss or manager.

The second type of achievement motivation is *Acquisitiveness,* which is the desire to acquire something tangible, such as a fixed sum of money, a new BMW, or a cabin cruiser. Many people live for the things they love, and they also hate to lose those things.

I once heard about a young man in Phoenix who came home from work exhausted and ready to wind down. If someone had told him he would be spending the night digging up his yard, he would have laughed and said, "There's no way I'm going to do anything but relax." But that was before his new bride told him she had accidentally flushed her $1,800 diamond engagement ring down the drain!

Immediately, his priorities changed. Possibly influenced by the $1,000 he still owed on the ring and the fact that it wasn't insured, he became motivated to acquire the ring—whatever it took. While he spent the night digging up and taking apart the plumbing in search of the ring, his wife spent the night with a relative to escape his foul mood.

After searching all night, the young husband was convinced the ring had departed from their property, so he called the water department, and out came Phoenix's "lost diamond crew" to pick up the hunt. They installed a trap at a downstream manhole, then sent a high-pressure stream of water down the sewer pipe to flush it. One of the crew members crawled down into the manhole and fished the diamond ring out of the sewage.

Now *that* illustrates motivation to acquire! One small possession completely dominated this young man's being for twenty-four hours, without distraction. How strong a force is motivation to acquire in your life?

The third type of achievement motivation is *Achievement via Independence,* which is the desire to achieve on your own skill and merit. This could involve going through the demanding academic training to become a neurosurgeon, scientist, attorney, or any other profession where you are sought after for your ability.

The fourth type of achievement motivation is *Status with Peers.* This is different from Status with the Experts because, to put it bluntly, your peers may not be the experts. Many of us are motivated by how we are regarded by our friends or our fellow employees at work.

The fifth type of achievement motivation is *Competitiveness,* something we all know about. NBC founder David Sarnoff said,"Competition brings out the best in products and the worst in people." How important is winning to you?

The sixth and final type of achievement motivation is *Concern for Excellence.* Vince Lombardi, the legendary coach of the Green Bay Packers during their pro football dynasty, believed that "the quality of a person's life is in direct proportion to their commitment to excellence, regardless of their chosen field of endeavor." Concern for excellence means that you are motivated every day to be the best you can possibly be in whatever you do.

Of the six motivation types we've covered, only two—Achievement via Independence and Concern with Excellence—are true intrinsic motivations. Not coincidentally, scientists also have found that these two motivations are the most effective in leading to significant achievement.

(Leaders and managers should take special note of this.

You need to be careful in your use of extrinsic motivators in trying to inspire your employees over the long run. Remember, enduring motivation must ultimately come from within the individual. That is why the words *empower* and *envision* are so vital to team performance and quality. It must be *their* power and vision that compels them, not that of the leader.)

The success of our efforts depends not so much on the efforts themselves, but rather on our motive for doing them. The greatest companies and the greatest men and women in all walks of life have achieved their greatness out of a desire to express something within themselves that had to be expressed, a desire to solve a problem using their skills as best they could.

This is not to say that many of these individuals did not earn a great deal of money and prestige for what they produced. Many did. But the key to their successes is to be found in the fact that they were motivated more by providing excellence in a product or service to fill a need than by any thought of profit. William Shakespeare, Thomas Edison, and Estee Lauder all became wealthy. Separated as they were in time and type of talent, they all were motivated by the same thing: to produce the very best, to express the very best that was in them.

Dr. Martin Luther King, Jr. spoke about this as eloquently as anyone ever has when he said, "If an individual is called to be a streetsweeper, he or she should sweep streets even as Michelangelo painted, or Beethoven composed music, or Shakespeare wrote poetry. He should sweep streets so well, that all the hosts of Heaven and Earth will pause and say, here lived a great streetsweeper who did his job well."

A Motivation Self-Evaluation

Following are fifteen statements about motivation taken from three of the categories of achievement motivation in the previous chapter: Concern for Excellence, Achievement via Independence, and Competitiveness.

After reading each statement, please assign it a number between 1 and 5 based on how much thc statement corresponds with your own life. If you strongly agree with the statement, give it a 5; if you strongly disagree with it, assign it a 1. If your feelings fall somewhere in between, decide on a numerical value between 1 and 5 that best expresses your opinion.

When you have finished responding to all fifteen questions, add up your totals for each of the three achievement motivation categories, and continue reading about how what you learn from this self-evaluation can help you.

Category One: Concern for Excellence

1. It's important to me to do my work as well as I can, even if it isn't popular with my coworkers.

2. I find satisfaction in working to my highest ability.

3. There is satisfaction in a job well done.

4. I find satisfaction in exceeding my previous performance, even if I don't outperform others.

5. I like to work hard.

Category Two: Achievement via Independence

1. I would rather rise to a new challenge than do the same thing over and over.

2. When a group to which I belong plans an activity, I would rather direct it myself than have someone else organize it and just help out.

3. If I am not good at something, I would rather keep struggling to master it than move on to something I may find easier to do.

4. Once I undertake a task, I persist until it's completed.

5. I prefer to work in situations that require a high level of skill.

Category Three: Competitiveness

1. I enjoy working in situations involving competition with other people.

2. It is important to me to perform better than others on any given task.

3. I feel that winning is important in both work and games.

4. It annoys me when other people outperform me.

5. I try harder when I am competing with other people.

Now add up your scores in each of the three categories and compare them. What do you think the scores tell you about yourself?

This test was administered by a group of psychologists to a wide demographic range of individuals, including college students and a variety of businesspeople. Using the results, it was discovered that, on a consistent basis, those subjects who scored significantly higher in the first two categories, Concern for Excellence and Achievement via Independence, were much more successful—in terms of objective measures such as grades and salaries—than those who have a similar or higher motivational base in Competitiveness.

If this sounds foreign to everything you've ever been taught, don't worry. It will make sense to you by the end of this book.

A Concern for Excellence

Dr. D.N. Jackson's achievement motivation study reminded me of a very goal-oriented young man named George. His twelve-year goal was to compete in the decathlon event of the Olympic Games. To work his way up to this, George had also developed numerous sub-goals, which included the times he wanted set in each of the decathlon's ten events and the dates by which he hoped to achieve those times. He also arranged his work, financial, and scholastic goals to allow himself to spend eight hours every day in training. Throughout high school and college, he seemed to be right on schedule, winning every competition, and after college, he competed through the Amateur Athletic Union.

George's sister Georgene was his number one fan. Whenever he participated in an out-of-state event she couldn't attend, she always called him to ask how he did rather than wait to read about it in the next day's newspaper.

After one especially important event, Georgene called and found George in the depths of depression. "I was just terrible," he told her. "I can't believe how bad I was."

All Georgene's attempts to console him seemed worthless. She assumed he'd fallen down or failed to finish one of the events.

But the next day, Georgene was amazed to read in the newspaper that George had won the AAU decathlon! "I know I won and that I broke a record," George told her later. "But I set a personal goal of cutting one second off my best time, and I didn't do it. That's why I was disappointed."

George's goals were so tied into his intrinsic motivation that he didn't even consider the extrinsic motivators of winning the meet. We can analyze this example further by looking back at the six types of achievement motivation.

Status with Experts, and Status with Peers: Everyone thought George did great. But he was disappointed in his performance.

Acquisitiveness: George acquired a gold medal. The medal may have been the only motivation for the athletes he was competing against, but it meant nothing to George.

Achievement via Independence: George was motivated to achieve based on his own skill and discipline. No one else could do it for him. He was the one who devoted eight hours a day to working out.

Competitiveness: To George, winning meant nothing. He could never be motivated by competing against others. He only competed with himself. If George made it to the Olympics, competition might have been a higher motivator, but he never expressed a goal of being the world champion. His goal was merely to be in the Olympics.

Concern with Excellence: Now this is what motivated George. His goal was to be the best in every event of the decathlon so he could compete in the Olympics.

George's intrinsic motivation is a model for all those who wish to achieve. Remember, there's only one person you truly have to please: yourself!

No other person and no external reward can motivate you more than your own desire to do the best you can do and be the best you can be.

The most powerful of intrinsic motivators, a concern for excellence will spur you far beyond any extrinsic factor. George's dream was to compete in the Olympics . . . what is yours?

Creating Your Own Motivation

A friend of mine named Natalie worked for a large family-owned company that seemed to specialize in demotivating its own employees. Although there were no women in management positions within this company, Natalie set a goal of becoming a manager. Without being asked, and on her own time after work, Natalie did an analysis of the company's marketing strategies. Then she formulated a plan to set up an additional marketing division designed to target a segment of the market not currently being reached. She felt that if the strategy were successful, she would be appointed manager of the new division.

Natalie worked out a proposed income and expense statement for one year based on various projections, together with a plan for test marketing without using a single dollar from the company budget.

Armed with budgets, charts, and her written proposal,

she asked for an appointment with the president of the company.

Natalie made her presentation, closing by saying, "What could we possibly lose by trying this? Test marketing won't cost us a penny!" The president was silent for about a minute.

Finally, he looked her directly in the eye and said, "Couldn't you make more money if you worked someplace else?"

And that was the end of the discussion.

If you were Natalie, what would that do to you? Would this motivate or demotivate you? Would you adjust your goal of holding a management position in that company . . . or maybe think about leaving altogether?

Well, the president's reaction gave Natalie a reason to go over the president's head to the CEO, who happened to be the president's father.

Now, I'm not recommending that you go over your boss's head without seriously considering the ramifications, but Natalie felt her idea was extremely valid. Furthermore, the president hadn't told her no, he had just ignored her.

When Natalie gave the same presentation to the CEO, he didn't even let her finish talking. He called the director of marketing and said, "Drop everything! I want you to hear these ideas!" Within thirty minutes, Natalie had approval from the director of marketing and the CEO to implement her plan.

Admittedly, Natalie was now in a tight spot with the president, but we have to understand his goals and motivation as well as Natalie's.

While Natalie was spurred on by her dream of creating

her own management position in which she could utilize her as-yet-untapped potential, the president's motivation in this instance was entirely different.

Everyone in the company knew he was president by birthright. This put him in a tight spot, too. Even if he were competent, everyone would think he had the job because his father gave it to him. So he was always on the defensive, trying to display abilities he didn't really have. He wouldn't take a chance in implementing someone else's idea regardless of its merit. He was highly motivated just to "run in place," maintaining the status quo that paid him $500,000 a year. After all, he had three other siblings waiting in the wings in case he makes a major blunder!

Natalie's encounter with the president illustrates how we create our own motivation based on our goals, desires, perceptions, and mind-set. And as is so often the case, our motivation also determines what we achieve and whether we deserve what we get.

The Support Beams of Motivation

Most of us spend our lives doing what I call "peak-and-valley" living. This is the old New Year's resolution or yo-yo diet scenario in which we get excited about changing or improving, we are pumped up and motivated, we set the goal and start pursuing it with excitement. Things start off great, but then the motivation starts to wear off, or we hit a challenge or a setback. Suddenly, we start sliding back down toward the old habits and mediocrity, and before long, we get frustrated, throw up our hands, and say, "I didn't really want that goal anyway."

I had a client make a very astute observation when he was setting some new goals and objectives for himself. He said, "When I die, I want to die a perfect man, so I'm going to make sure that I die on January second! I always set my new goals on the first and do them perfectly on the second, then I start sliding back." How true this is for most of us! To achieve long-term success, we need to develop a support system to carry us through the tough spots.

In my work, I have had the chance to coach, observe, and monitor top achievers and peak performers from all walks of life, and I have found that most of them possess three common qualities that could be called "support beams" for excellence and long-term success.

The first support beam of motivation is *education.* All of the top achievers I know are life-long learners. They are constantly looking for new skills, insights, and ideas. They recognize that if they are not learning, they are not growing, and if they aren't growing, they are not moving toward excellence. They also understand that new knowledge and education can provide them the necessary information to overcome new challenges in their personal or professional lives. In our rapidly changing, ever challenging world, you cannot stand still anymore. You are either moving toward or away from excellence. Here are six quick strategies to develop your motivational support beam of education:

1. Learn by listening to educational or motivational audio tapes or CDs, or by watching videos.

2. Gain insight by attending seminars and workshops.

3. Obtain more understanding of your industry or goals by reading magazines and trade publications.

4. Enroll in continuing education at your local community college or university.

5. Tap into the Internet and the incredible array of knowledge available there.

6. Finally, and perhaps most importantly, if you haven't been to your local library lately I strongly suggest you go. Your library card is much more important than your credit card!

However you choose to go about gaining education, make sure that you do it, and do it now. With education, you are adding "skillpower" to go along with your willpower. You see, the more you learn, the more ammunition you will have to combat trials and challenges that have the power of blocking you from achieving your goals. Developing and cultivating your knowledge is one of the most effective ways of bolstering your motivation.

The second support beam of motivation is *internalization*. Internalization is going beyond the mere *understanding* of what it takes to achieve your goal; it is making those concepts a part of who you are and a part of what you do every day. To internalize new principles and concepts, you must get repetitious. A musician must practice and repeat over and over again those tedious notes and monotonous scales until they are internalized and become reflex habits. We have to do the same thing with our learning and education. The skills and strategies for achieving excellence must become reflex habits like brushing your teeth or driving your car. As you deepen the internalization, it will become easier for you to quickly tap into your knowledge when you face difficult challenges.

Research studies suggest that it takes you a minimum of eight repetitions to really internalize and master new concepts and strategies. So if you are getting most of your education from written materials—books, magazines, trade publications, et cetera—you must go beyond just using your highlighting pen and marking key principles. Most of us mark and highlight pretty well, but then what do we do? We put the books up on the shelf and the articles into the filing cabinet, and we never go back. Zero repetitions.

I suggest that you take those key principles and write them down on three-by-five cards and carry them with you in your pocket, purse, or briefcase. When you are waiting for a meeting or stuck in traffic, just pull them out and start getting in a few repetitions. You could also take those key principles and enter them into your computer for quick reference. There are even some great screen-saver programs available that allow you to enter in your own messages, which will then flash on your computer screen during the day. This is a fantastic way to internalize the principles of excellence in your field, and it also constantly spurs your achievement motivation.

As you may be aware, one of the best ways to internalize new information is through audio-based learning. It is the quickest and easiest way to get your repetitions in. You can listen to educational or motivational tapes in your car, when you are exercising, or when you are working around the house or in the yard. In fact, if you spend just thirty minutes a day at any of these activities (which equals about 130 hours per year), think of all you could learn and internalize in that time!

Education is a powerful support beam of achievement

motivation, but it is also extremely important to internalize what you learn in your quest for excellence.

The third support beam of motivation is *continuation.* It is the ability to sustain motivation over the long term that is the challenge of life. Here are a few practical suggestions for the implementation of the continuation support beam.

Participate in a "mastermind" group. This group of four or five people should get together once a month in an informal meeting. This meeting can take place after work or over breakfast or lunch. During the meeting, talk about goals, challenges, and possibilities. Brainstorm together. Read an article or listen to a portion of a tape together, and discuss how to apply it to your lives. This type of group is a great way to make sure that you are staying focused, motivated, and on track each month.

Establish a good library for yourself. This is simply a collection of all of the books, tapes, videos, magazines, and resources that will help achieve excellence. I would like to point out that a box of books in the garage doesn't qualify as a library! They must be accessible, so when you are having a bad day or you encounter a setback, you can go and review your education. This will help to remotivate and refocus you and keep you moving forward.

Keep a "success" journal. This can be a great source of continued achievement motivation. Often, personal growth is incremental, so you may not even realize that you are doing well or improving. It is easy to get discouraged and lose motivation when you feel that you aren't accomplishing your goals and dreams. Your success journal will help you draw confidence from the positive action and positive performance of your past, which will give you the courage to meet current and future challenges.

Use "instant replay." Much like your success journal, instant reply can be an important part of your continuation support beam. For years, coaches have used the concept of a "personal highlight" film to reinforce positive performance. Rather than having the athletes watch their mistakes on video, they watch a highlight film of all their greatest moves, best shots, and peak performances. This reinforces the mindset that they can rise to the highest level of competition. While you may not have a handy compilation video of all your past successes, you can replay them mentally or recall them by spending a few minutes a day with momentoes of your triumphs.

The motivational support beam of continuation is perhaps the hardest of the three to keep in place, but it is also the most critical. Without being replenished by continuing motivation to achieve, your goals will quickly lose their pulling power, and your education and internalization will have been for nothing. Without the support beam of continuation, your life will be an inconstant series of peaks and valleys. And few of us get to die on January second.

Your Magnificent Obsession

Another important bolster for continued motivation is having a "magnificent obsession." Far too many people have disconnected their person from their profession. It is crucial to your long-term motivation to feel the power of purpose and to recognize the difference that you make in your work, your company, or in the lives of those you serve.

Let me ask you a question: Would you be interested doing my job? Would you like to fly almost every day of the week, spend half your life in airports hearing those wonderful words "Your flight has been canceled," sleep in hotels with lumpy beds, eat high-priced, low-quality meals in greasy spoon cafes, be away from family and friends for long stretches of time, deal with difficult hotel staff, and eat more rubber chickens than anyone else in the country? Interested?

Maybe you would rather take a job that would send you to travel to some of the greatest places in the world and meet some of the finest people. This job would allow you to learn about many different cultures and philosophies and try wonderful cuisine. It will also give you the chance to have a flexible schedule and even take your family traveling with you if you like. The great benefit of this job is that it gives you the chance to make a difference in the personal and professional lives of those with whom you work. And you would be paid well for your services. How does *this* job sound?

The reality is that both of these job definitions describe the exact same job! You see, there are good and bad aspects to every business. What you must do is connect with the positives of your career. This will help you focus on your purpose and the difference you make to those with whom you come into contact. When this happens, work becomes exciting and fulfilling. Without purpose and connection, work is drudgery.

I'm sure you remember the disastrous floods that devastated the American Midwest in 1993. As the flood waters rose, citizens and volunteers from around the country rallied to save communities. They filled sandbags day and night, trying desperately to preserve homes, schools, and entire towns. These volunteers found themselves with unlikely help from convicts involved in a Green County, Illinois prison program. Convicts and citizens worked side by side in an attempt to save the little town of Inota.

Many were amazed at the effort the convicts put into their work. They refused to stop working, even to sleep or eat. They pressed on around the clock, endeavoring to stay the waters and preserve the town. Despite their best efforts,

What is your magnificent obsession? You may not have the urgency of helping save a town by filling sandbags, but your connection to your own work may in the end be just as vital to you.

the levee gave way, and the town of Inota and its two hundred homes were destroyed.

The prisoners wept as they realized that they hadn't saved the town. They also expressed their sadness and condolences to the people who had lost their homes. What an amazing turn around from begrudging convict on a forced labor project to good Samaritans with genuine feelings of compassion and empathy toward people they had never met! How did this transformation take place? The convicts had tapped into the power of a magnificent obsession and had become personally connected to their work. Their purpose was to save a town, and they knew that if they didn't do it, destruction was the inevitable end.

Take some time to identify your own magnificent obsession for your work and career. Connect yourself to what you do by identifying the impact your performance has on others. Ask yourself, "How does my performance effect the company or business? What is its impact on my customers and clients? How does it effect my family and loved ones?" You'll be amazed at how much easier it is to stay focused and motivated when you find your magnificent obsession and connect yourself to what you do every day.

Many people tell me that they have big dreams. Some even claim that they do have a magnificent obsession. Yet far too often, these are casually conceived, for-the-moment, temporary whims.

These may be things that you react to after watching a movie or television, thinking, "Oh, If only I could..." Your adrenaline gets pumping, and you start imagining your new life with more money, a better body, or that new house in the country. Unfortunately, however, these whims or daydreams have very little staying power, and usually by the next morning, you are justifying to yourself and everyone else why it won't work for you. You simply have not tapped into your magnificent obsession.

A magnificent obsession is the way you want to live, not just the things you want to own. A magnificent obsession is the person you want to be, not just the title you want to see under your name on the door. A magnificent obsession is the mind-set that you have, not the degrees you earn. A magnificent obsession is the worldview that you claim as your own, not the collection of stamps in your passport.

Your magnificent obsession will cover all areas of your life including how you want to live, to think, to work, to play, to grow, to love, to worship, to create, and to spend your precious hours and days and years on this earth.

Ask yourself the following questions to help you find your magnificent obsession:

If it weren't for money, time and personal responsibilities, what would I really love to do with my life?

What do I really get excited about?

Five years from now, what will my days be like? What will I be doing? Where will my focus be professionally? What will I be spending my time on? Who will I be spending my time with? What will be different about my life then? Where will I live? What will I have accomplished?

Take a look back at your childhood dreams. What were the things that you dreamed of doing or becoming when you were young?

Many of the world's top achievers didn't overcome their personal challenges or problems or become successful until they went back to the magnificent obsessions of their childhood. This concept will be discussed further in a later chapter of this book.

You can talk to all the successful people in the world, and most of them would tell you that one of the main reasons for their success and ongoing motivation is that they love what they do and that, early on, they decided to pursue their magnificent obsession. They chose the road less traveled, which is usually the road *best* traveled . . . the road to riches, happiness, and fulfillment.

Finding a Compelling 'Why'

I have for you a suitcase. In that suitcase there is one million dollars in cash. The suitcase is sitting in a building that is about an hour's drive from where you are right now.

Here is the deal: All you have to do is get to this building in the next seven hours. If you get there before the end of seven hours, I will hand you the suitcase, and you will be a million dollars richer.

There is one catch, however, and that is, if you are even one second late, our deal is off, and you will not get a dime. No exceptions! With that in mind, what time would you like to leave?

Most people would respond to that scenario by saying that they would leave right now. Wouldn't you?

So off you go. You jump into your car and start driving for the building. You are excited and are already starting to plan how you are going to spend your million dollars. Then, suddenly, the traffic comes to a complete stop. You turn on the radio and find that there has been a series of freak accidents all around the building, and there is no way to get there!

Now what would you do? Would you give up and go back home? Or would you get out of your car and walk, run, hire a helicopter, or find some other way of getting to the building on time?

Now let's suppose for a minute that you are driving to an appointment at your dentist's office. The traffic again comes to a stop. Amazingly, there have been freak accidents all the way around your dentists office. What would you do now? Probably give up, go home, and reschedule!

What is the difference between these two situations? I think it all comes down to *why*. I firmly believe that if the *why* is big enough, the *how* is usually not a problem. This compelling why will usually be connected to your personal mission statement or your magnificent obsession. It will be the basis of your motivational support beam of continuation. Truly motivated people are able to identify and tap into the power of a compelling why.

ACHIEVING WITH OTHERS

Stimulating Children's Motivation • The Power of High Expectations • Motivation from Mentors • Finding Support in Coaches and Mentors • The Process of Selecting a Mentor • Being a Good Role Model • The Best Sources of Feedback • The True Nature of Competition • Avoiding Futile Competition • Leading with Relationship Power

"If I could live my life again, I would give my children roots and wings, instead of loot and things. I would first and always offer them unconditional love. I would help them build their own internal standards by setting an example with a family code of honor, integrity, and ethics."

"People become conditioned, through failures and successes, to perform at a level consistent with their expectations and the expectations others have for them. Unfortunately, most of their limits are caused by past experience or negative conditioning, when in actuality, there are no actual boundaries to their current or future achievements."

"According to the research, one of the most interesting qualities of motivated individuals is their ability to recognize potential sources of support in other people, to look beyond the walls of their homes to find relatives, friends, teachers, or other role models who can provide help."

"Don't seek feedback from fair-weather friends, competitive peers, or any person who doesn't have your best interest at heart. Neutral doesn't count. Get feedback from someone who is on your side but will still be objective and honest with you."

Stimulating Children's Motivation

The educational system in the United States today is undergoing tremendous upheaval because we seem to have stifled the students' curiosity and the inner desire to learn in favor of immediate, external gratification.

Educational psychologists have examined in depth the question of whether extrinsic motivations—like the desire for good grades—reinforces the students' intrinsic motivation to learn for the satisfaction of mastering new knowledge; or conversely, whether extrinsic rewards might possibly weaken the inner motivation to learn. In several studies, students who were given strong extrinsic incentives, such as cash rewards for high marks, did extremely well. They did better than their counterparts who were given no special extrinsic incentives to learn. But for how long? As soon as the incentives were withdrawn, the extrinsically motivated students' performance started to decline, and they soon fell behind the students who had never been given any special reason to exert extra effort. When students had found their primary motivation to be in the extrinsic rewards offered, they had trouble seeing the task as worthy in and of itself.

I remember lecturing my children on the fact that their adopted sister from Mexico, who came from a very humble, disadvantaged environment, seemed to be succeeding more rapidly than several of them, who'd had the benefit of a much grander socioeconomic head start. My biological children thought for a moment and volunteered their justification: "I guess it's because we have your genes, Dad!" Lately, I've stopped lecturing my family and started listening more openly to their individual desires and motivations.

If I could live my life again, I would give my children roots and wings, instead of loot and things. I would first and always offer them unconditional love. I would help them build their own internal standards by setting an example with a family code of honor, integrity, and ethics. I would teach them to explore and to be curious about everything they were doing at the time, rather than harping so much about the payoffs and rewards later in life. I would stimulate their imaginations with great books, more museums, more do-it-yourself projects, and more problem-solving opportunities. And I would help them learn that happiness is a decision and a way of traveling, not wrapped up in future results and put on layaway. These are the things that stimulate intrinsic motivation in children.

The Power of High Expectations

The home environment is by far the most significant factor in determining a child's success in the external world. Children rise to the expectations of the significant adult role models in their lives. The late Lawrence Kohlberg, the famous Harvard psychologist who studied child development, was fond of saying that positive values are "caught"—not taught. By that, he meant that children are more likely to store and absorb their parents' values by being around them constantly. Instead of preaching, parents are much better advised to be teaching by example.

Recently, I read about the impact of the low expectations that parents have for their children. Two young boys had been caught stealing handcuffs and other items from a police car. The officer related that the two kids told him that, on the day of the theft, their mother had reminded them over and over again how bad they were and told them they would end up in jail one day for stealing or doing some other unlawful activity. Here is the self-fulfilling power of low expectations in action.

Positive expectations are self-fulfilling, too. I'd like to share with you some characteristics of personal environments that foster positive expectations. These principles can apply in any business as well as they do in the climate in a home:

There is emphasis on building the self-worth and self-respect of each family member. Each member respects the needs, dignity, and individuality of every other member. Relationships are characterized by loving, caring, trust, and affection. The family unit is secure and cohesive, with pride in its members and their accomplishments. There is a feeling of "ownership" and opportunities for involvement and participation in family affairs. Fault finding, bickering, and quarreling are kept to a minimum. Differences are settled reasonably, fairly, and amicably. Communications are free and open. Family members are encouraged to express their opinions and feelings without fear of recrimination or reprisal. Expectations for each family member are high, and there is cooperative effort to help each achieve his or her goals.

While visiting Sea World in Florida, my grandchildren were amazed to see four-ton whales jumping out of the water and over a rope positioned ten feet above the surface. We learned from the trainers that they begin by placing a rope on the bottom of the pool and rewarding the whales when they pass over it. Incrementally, the rope is raised until it is completely out of the water, and the whale is required to jump out of the water to cross over the rope.

People also become conditioned, through failures and successes, to perform at a level consistent with their expectations and the expectations others have for them. Unfortunately, most of their limits are caused by past experience or negative conditioning, when in actuality, there are no actual boundaries to their current or future achievements.

When we are subjected to continuous criticism, failure, or disappointment, we lower our level of expectations and performance. Just as the whales were encouraged through positive reinforcement, people respond to rewards, appreciation, recognition, and praise. Unlike animals, however, we have the power to choose and control, to a large degree, the conditioning of our lives. It is a power we should put to good use . . . both in our own lives and in the lives of those who look to us for wisdom and support.

Motivation from Mentors

By extolling the power of intrinsic motivation, I'm not suggesting we should get carried away and and throw the baby out with the bathwater. Extrinsic motivators can be powerful and helpful, especially when they function to pull us toward sub-goals and objectives along the road to an intrinsically motivated long-term goal. One category of extrinsic motivation that is especially valuable is that of the mentor-protégé relationship.

In a healthy relationship, the protégé will want to gain status with his or her mentor by excelling and meeting the more experienced individual's expectations. People not only rise to their own expectations, they rise to the expectations of significant role models in their lives.

The mentor may initially expect more from the younger protégé than the protégé does from himself or herself. In this way, the first achievement motivation from Section One,

Status with the Experts, plays a positive role in the ability of the individual to gain intrinsic motivation for a lifetime. Having a good mentor or role model who expects a lot out of you is great if you learn to expect a lot out of yourself.

One of my role models is someone I've only read about and heard about from my teachers. I can never meet him. He can never be there to coach me in person. But in his example, I have learned to expect a great deal more from myself and that it's never too late to become inventive and imaginative. When I go to the library to read or check out a great book, I think of him. He founded America's first library at the age of twenty-five. When I mail a letter, I recall that he founded the U.S. Mail at the age of thirty-one. When I hear the siren of a fire engine heading for another California brush fire, I silently thank him, because he started the first fire department, also at the age of thirty-one.

When I put some kindling wood in our old pot-bellied stove on a crisp evening in our mountain retreat, I'm warmed by the fact that he designed it when he was thirty-six years old. When I flip the "on" switch and my personal computer hums into action, I'm grateful that he harnessed the power of electricity at the age of forty. Lightning hit our barn recently and knocked out our electrical and phone service for two days. The barn survived, thanks to the lightning rod he invented at age forty-three. Several of my kids got an education at one of the Ivy League universities, which he founded at age forty-five.

And when I try to read the menu in the ambience of an intimate, candle-lit French restaurant, I reach for my bifocals, which he invented at age seventy-nine.

With two years of formal schooling, he was an international wit, conversationalist, economist, philosopher, diplomat, inventor, statesman, printer, publisher, and linguist who spoke and wrote five languages. He even conceived the idea of paratroopers—from balloons—a century before the airplane was invented. He expected a great deal of himself and lived every day looking for more problems to solve, more mysteries to understand, more questions to ask, for eighty-four highly motivated years. May I take the lid off my creativity and act more like Ben Franklin, instead of talking about him!

We all need extrinsic mentors to move us forward. Frank Sinatra learned his superb breath control in singing from his band leader, Tommy Dorsey. Helen Keller, though blind and deaf, became an educated, contributing person because of the nurturing and expectations of Anne Sullivan. Plato had Socrates as his mentor. And Olympic sprinter and world-record holder in the long jump, Carl Lewis, had his father and the late Jesse Owens as his role models.

Usually, the protégé will do everything possible to please the mentor. Several people told me that the worst thing their mentor could ever say to them was: "I'm disappointed in you." If this happened to them, it was motivation to totally turn their behavior around so they could regain the approval of their mentor and role model.

Finding Support in Coaches and Mentors

Throughout history, most of the great achievements and incredible comebacks have been the result of an individual whose motivation to persevere was influenced by a coach or mentor. In science, art, politics, sports, and business, there is a common thread of having been coached among those who achieve greatness. A coach doesn't need to be a professional consultant or counselor. He or she could be someone within your organization or industry, or it could be someone from your personal life that you respect or admire.

A study was undertaken on the Hawaiian island of Kauai by two researchers named Emily Werner and Ruth Smith. This study, which followed more than 450 men from childhood through their adult lives, was an attempt to learn why some people are motivated to overcome severe disadvantages while others from the same background seem to have been overwhelmed by their problems. This research continued for an incredible length of time: forty years, to be exact.

According to the research, one of the most interesting qualities of these motivated individuals is their ability to recognize potential sources of support in other people, to look beyond the walls of their homes to find relatives, friends, teachers, or other role models who can provide help. This very important finding illustrates the benefits of a forming mentor relationships to encourage achievement motivation.

Choosing a coach or mentor is really like having an additional correctional device to keep you on target. An analogy of this premise comes from aerospace technology. Years ago, the military used inertial guidance systems on missiles. Unfortunately, once the course of an inertially guided missile is set, it proceeds along that path with no capability for adjustments. It's like a bullet fired from a rifle. Even when the aim is good at the outset, if the target moves unexpectedly once the projectile is in flight, the shot is going to miss. And if there's one thing you can count on in life, it's that the target is going to be moving! In the Gulf War of 1992, the Patriot missiles that defended Israel and Saudi Arabia were not inertially guided. Instead, the Patriots had an advanced self-adjusting navigation system that continuously monitored the missiles trajectory as well as the path of its swiftly moving target. The Patriot was able to make whatever corrections were necessary, regardless of changes in the position or speed of its objective.

A highly motivated person uses a coach or mentor in the same way when he or she has targeted a worthwhile goal. A coach or mentor can assist you in making adjustments and navigating through difficult times.

Who can forget the amazing display of achievement motivation from the 1996 Summer Olympics in Atlanta. The U.S. Women's Gymnastic team held a slim lead going into the final rotation, but their performance seemed to be falling apart. Finally it came down to Kerri Strugg's performance on the vault. She would be the determining factor for a team gold medal. As she landed her first vault, she heard a pop in her ankle. She knew she had injured it. What would she do? The team and the country were looking to her to save the victory. As everyone turned their eyes to Kerri, Kerri turned to her coach, Bella Karoly. Bella had coached the best: Nadia Cominice and Mary Lou Retton. Coach Bella's piercing eyes connected with Kerri's, comprehending her situation. And he pumped his fist and shouted, "You can do it!"

With that prompt from her coach, Kerri gazed down the runway at the vault. Then mustering all the motivation she had, she sprinted down the runway, sprang off the board, over the vault in a rotating, twisting blur, and kept her balance when she landed on just one foot. She'd done it! The gold medal and the lasting respect of the world was hers. And who was there to carry her up to the top platform to receive her gold medal? Her coach, of course.

High achievers are able to these find coaches and role models, even if they have to look far afield for them. Have you had people in your life who provided strength when support from other sources was lacking? If so, you've not only been very fortunate, but in cultivating those relationships, you've also displayed an important aspect of a motivated high achiever.

The Process of Selecting a Mentor

Finding coaches and mentors is an important mission. You will no doubt have several over the course of your life, and it is critical that you choose them wisely. Your mentor is someone to whom you'll be committing a great deal of time and attention, and who ideally will take a very focused interest in you as well.

The process of selecting a mentor begins, first of all, with a clear-sighted view of what your life's goals really are, both for your career and your personal life.

If you're just starting out as an associate in a large law firm, you might choose one of the senior partners as your mentor, or perhaps a partner in another firm you're familiar with. If you're just starting a family, and you're facing the lifestyle adjustments that kids require, your mentor could very likely be someone who is reaching the other end of this very exciting, but demanding, process. In any case, your mentors should be people whose experience can serve as a model for reaching your most significant goals in the most important areas of your life.

Selecting a mentor is not just a matter of finding someone you like or feel comfortable identifying with. Make sure that the mentors you choose have a genuine history of success. I'm continually amazed by the number of people who look to only superficially successful people as role models for achievement. Even experts can make conspicuous mistakes of judgment in this area. The next time you're in a bookstore or library, take a look at the bestselling books on business and management from four or five years ago. There's an excellent chance that some of the companies cited as models of efficiency are now out of business. I don't bring this up to disparage anyone's business expertise, but simply to point out the need for great care in selecting a coach whose success will stand the test of time.

In addition to selecting your coaches based on their ability to achieve goals similar to your own, choose mentors who in the process have overcome some of the same obstacles you're facing. Ideally, a mentor really represents both what you want to become in a particular area of life and what you want to do. Seeing your mentor today is like seeing what you intend to be. The coach has arrived at or been to places similar to where you want to go.

Choosing a celebrity or public figure as a mentor is a very questionable decision. A mentor should not be someone unapproachable. If at all possible, select a mentor with whom you can actually spend time and with whom you enjoy having conversations and exploring ideas with.

Of course, you can have favorite historical personages,

authors, educators, or artists as role models or what might be called "specialist coaches." You can learn a great deal from people whose work is published and whose ideas are available in print, audio, or video form. If you discover someone with whom you feel a special affinity, make an effort to obtain everything they've written or said. Really become a student of their work and their lives. Don't just admire them, genuinely *learn* from them, as I have learned from the life and wisdom of Benjamin Franklin.

One of the most interesting aspects of selecting a mentor is the fact that, for me at least, one can rarely separate a person's tangible achievements from the qualities of their character. More than their bank accounts or their real estate holdings, role models prove by the conduct of their lives that they're worth emulating.

Selecting a mentor, coach, or role model is an important step in your path to success, whatever your field of endeavor. By sharing the secrets that led to his or her success and encouraging your development, your mentor can help you achieve your own dreams far more quickly than you might on your own.

Being a Good Role Model

It always amazes me that so many young people have as their goal to be anything other than like their parents or what their parents would like them to be. This could be that parents are viewed by many young people today as flawed inn keepers and wardens rather than as nourishing role models.

One of my wife's friends, Suzanne, has a workaholic for a mother. Suzanne and her four sisters pretty much took care of themselves because their mother worked a minimum of twelve hours a day outside of the home. It's interesting that now, twenty years later, Suzanne and her four sisters are all full-time housewives and mothers in a society where there are more working women than men. Not one of them will consider taking a job outside the home.

And yet, my friend and mentor Mary Kay Ash also had a mother that worked a minimum of twelve hours a day outside the home, and Mary Kay went on to build one of the most successful cosmetic firms in the world.

And then there's Sarah, whose mother never worked outside the home. Every day of her life, Sarah saw her mother work diligently preparing three meals a day for her family, doing the laundry, cleaning house, and taking care of babies. What goals do you think Sarah set for herself? Sarah decided that she would be anything but a housewife. She consciously has rejected all attempts to learn to cook and has had no interest whatsoever in any traditional domestic chores. Sarah became a total career woman.

Now Sarah has a daughter in college who is setting goals for herself. Although her daughter is dutifully working toward a career, deep in her heart, she wants to be a mother and full-time housewife with a career to fall back on in case something unforeseen happens to her husband.

What we can learn from all this is that sometimes our actions and motivations lead others to follow in our footsteps, and other times they cause others to take a totally different course.

What an awesome responsibility we have as mentors and parents. Do those around us see someone to emulate? Or by being too close to us, do they see a person whose life is unbalanced or unfulfilled? Think about it.

The Best Sources of Feedback

Although your own internal measurements are the most important, you will occasionally need to seek external feedback on your progress toward your goals. When you do so, be sure it is from people who are truly interested in seeing you succeed. Don't seek feedback from fair-weather friends, competitive peers, or any person who doesn't have your best interest at heart. Neutral doesn't count. Get feedback from someone who is on your side but will still be objective and honest with you.

I've observed time and again that misery truly does love company. Jealousy creates some of the most miserable people I know of. Surpass the achievements of your particular social crowd or your business colleagues, and look out for the slings and arrows of those who wish you were back where they are.

You have to dodge the snide remarks and catty

comments. Let them roll right off you. Don't internalize them. Only pay attention to feedback from those who have similar goals or who are working actively alongside you to achieve goals of their own.

Motives and fears run deep. Study them in others. The manager who supports you and comforts you when you're down may like you best when you are in just that state: down and dependent. When you start succeeding beyond his expectations and comfort level, he may be among the first to get you to back off, limit your horizons, and lower your goals. Recognize this feedback for the insecurity it is. It will rarely be objective or well-intentioned.

Even parents and significant family members aren't immune to emotional conflicts that can pollute their feedback. Many relatives and siblings have difficulty accepting the success of others in the family or encouraging further success.

Ultimately, nobody else is responsible for your life but you. Nobody else is accountable for your actions but you. Therefore, nobody's expectations for you and opinions about you are as important as your own. So make sure those take precedence in your mind over all others, and if you do need to consult with someone else, think very carefully before you choose exactly who.

The True Nature of Competition

In its purest form, competitiveness is the ultimate extrinsic motivation. The competitive person does not necessarily care about his own inner satisfaction in doing a job well; he cares most about other people's perception of him as superior. In a way, although somewhat more difficult to comprehend, he is like the person who acts—or chooses not to act—out of a fear of failure. Both the failure avoider and the competitor seem to be running away from real self-knowledge and self-discovery—the failure avoider by not engaging in projects that would give him information about his own ability to struggle and succeed, and the overly competitive person by concentrating on the manipulation other people's perceptions, rather than concentrating on the building of self-esteem and self-efficacy by working toward goals that are personally meaningful and important. (All of these topics will be covered more fully in later chapters.)

Competitiveness also handicaps individuals in the area of teamwork and cooperation. Those two concepts are absolutes for survival and success in today's world economy of the "Asian Tigers," the "United States of Europe," and the members of the NAFTA agreement. The overly competitive person hesitates to join a team effort because he knows he'll have to share the glory of achievement rather than having it all for himself. Others, sensing this dominant drive in him, hesitate to fully cooperate because his competitive nature makes it difficult to grant him complete trust and confidence.

Does this sound like heresy? What's wrong with Avis versus Hertz, McDonald's versus Burger King, and AT&T and IBM against all newcomers? Am I denying the benefits of healthy competition? Of course not. But let's frame competition in its proper perspective.

We all know that competition provides the soil in which free enterprise takes root. And we all know what happens when a company or group has no competition. We need only look at the economies of the former Eastern Bloc nations to get our answer. Seldom does lack of competition result in reasonable prices or good service. The word *competition* is not the culprit. The real motivational culprits that form the dark side of competition are the insatiable drives for status and power that go with the territory.

We can see the evidence all around us. In our extrinsic-status-oriented culture, achieving at the expense of others is more in fashion than winning by sharing and caring. Healthy competition to ensure quality in a free market has given way to "putting other people down" and "knocking the other guy" in order to look good. The trend toward "dirty politics" in our national, state, and local elections combined with dirty internal politics within our companies and institutions has distorted our basic values.

Success at any price is the order of the day. We have become so addicted to extrinsic values and skin-deep rewards, we live in a constant anxiety that can only be relieved by some public accomplishment, adornment, or status symbol.

A look at the word *compete* is revealing and even surprising. The Latin source is *competere,* meaning "to come together, agree, be suitable, belong." Nothing in the original definition of *competing* suggests the need for a killer instinct. We have added that little feature by defining excellence only in comparison to and at the expense of others.

In the final analysis, one person, or a small group of people, has to be "the winner" in the sense that they do a superior job and move up to a higher level of management. But in the long run, the right approach to competition should mean that everybody is better off just for having run the race.

Avoiding Futile Competition

Seeing everyone as your competitor has two negative consequences. First, it isolates you and your efforts, putting a full burden on your shoulders that others could help you bear; and second, it means you waste energy trying to set others back rather than using that energy to push yourself forward.

Consider the following true story by Frank Koch in an issue of *Proceedings*, the magazine of the of the United States Naval Institute. Two battleships assigned to the training squadron had been at sea on maneuvers in heavy weather for several days. Koch was serving on the lead battleship and was standing watch on the bridge as night fell.

"The visibility was extremely poor with patchy fog, so the captain remained on the bridge, keeping an eye on our navigation activities.

"Shortly after dark, the lookout on the wing of the bridge reported, 'Light, bearing on the starboard bow!'"

"The captain called out, 'Is it steady or moving astern?'

"The lookout replied, 'Steady, captain,' which meant that we were on a collision course with that source of light.

"The captain then called to the signalman, 'Signal that ship: We are on a collision course . . . advise you change course twenty degrees.'

"Back came the signal from the other ship. 'Advisable for you to change course twenty degrees!'

"The captain barked, 'Send, I'm a captain . . . change course twenty degrees immediately."

"'I'm a seaman second class,' came the reply. 'You had better change course twenty degrees!'

"By this time, the captain was furious. He spat out, 'Send, I'm a battleship. Change course twenty degrees.'

"Back came the signal from the flashing light, 'I'm a lighthouse.'

"The captain changed course."

The moral of the story is that it is futile to try to set others back when you could turn yourself twenty degrees and go forward!

Leading with Relationship Power

The most effective models for business relationships these days resemble a family or network rather than a hierarchy or top-down organizational chart. Competition remains an important business motivator, but it works best when it inspires people to greater heights rather than badgering them to avoid failure and falling behind.

My friend Pat Riley, one of the most successful coaches in the history of professional basketball, provides a case in point. Riley says that his mission is to create a system in which the individual talents of his players will be free to develop to their full potential, because when those various individual talents flourish, the team as a whole will succeed. Coaches like Pat Riley set a standard for leaders in every field. They don't rant and rave. The don't intimidate. They teach excellence and inspire confidence.

In the past, businesses expected people to perform

according to a specific job description. Today, success depends on teams responding quickly and creatively to challenges and opportunities that surface daily, which requires empowered decision making at all levels in an organization. Effective leadership must promote team and individual responsibility, and this can't be done by finger pointing and presuming to know what is best for others. Leaders must learn the fine art of retaining accountability for success without trying to rigidly control others or saddle them with specified codes of behavior. By shifting the spotlight to the people who are actually accomplishing the work, a leader fosters individual and team motivation and a sense of shared ownership.

The Mirage Hotel Resorts, headquartered in Las Vegas, was named in a *Fortune* magazine survey as the second most admired company in America, after Coca-Cola. This is an outstanding accomplishment in that The Mirage is the first service organization ever to be in the Top Ten. The Mirage has climbed steadily in recent years to become more admired than Procter and Gamble, RubberMaid, Johnson and Johnson, Microsoft, Intel, Hewlett-Packard, Merck, and Kodak. How could a Las Vegas gaming resort company accomplish that?

First, the company has a clear and elevating mission of outstanding service to its customers. Second, every employee has a clear individual mission of how his or her specific service dovetails with and supports that corporate mission. Third, and most important, each employee is encouraged to develop personal images of achievement in the form of life goals that have nothing to do with the corporate bottom line. By doing this, The Mirage is demonstrating to its family of employees that it cares about them as human beings, not just profit centers.

This nurturing of personal development has created an *esprit de corps* unparalleled in a company with over thirty thousand employees and makes it a place where those who work there trust one another. If you were to interview a waitress at The Mirage, you might discover someone who is being encouraged and helped to complete her college degree in marketing, her personal goal that goes well beyond functioning in her day-to-day role at the resort. When people believe that you have their best interests at heart, not just your own motives, they perform at the highest level possible.

MAPPING YOUR STRATEGY

The Power of Imagination • Developing Your Imagination • Getting Your Imagination to Work for You • Feedback from Cognitive Maps • Creating Positive Mental Images • Programming Your Inner Computer • Creating a Cognitive Map from One Idea • Expected Probability of Success • Cognitive Maps vs. Check-Off Lists • Visualization and Simulation

"Start thinking of your imagination as a skill you can develop rather than as an inborn level of ability that you're stuck with, that you either have or you don't."

"Unfortunately, the mind doesn't automatically gravitate toward truth, justice, and the best of everything. It gravitates toward what it is exposed to the most. The development or nondevelopment of your potential is linked directly to what you allow yourself to be exposed to."

"When you hold a strong, positive, relaxing image in your mind, your body responds with a lowered heart rate and decreased blood pressure, and all your muscles tend to relax. These functions take place automatically, unconsciously, and you're seldom aware their cause. You think they 'just happened.'"

"Unlike a kite, there is no string attached to how high and how far your goals may take you. They are limited only by the power of your imagination and the strength of your cognitive maps."

The Power of Imagination

The key to developing and maintaining your motivation is devising a strategy for accomplishing your goals. Goal setting and strategizing are pursuits that require a vivid imagination. How do we know this? Let's consider the theory of motivation developed by Dr. David McClelland of Harvard University.

McClelland began to formulate his theory based on the theory that all motivation comes from internal images. He wondered if highly motivated achievers actually imagined things differently from other people. To find the answer, he devised an ingenious study built around experiments he called "projective tests."

In these projective tests, McClelland used photographs or drawings depicting very basic scenes. For instance, in one photograph, a man is lying in bed with his eyes closed. His hand is raised and extended over an alarm clock on the table next to the bed. A window in the background is bright with the rays of early morning sunlight. McClelland asked his subjects to either describe the scene or tell a story about the person in the picture. To be sure that the responses were solely a function of motivational levels, the subjects for each test were people of the same sex, age, social background, and level of education.

This was McClelland's hypothesis: Since all motivation comes from internal images, the subjects in the study who demonstrated the highest and most active levels of imaginative power would become the most successful in achieving their personal goals. McClelland called these people "highly motivated achievers."

His experiments confirmed his hypothesis. He found that highly motivated achievers told action-filled, goal-oriented stories about the scenes. People with a lower motivational level generally gave bland, passive descriptions of the images.

For example, after viewing the photo of the man in bed holding out his hand toward the clock, a highly motivated achiever might describe a man who has to wake up early and get back to work on an important project that kept him up late the night before. Since highly motivated achievers imagine things so precisely, they would even describe details of the project.

On the other hand, McClelland's less-motivated subjects tended toward a passive interpretation of the scene. Many described a sleeping man who is reaching to turn off the alarm because it's Saturday and he doesn't have to go to work.

David McClelland was not content to accept the results

What does this picture suggest to you? Developing your imagination and allowing it to become an active part of your daily life is a sure way of becoming a highly motivated achiever.

of his first study at face value. He continued to ask himself the following question: What if individuals don't start off with a vivid imagination, but their professional position demands a vivid imagination? If, in fact, highly motivated achievers developed their imaginative abilities in response to their jobs, it would mean that their imaginative powers might not have played a role in motivating them to their level of extraordinary success.

In other words, how could McClelland be certain that the vivid imagination of these individuals was a *cause* of success and not a *result* of it?

He solved the problem by devising a second study that took fourteen years to complete. For four years, he gave his projective tests to college students. After giving the last projective test, he compiled the results and divided the students into two groups. The first group comprised those who showed the same traits as the highly motivated achievers of his earlier study, and the second group included those who were, at best, of only average motivation.

McClelland then had to wait ten years before he could complete his study, giving the students time to establish careers. He knew that if those with the most vivid imaginations were the same ones who had advanced furthest up the corporate ladder, he would have proof that a vivid, action-oriented imagination was a cause, a prerequisite in maintaining a highly motivated state, not just a result of success.

Ultimately, McClelland's findings confirmed his expectations. The highly motivated achievers, those students who told the most vivid, action-oriented stories in the projective tests, had most often chosen entrepreneurial careers involving a large amount of personal responsibility, initiative, and personal risk. The other students gravitated to nonentrepreneurial fields that required much less personal initiative. From the fourteen-year study, McClelland concluded that highly motivated achievers find the strength of their motivation in the power of their imagination.

McClelland's research may seem complex, but remember that there's one principle woven throughout all of his studies: The more vivid and real the image that motivates you, the stronger the motivation.

Developing Your Imagination

How can you benefit from the scientifically proven knowledge that imagination leads to success? First of all, you can start thinking of your imagination as a skill you can develop rather than as an inborn level of ability that you're stuck with, that you either have or you don't.

There is a universal law that teaches us: "If you don't use a skill, you lose it." If you've ever had a broken bone, you'll recall how the muscles were weak when the cast was removed, and it took weeks of exercise to bring strength back to those muscles.

If this is the result of a lack of use for six weeks, think of what will happen if you don't use those muscles for several months or several years? But just as you can bring back the strength to those muscles, you can cultivate the power of your creative imagination.

* * *

Here are a few exercises to stimulate your imagination:

1. Starting now, become acutely aware of your senses. Take in as many sights, sounds, smells, textures, and tastes as you can. Feel the texture of wet sand, cool grass, or plush carpet between your toes. Smell the countryside, the sea breeze, the fragrance of the trees and flowers, the aromas of a restaurant or bakery. Notice all the shapes and colors as you walk from one business appointment to another or relax on a weekend. Be more curious and aware about everything in the environment.

2. At business and social meetings, when you're listening to someone talk, try to form a mental image of the situation he or she describes. Allow the words to form images, feelings, and sensations.

3. When you speak, use words that are rich in visual imagery. Describe events and plans in more descriptive detail and with more enthusiasm. You'll enjoy a side benefit of becoming a better conversationalist and public speaker if you do.

4. Sit comfortably in a chair. Relax for a few seconds. Look at the objects around you. Now close your eyes. With your eyes closed, try to recall as many objects the room as you can. You'll be surprised at how many objects you will fail to recall. Continue this exercise as often as you can. As you recall an object, try to remember its color, shape, texture, and size. The key is to recall the object by its image, not its name.

5. Close your eyes and hold an object in your hand. Feel the object as you move it from one hand to the other. Trace the shape of the object with your fingers, and picture its shape at the same time in your mind.

6. In addition to listening to nonfiction audio tapes, purchase a fiction book on tape in which the narration has accompanying sound effects and is dramatized with actors and actresses. Put yourself in the plot as you listen. Next, buy a book on tape that is read by a narrator and add your own sounds, sights, and settings with your imagination. I do this when I read fiction novels and when I listen to drama on the radio.

7. Try watching television with your eyes closed. (Actually, this is the best way to watch most television!) It may sound silly, but this is the best way to exercise your imagination with that medium. That's why creativity in children is stifled so early in their lives. TV gives them little or no interaction and opportunity to stimulate their own power of imagination. All the images are provided.

8. Write your thoughts down on a regular basis. The best way is to buy a bound book with lined pages at a stationery store. You don't need to view it as a diary because most people have a stereotyped response to diaries. If you have a diary, they think, you are (a) writing your life story, (b) in love, (c) rebounding from a lost love, or (d) gathering evidence for a lawsuit. I carry a notebook in my briefcase and fill it with brainstorming ideas in the waiting lounge at airports, while at the same

time taking mental notes of everything and everyone I see during that so-called idle time.

With some effort, you can enhance and sharpen your imaginative skills and place yourself among the top five percent of achievers in the world who use their thoughts as a software library of rich memories and as a weather satellite to map and forecast a bright future.

Getting Your Imagination to Work for You

One of the wonderful aspects about human imagination is that it can break through the barriers of time and space; it can fly away to foreign lands and beyond; it can see things not as they are now, but as they can be; it can foretell the future, based upon our beliefs and expectations, in an almost uncanny way; it can draw the colorful mental images that we hope someday to turn into reality. Imagination is the beginning of creation. Whatever our imaginations become fixed upon will ultimately become real in our lives.

This can work for us or against us. Unfortunately, the mind doesn't automatically gravitate toward truth, justice, and the best of everything. It gravitates toward what it is exposed to the most. The development or nondevelopment of your potential is linked directly to what you allow yourself to be exposed to.

One of the most critical aspects of human development

is the influence of repeated viewing, listening, and verbalizing in shaping our lives. The information is processed by our brains, almost unnoticed. We don't react to it at first. But we do react later, when we aren't able to realize the basis for our reactions. In other words, our value systems are being formed whether we realize it or not.

That's why control of the imagination is so important. I mean "control" as in the way we drive a car. We want it to take us where we want to go; we don't want it to take us into a ditch or into another car, so we control its speed and direction. It's the only way to drive successfully.

Controlling the imagination—or freeing it along positive, growth-directed lines—will take us where we want to go. If we decide upon a goal we think is right and worthy of us, our imagination becomes like a pair of hands holding the picture in our minds, feeling every part of it, exploring it, examining every detail. And as we hold that picture in the hands of our imagination, the enormous power of our minds is set on achieving it. Soon, depending upon the difficulty and complexity of the image, it is ours . . . it is a reality, where before it was only a picture in our imagination.

You really can make your imagination a kind of genie to bring you almost anything you seriously decide upon. You imagine what you desire, you will what you imagine, and finally, you create what you will.

Feedback from Cognitive Maps

In his research, David McClelland discovered that another attribute shared by successful entrepreneurs and business executives was their insistence on frequent status reports to measure their progress. But this does not hold true in all fields. In creative professions, such as scientific research or the arts, achievers often work for long periods of time without knowing how or if their efforts are truly progressing toward their goal.

The American novelist Walker Percy said that he often labored over an idea for six months or more without realizing that it couldn't work out, and he would have to abandon it. And think about all the medical scientists dedicating their efforts seeking a cure for cancer and other life-threatening diseases. Consider how many false starts and blind alleys there have been. Many more hours have been devoted to imagined cures that did not prove to be viable than on the ones that did. Nonetheless, if these scientists had never explored every avenue seeking the truth, the one who finally won the Nobel Prize may also have travelled the same dead-end path and never made the important discovery. In a real sense, the other scientists were all the Nobel laureate's collaborators. The success belongs to them all. Researchers and artists have to pursue their goals without frequent feedback and inputs on how well they are doing, and this takes a special kind of intrinsic motivation.

In business, sales, law, and the majority of other fields, highly motivated achievers desire as much information on their own progress as they can obtain, and they want this information to be as concrete and specific as possible. It doesn't have to be external feedback or a progress report from someone else. Most often, this monitoring of progress is purely internal. In addition to using vivid images to formulate and set their ultimate achievements, they employ these same vivid images all along the road to achievement as directional signs.

Imagine that you're driving home. Think about the steps you take. You start the car, turn left at the light on Main Street, take a right to the expressway, and head west to the foothills. These interim steps break down your final objective, in this case reaching home for supper, into easily segmented steps.

Psychologists call this interior model or template a "cognitive map."

The cognitive map gives you an image by which to check progress at every moment. If you expect to reach a landmark in less time than you are taking on this particular trip, you might speed up a little to get back on pace.

Scientists refer to the process of adjusting your actions to fit your image of what is right as using a "negative feedback loop." For example, an opera singer has an audial image in her mind of what C-sharp sounds like. As she sings, she adjusts the pitch of her vocalized note to match the note in her head. Every day, you use these negative feedback loops to direct your behavior according to the cognitive map in your mind.

Gary Player, one of golf's immortals, gave an impromptu demonstration of this process during the Masters Tournament a number of years ago. He lined up his shot, hit a solid seven iron, and laid the ball down softly thirty feet past the pin. For me, that would have been a sensational shot. For Player, it was a long putt for a birdie, and he wanted to correct his error.

Without changing his expression, he looked at his caddie, who handed him his eight iron. Player walked back to where the ball had been, went into his stance, glanced at his target, and then swung through, watching the imaginary ball land dead to the pin. You could almost see him thinking to himself, "That's the way to play this shot. The eight iron was the proper club. Next time, I'll put it right there."

Creating Positive Mental Images

Much of the visual, audial, and sensory information fed into your cognitive map stays there. Billions of integrated and separate items of input over a lifetime are all there awaiting retrieval.

They can never be willfully erased. You can override them with stronger, more vivid messages or modify their effects over a period of time. What has always amazed me is the research reported during brain surgery, in which patients whose brain cells were stimulated with a thin electrode described the sensation of reliving scenes from the past. Their recall was so strong and vivid that all details were there again—sounds, colors, people, shapes, places, and odors. They were not just remembering, but reliving the experiences!

Just as our bodies react to images from the external world, they also react to mental images. The American physiologist Edmund Jacobsen has done studies showing that when a person imagines running, small but measurable amounts of contraction actually take place in the leg muscles.

In the same way, when you create a vivid, frightening image in your mind, your body responds with a quickened pulse, elevated blood pressure, sweating, goosebumps, and dryness of the mouth.

I remember feeling all of those symptoms when I was twelve years old and my friends dared me to run through a farmer's pasture that had the biggest, ugliest, meanest bull I'd ever seen corralled there. Above the fence that we were supposed to crawl through before sprinting safely to the other side was a cryptic sign for us would-be trespassers: "Don't attempt to cross this field unless you can do it in 9.9 seconds. The bull can do it in 10!" That sign motivated several involuntary muscle spasms in me.

Conversely, when you hold a strong, positive, relaxing image in your mind, your body responds with a lowered heart rate and decreased blood pressure, and all your muscles tend to relax. These functions take place automatically, unconsciously, and you're seldom aware their cause. You think they "just happened."

Our motivations arise from every part of the brain, but they all involve just two mental functions: memory and imagination. A strong emotional reaction, such as fear, results from events we remember from the past that upset us, or when we anticipate that something bad will happen in the future. Fear often motivates us to stay where we are—to freeze—or to move away from the cause of the fear. But a strong memory or anticipation of well-being will attract us, motivating us to move toward the source.

If you put your hand on a hot stove, you instinctively recoil and snatch it away. You don't even think about it. The same thing occurs when someone throws a ball at you. Even if the thrower says "Think fast," you have already made the decision to duck or catch the ball without consciously thinking. We take reflexive reactions for granted, and indeed, we would have a difficult time surviving without them.

Programming Your Inner Computer

When we speak about cognition and the cognitive map, we are talking about the most rational, most conscious actions of the human mind. Most of our mind's operation does not involve cognition. It involves instincts, emotions, and regulation of involuntary body functions.

Cognition is unique. It is the only type of thinking which we can direct. When psychologists talk about our cognitive maps, they stress that when motivation is vivid and strong, we actively direct our cognitive powers.

We can direct our reason to begin working on a solution to a problem. We can direct our imagination to begin to formulate and shape a concept. And we can direct our memory to try to remember what happened on a certain day at a certain time.

Cognitive mapmaking is fundamental to directing inner processes for goal achievement. The instructions don't have to be memorized, but we need to have a sense of their meaning in words and images that we can repeat internally.

What we are doing is programming our own on-board navigational computers. In the future, all commercial and private vehicles will have navigational guidance computers so we won't drive around in circles during a family outing. (Like most men, I'm too proud to stop at a service station and ask for directions. We just keep driving until the fuel gauge reads "Empty," and then we use the excuse of needing gas to casually ask the attendant how to get back to the main road.)

I view my cognitive maps as a chef might look at an interesting recipe. If I am unfamiliar with the process, I'll either get a recipe book or watch another chef prepare the dish and observe and take notes. After I have read the instructions and experimented a number of times, I might be able to recall the words: *start with a tortilla shell, add refried beans, shredded beef or turkey, add tomatoes, lettuce, jalapenos, sour cream, guacamole, cilantro and grated cheese on top.* Eventually, I might not see or hear any detailed instructions at all. I might simply see all of the ingredients coming together in the completed Tostada Salad Supreme.

When I cook anything except steak, chicken, or fish, I need to follow the recipes closely. But my wife, Susan, is a marvelous gourmet cook, so she alters ingredients and amounts, improvises when she discovers she is out of one particular item, and keeps improving as she goes. She has a vivid, creative cognitive map when it comes to cooking or any aspect of interior design of buildings and homes. Instead of going down a list of procedures, she sees the completed room or house in advance, from a combination of recollections she has observed in her travels or in magazines; and from an active imagination, from the inspiration of what the room or home could be like.

These are all intuitive powers that stem from the usage of cognitive maps to envision your final goal and the steps you need to accomplish it. Summoning motivation is easy when the target is in plain sight.

Creating a Cognitive Map from One Idea

When I was researching the history of the building of the Brooklyn Bridge as a major illustration for the ideas in this book, I became engrossed with the story of how the first bridge was built over Niagara Falls. To build a bridge over a giant gorge, first you have to get a line over the canyon, from one side to the other. Easier said than done at Niagara Falls.

The engineers couldn't cross the falls in a boat to take the line from one side to the other because the boat would go over the falls. And the airplane hadn't been invented yet. The distance also was beyond the bow-and-arrow range, which had been a common method at the time of getting the first line across to build a bridge.

The designing engineer, Charles Ellet, pondered the question until his cognitive powers created a map. He decided that, while solving the problem, he also would have some fun and generate some publicity for the project. Ellet sponsored a kite flying contest and offered five dollars to the first person who could fly a kite across the gorge and let it go low enough to the ground for someone to be able to grab the string. In 1849, five dollars was a prize similar to winning the lottery today. The boy who won the prize relished his accomplishment until his death, nearly 80 years later.

It all began with an idea and one thin kite string across the gorge. The kite string was used to pull a cord across, then a line, and then a rope. Next came an iron-wire cable and then steel cables, until a structure strong enough to build a suspension bridge was in place.

Think of that kite string as a single thought in your mind. The more vivid and clear the thought, and the more you come back to it, the stronger it becomes—like a string to a rope to a cable. Each time you rethink it or dwell on it or layer it with other thoughts, you are creating a cognitive map, like building a bridge over Niagara Falls. That map will become so strong and real that your mind and body will automatically respond to it and improvise when the ravine widens suddenly or the environment changes.

But unlike a kite, there is no string attached to how high and how far your goals may take you. They are limited only by the power of your imagination and the strength of your cognitive maps.

Expected Probability of Success

Imagine that your goal is to drive from St. Louis to Houston to see someone very special to you. Imagine that you are armed with a road map that shows you the alternate routes between the two cities. According to my pocket road atlas, there are 780 miles between St. Louis and Houston. That's a long way to drive, and there are innumerable turns and highway changes you would have to make to complete the trip successfully. It would be very easy to get lost and end up in the middle of the Texas desert.

But don't forget: You have a map!

Obviously, the map is not your motivating force to travel, but it definitely strengthens your motivation considerably. The map gives you confidence.

No matter how much you may want to see your friend or relative, you're not going to set out on the highway until you confidently believe you can actually reach Houston. The map enables you to believe that.

Let me be a little more specific about maps, because this is a very important concept.

You see, all useful maps have two elements in common. First, a map shows your destination—the place that will require your motivation, effort, and time to reach. Second, and this is crucial, most maps illustrate more than one way to get there.

If the Interstate is closed, the map shows how you can take a detour. With the map, you always know where Houston is; you know you'll arrive eventually, and this motivates you to stay on the road.

The confidence you get from having a map reinforces the theme of intrinsic motivation. The stronger the power of the motivating image, the more powerful the force of the motivation. A large part of the power of the image lies in it being real to you—that is, in your own belief that you'll be able to take successful action toward your goal.

Think about that the next time you're facing a challenge. See the positive result you want to achieve. Know the result is within your reach the way you know you can drive to a distant city.

Once again, the power of this kind of thinking has been scientifically proven. Researcher John Atkinson found that a high correlation exists between the strength of a motivation and the expected probability of success.

Notice the word *expected.* The strength of a motivation has little to do with the actual probability of success. It all depends on whether you *believe* you'll be successful.

Atkinson described the relationship between motivation and expectation with a phrase he coined: "Expected Utility of Success." He explained that our true motivation was equal to the strength of our desire, which he termed "Utility of Success," multiplied by our expected probability of success. You can express it as a formula:

Desire x Expectation = Motivation.

Until you study the map showing the way from St. Louis to Houston, the probability of success will seem much lower to you than it will after you have seen the different roads that lead to your destination. This indicates that no matter how badly we want something, the motivation to try for it will remain very low until we believe we have a good chance of actually attaining it.

Cognitive Maps vs. Check-Off Lists

For most people, goals exist in the form of a check-off list, a series of commands to be carried out in a particular order, with the successful completion of each command necessary for the initiation of the next. This can work fine . . . until something goes wrong; until there's a road block or a detour, and it is impossible to check off the next item on the list.

This has happened to me several times when I have rented a car and received a computerized printout with specific directions to a destination.

When one of the items has changed because of an accident on the road, a flooded area after a heavy rain, or construction, I find myself hopelessly lost and have to pull out my trusty road atlas.

A map is better than a check-off list. Maps reorient you and offer you alternate routes. As long as you can place yourself on the map, it will show you where you are both in relation to your starting point and your destination.

The same is true with any goal. If the way is blocked, you can consult the cognitive map in your mind and pick a different direction to the goal. That is the value of experience.

When you have successfully weathered a difficult or challenging ordeal, you not only have a reservoir of vivid cognitive maps to use again, you also know you can get through the next challenge and achieve the next goal.

Visualization and Simulation

Visualization requires active use of your imagination. When a person holds a vivid, fearful picture in his or her imagination, the body responds through the autonomic nervous system with a feeling of uneasiness, upset stomach, elevated pulse and blood pressure, sweating, and dryness of mouth. Conversely, when an individual holds a pleasant, relaxing image in his or her mind, the body responds with a lowered heart rate, decreased blood pressure, and relaxed muscles. That's why, in my work with Olympic athletes and astronauts, we used the technique of VMBR, which stands for "Visuo-Motor Behavior Rehearsal." Because of the direct relationship between visualization and actual performance, we taught the Olympians and astronauts to be masters in the art of simulation.

I'll never forget what the great Russian sprinter and Olympic gold medalist Valeri Borzov told me in an interview about his approach to the hundred-meter sprint finals. Borzov said, "By learning to draw a mental picture of the race while I was still in the starting blocks, I was able to react to the starting gun with split-second speed. And when the shot was fired, my inner computer—programmed to get me out of the motionless state—switched on and took over, projecting me forward about ten meters ahead of where I was actually running."

If you would like a vivid example of how simulation works, you might visit a NASA center or an airline pilot training facility. One such facility, operated by American Airlines in Dallas, is open for public tours. Through the use of interactive video and computer technology, the pilots "fly" the simulator through every type of weather condition and foreseeable emergency. They taxi from the ramp, take off, fly to a city, and land—never leaving the ground, of course, but experiencing nearly every physical and emotional sensation that could be encountered on a actual flight.

Trial lawyers and sales representatives simulate by going through their presentations in front of peers in as realistic a setting as possible. Seminar leaders, teachers, actors, and other performers also learn to perfect the art of visualization. The beauty of the simulation skills is that it allows you to perform and get it right without the fear of failure creating stifling or choking pressure. When you face actual high-performance achievement (the real thing), it will be almost like another simulation drill.

With visualization, setting new sights and reaching for new heights is no longer an uncomfortable prospect; it's an exciting, stimulating challenge.

SETTING YOUR GOALS

Focusing Your Energy • Following Your Dreams and Goals • Gathering Information for Goals • Creating Effective Sub-Goals • Goals and Intrinsic Motivation • Goal Setting and Job Satisfaction • Mistakes in Goal Setting • Three Profound Truths • Evaluating Your Goals • Creating Focused Goals • Resource Allocation • Putting Your Goals in Writing • Setting Goals so Everyone Wins • A Life of Creative Goal Setting

"When goals are focused and in logical progression, they produce a driving force in the human mind with awesome creativity and power of accomplishment."

"One of the most important lessons I've learned is that, while we all say we don't have enough time to do justice to our personal goals, each of us has all the time there is."

"By breaking down our long-term goals into more easily realizable sub-goals, we can maintain a high expected probability of success for each segment of the task. The initial sub-goal seems within reach, so we keep moving toward it."

"Achievement is a motivator because achievement is its own best reward. When we set and reach a goal, the payoff is the internal sense of accomplishment."

"People who passively assume that everything will somehow work out in the end can hardly be termed creative. They're not creating their lives, they're just hoping that something good will happen to them."

Focusing Your Energy

Without clear, specific goals, we toil in a job but never build a career. Without goals, work becomes a necessary interruption between weekends. Weekends, to many people, are an escape from a weekly prison of purposelessness. Goals provide the the energy source—the motivation—that powers our lives. One of the best ways we can get the most from the energy we have is to focus it. That's what goals can do for us: concentrate our energy.

Philosopher Harry Emerson Fosdick said: "No horse gets anywhere until it is harnessed. No stream or gas ever drives anything until it is confined. No Niagara is ever turned into light and power until it is tunneled. And no life ever grows great until it is focused, dedicated, and disciplined."

No better example of focused energy can be found than that of laser technology. A laser is an example of a powerfully concentrated form of energy. The word *laser* is an acronym for "Light Amplification by Stimulated Emission of Radiation." Basically, it's a rod of light that amplifies, or strengthens, light energy. A laser produces a beam of very pure light in which all the waves are exactly in step and of exactly the same wavelength.

In contrast, a floodlight, being unfocused and nondirectional, illuminates a general area, but it has no real power to do anything more than flood that general area with light. With vague, nonspecific goals, individuals may be likened to floodlights, each trying to find his or her way somewhere, somehow, and hoping to project enough light to be noticed and appreciated for being there.

An person with focused, concentrated goals is like a laser. A laser, compared to a floodlight, can do a variety of spectacular things, from performing delicate eye surgery to triggering a thermonuclear explosion. It can carry over a hundred thousand times more information than a telephone line and can produce twenty thousand lines of print in sixty seconds. It can drill through something as hard as a diamond or as soft as rubber.

Scientists believe that in the future, lasers will help us communicate with distant galaxies and propel rockets and starships faster than we can imagine and more economically than today's airplanes transport us around the country. Thirty years ago, no one had ever seen a laser beam. But in the twenty-first century, through laser fusion, this concentrated form of light may provide the world with unlimited energy to meet every human need for survival and growth.

Laser technology and goal technology are based upon the same scientific principles. When light waves are concentrated and in step, they produce a beam of pure light with incredible power. When goals are focused and in logical progression, they produce a driving force in the human mind with awesome creativity and power of accomplishment.

Following Your Dreams and Goals

Perhaps the greatest torture that could be devised would be for us to be forced, in our later years, to watch a continuously repeating videotape of the lives we could have led had we dared to believe in and pursue the dreams and goals that were available and attainable in our lifetimes.

One of the most important lessons I've learned is that, while we all say we don't have enough time to do justice to our personal goals, each of us has all the time there is. I also learned that none of us really has a time-management problem. We really have a dream- and goal-focus problem. We spend too much energy worrying about the things we want to do but can't instead of concentrating on doing the things we can do but don't. It is the regret for something we did or didn't do yesterday and the apprehension of what tomorrow may bring that's the biggest energy drain on our life force.

A dream is your creative vision for your life in the future.

It's what you would like your life to become. A goal is what, specifically, you intend to make happen. Goals should be just out of your present reach, but not out of sight. Two great tragedies in life are to have never had great goals for yourself and to have fully reached them, so tomorrow holds no eager anticipation of challenge.

Many individuals become spectators, resigned to experience success vicariously through others' accomplishments. They can see success for others, but they can't imagine it for themselves. Dreams and goals are previews of coming attractions in your life. You can be either the script writer, the star performer, and the producer of an Oscar-winning epic life or an extra in "B" movie that someone else wrote and directed for you. Which is it to be?

Gathering Information for Goals

Deciding upon and achieving your goals both require much outside information and planning. Here are some practical guidelines for gathering and checking sources of information in your quest to realize your goals:

1. *Network with proven experience.* Always check the track record of your mentors. Make sure they've actually succeeded in the field you're in, not just succeeded in writing or lecturing about it. Track records don't mean how much money they have made, how popular they are, and how many TV infomercials they have done. If possible, determine if the mentor or role model has actually done what you want to do.

2. *Check your own information sources.* Most people rely on their parents, friends, the media, and a variety of indi-

viduals with questionable credentials for their knowledge base on goal achievement. You will be amazed at how frequently you ingest information from the environment that is no more than speculation based upon biased opinion.

3. *Use idle time to learn.* Listen to audio books and seminars in your car during commute time. Watch how-to videos or use educational multimedia software during breaks from work. Read books and browse through magazines looking for breakthrough ideas from other fields you can apply to your own. Many innovations and inventions are applications borrowed from other industries.

4. *Consider investing in a laptop computer.* You should have a central repository for all of your ideas.

5. *Seek out idea-oriented colleagues.* Highly motivated achievers draw out the creativity of others at every opportunity. They're listeners who ask questions and then absorb knowledge like sponges. There is always someone who knows where or how to find out what you need to know.

6. *Develop a relationship with the finest university near your home or business.* Get on the list for continuing education seminars and courses. Become a frequent face at the university library.

7. *If you're young and relatively inexperienced, network*

with more mature, seasoned entrepreneurs. Your enthusiasm and desire, combined with their richness and experience in cognitive mapmaking can be very powerful. If you're a veteran executive with a lot of experience, seek out a young entrepreneur who may be more open to new ways to achieving their goal and who hasn't learned the meaning of setbacks and defeats. Providing them with your valuable input and advice may make all the difference in his or her life . . . and your own!

A commitment to researching the information that will help you create and achieve your goals is very important. Become an avid learner, soaking up knowledge in all of its forms, from books and audio tapes to the experience of seasoned professionals.

Creating Effective Sub-Goals

Highly motivated achievers know their destination and the sub-goals they need to reach along the way, and they continually refer to their cognitive maps to make sure they taking the best road to success. They leave themselves great flexibility in dealing with the day-to-day obstacles and distractions that inevitably arise.

By breaking down our long-term goals into more easily realizable sub-goals, we can maintain a high expected probability of success for each segment of the task. The initial sub-goal seems within reach, so we keep moving toward it.

As we reach each of our sub-goals, we begin to see that we can achieve our more complex, long-term objective. The perceived probability of success for the whole enterprise is rises accordingly.

Motivationalists in sports and industry have studied goal setting carefully. In our many years in working with Olympic athletes, for example, my colleagues and I emphasized that the decathlon was a series of ten sub-goals, and a marathon race had a multiple number of sub-goals and benchmarks along the route. Every gold-medal winner, whether in sports or in business, uses his or her cognitive map as an aerial view of the race and then uses sub-goals as both progress guides and positive motivational reinforcements.

For a goal or sub-goal to be vivid, meaningful, and have any real pulling power at all, it must be very specific. Even the most marvelous computer ever created, the human mind, cannot focus and act upon nebulous, general thoughts. The more specific the input into your mind, the more detailed and vivid the image creating the motivational force to achievement.

One of the most highly regarded scientists studying goals and motivation is Professor Edwin Locke of the University of Maryland. In one recent study, he found that ninety-six percent of test subjects did better if they were given specific and challenging goals than if they were simply instructed to do their best. Numerous other studies have confirmed this finding.

I find this particularly interesting in that it is very common today to try to motivate our children and employees by telling them simply to do the best they can. The problem is that children and many adults really don't know what their best is and therefore don't have a good idea of what they're aiming for.

A disturbing result discovered by these studies was that in society today, while most people are trying to "do their best," only about four percent of the population actually do perform near the top of their abilities. This is why it is important to be motivated intrinsically—out of love and belief in what you are doing—and then to arm yourself with a cognitive map and sub-goals showing specifically what you are going to do every step of the way.

So again, the more vividly we imagine something, the stronger the motivating force it exerts. Specific goals are stronger because they are more thoroughly imagined and more tangible. Telling a basketball player to try to pull in ten rebounds per game paints a much clearer target than telling him to go out on the court and do his best.

Professor Locke also has placed great emphasis on reaching the proper level of aspiration, which in this context refers to the difficulty of the goal. Locke has found that, over long periods of time, challenging goals are effective in maintaining motivation and raising performance if—and this is a big *if*—the goals are actually attainable.

He learned this by studying the use of goal setting in a United Way fundraising campaign. When United Way campaign managers set a goal of increasing the amount raised by twenty percent over the previous year, certainly a challenging assignment, the money raised actually went up an average of twenty-four percent. The goal was difficult to reach, but not impossible. On the other hand, a different group of managers who set much greater, virtually impossible, fundraising goals had much lower increases in performance, and some performances actually declined when the goals appeared especially outrageous.

These managers no doubt would have been happy to accept a twenty-five percent increase in productivity but thought that by setting the highest goals imaginable, they might motivate their workers to play over their heads. They failed to take into account the importance of perceived probability of success in the creation and maintenance of a high level of motivation. Their employees could see that the goals their supervisors set were unattainable, and the employees lost their motivation to try even for attainable improvements in their performance.

So set a specific goal that's ten to twenty-five percent beyond your current reach, and break it down into reinforcing sub-goals along the way. This is the easiest and most effective way to achieve your dreams.

Goals and Intrinsic Motivation

Professor Gary Latham, a frequent partner of Edwin Locke, has looked into the relationship between goal setting and intrinsic motivation. In several studies, the most famous of which involved truckers who haul lumber, Latham found that just goal setting alone can be enough to support an individual's intrinsic motivation. No extrinsic motivation had to be added: No bonuses. No contests. No perks.

The truck drivers in the study had tended to load their trucks to only sixty percent of capacity. This meant more runs than necessary and reduced profits. For a long time, the truckers' supervisors had exhorted them to load more fully, but this didn't result in any significant improvement in the truckers' performance.

Finally, the supervisors were instructed to give the truckers the goal of loading their trucks to ninety percent of legal capacity by weight.

The result: the truckers actually came closer to hitting ninety-four percent than the stipulated goal of ninety percent. The performance improvement not only was dramatic, it was sustained. Productivity steadily improved until the study was terminated almost a year after the goals were put in place.

The truck drivers had not been given any extrinsic incentive to improve; instead, the goal was set in a way that stimulated and brought out the power of their intrinsic motivation. With a specific goal firmly in place, the drivers knew at what level they would have to perform to reach professional competence. In this way, the company used goal setting to encourage intrinsic motivation.

Simple encouragement for the truckers to load their trucks more fully had no measurable effect at all. But using specific goals to tie the drivers' professional self-esteem to the attainment of a certain level of performance changed everything.

Goal Setting and Job Satisfaction

An important study of white-collar workers done by Frederick Herzberg and his associates led to the conclusion that the factors producing job satisfaction were entirely separate from those causing job *dis*satisfaction.

In other words, when it comes to motivation, *satisfaction* and *dissatisfaction* aren't opposites. The opposite of *satisfaction* is *no satisfaction.*

Herzberg called factors which produced satisfaction "motivators." He identified some of them as recognition, achievement, responsibility, chance for growth, opportunity for advancement, and feelings of increased competence. The factors that led to dissatisfaction were the extrinsic motivators, which he called "hygienic" factors: company policies, salary, fringe benefits, relationship with supervisors, working conditions, and job security.

Herzberg stated that motivation is present in direct

proportion to the inner satisfaction of a job. If there's no inner satisfaction, it doesn't necessarily lead to active dissatisfaction. The individual will probably continue to work for the company, but he or she won't be setting higher and higher goals.

Scott Meyers built on Herzberg's theory in a six-year study of Texas Instruments. The results were published in the *Harvard Business Review*. Texas Instruments commissioned the study in the belief that company goals could be best served by providing opportunities for employees to achieve their personal goals. An interesting concept, isn't it? Included in the study were scientists, engineers, manufacturing supervisors, hourly technicians, and assemblers.

Myers found that achievement is a motivator because achievement is its own best reward. When we set and reach a goal, the payoff is the internal sense of accomplishment. Only twenty-four percent of the participants were motivated by the prospect of recognition for reaching their goal. And the opposite of achievement, failure, was not a demotivator, but a dissatisfier. Only twelve percent felt failure was bad because it resulted in a lack of recognition.

The implications of these powerful studies are clear. For achieving work-related goals, there should be an opportunity to feel a sense of achievement, to feel that your efforts are being taken seriously and that you've been given responsibility. But if you feel you're being taken for granted or there's no chance for growth in your work, the environment is not conducive to the achievement of goals, yours or the company's.

Mistakes in Goal Setting

Three of the most common mistakes people make in goal-setting are misstating a goal, setting goals in negative terms, and concentrating on goals others set for them instead of self-set goals.

The misstating or ill-defining of goals is especially common when it comes to formulating sub-goals on the path to a larger goal. Suppose, for example, your goal is to drive home from work. In between you and home there is a big hill. You know you must get beyond the hill to reach home, and every day you travel on a beautiful, country road over the hill toward home.

You might misstate your sub-goal as "getting over the hill." But one day, the mountain road is closed due to a rock slide. Your sub-goal would have been better stated as "getting past the hill," which would include driving around it. By misstating goals and sub-goals, we often limit our horizons and alternatives when the first roadblocks occur.

The second common mistake is to set goals in negative terms. For example, an employee might set a goal of not being late so often.

Whether its a goal to lose weight, not talk so loud, or not get so upset so often when things go wrong, you need to stay away from "negative," or "reverse," goal setting. The mind can't focus on the reverse of a concept, so the negative, or reverse, of a goal becomes a fear. Being late reminds the employee of the problem, not the solution.

The properly stated goals should be "I'm an on-time person" or "I remain calm and relaxed under pressure." These are positive goals that pull us toward the desired result.

Finally, since we know all real motivation springs from within, it's important to set your own goals and to help those close to you to do the same. Don't try to buy into other people's goals, and don't expect anybody to buy into yours. Given the chance, a person will create more exciting and challenging goals for himself or herself than parents or company managers would ever dream of creating for them.

Avoiding these mistakes in goal setting can save you from spending weeks, months, and even years of your life going in frustrated, unmotivated circles. Your goals will be brought into clear focus, and your chances of achieving them will rise dramatically.

Three Profound Truths

There are three profound truths that are helpful when it is time to define your life-forming goals. I have written them in my personal journal, and I strongly recommend that you write them down in your own journal so they will always be strong motivating factors in your life.

First, make certain your goals are your own, not those of others. No goal set for you by others will ever be sought with the same passion, effort, and time commitment as one you set for yourself. The ones *you* want are those you will be more likely to achieve. Here is what actress Louise Fletcher says about this: "I'm doing what I should have done years ago, which is finding out who I am and what I want. I want to have a choice. And when I make decisions through choice, not duty, it has to be better for me and for the people who love me and the people I love."

Second, make certain your goals, though they are yours

alone, benefit others too. In his book *The Greatest Thing in the World,* Henry Drummond states that "there is no happiness in having or getting, but only in giving. Half of the world is on the wrong scent in the pursuit of happiness. They think it consists of having and getting and in being served by others. It consists of giving and serving others."

Or follow the advice of philosopher William James, who said simply: "The great use of life is to spend it for something that outlasts it."

Third, make certain that your goals are not measured in comparison to others. Avoid the tendency to measure your own progress by looking over the fence at greener pastures. There are many others who have started a little earlier than you, and you may become discouraged if you see them harvesting success when some of your seeds are barely in the ground. Comparison rarely benefits anyone. You'll always be able to find someone smarter, younger, older, wiser, richer, more clever, better looking, or working harder or more effectively than you are.

When you make comparisons in which you place yourself beneath others, you're in for discouragement that will keep you procrastinating and perhaps even from seriously pursuing your life goals. You can also find others who don't measure up to what you have become or are aspiring to be. Avoid the tendency to compare yourself to them as well. You'll lower your goals and settle for average when you could have excellence. You may come to think that you deserve more success than others or that success lies ahead for you no matter what you do. Both are false assumptions.

In truth, success isn't a pie with a limited number of pieces. The success of others has very little bearing on your own success. You and everyone you know can become successful without anyone suffering setbacks, harm, or downturns. Neither is your success measured by what others say or accomplish. Only you can truly define your success, and only you can measure it.

Evaluating Your Goals

Following are six important questions to ask yourself as you define and evaluate your goals.

First, as I've already discussed: *Are you sure that this is something you really want?* Or is it something you "ought to" want or even something that someone else wants for you? It's worth taking some time to think about this because often the answer is far from obvious. By being totally honest with yourself on this first all-important point, you'll immediately eliminate some of the biggest reasons why people fail to accomplish what they set out to do.

Second: *Is your goal specifically defined and stated?* By creating a vivid mental picture of exactly what you want to achieve, you make it possible for your mind to accept the goal on a subconscious level, thus working toward the goal even when you're not consciously thinking about it. Allow yourself to see the novel you're going to write, the house you're going to buy, or the distance you're going to run. By visualizing your goals in this way, you'll be using one of the most powerful new scientific discoveries on how the human mind really works.

Third: *Is my goal dynamic and flexible, or have I misstated it by defining it too narrowly?* This is the other side of the coin of the previous question. After all, one of the biggest breakthroughs in twentieth-century medicine—the discovery of penicillin by Alexander Fleming—was made by accident when a bit of mold fell into a culture dish where Fleming was routinely working with some common bacteria. Whatever Fleming's purpose may have been for his routine experiment, he certainly put it aside to pursue the dramatic new possibilities that had opened up. Fleming's ultimate goal was to make the greatest possible contribution to science, and his cognitive map provided him with the flexibility for doing that.

Fourth: *Is your goal set realistically? In other words, is it challenging but attainable?* Will this goal really help you to act effectively on your intrinsic motivation? For the vast majority of things in life, hard work and commitment can overcome virtually any limitation. On the other hand, it's also a fact that many people like to sing in the shower, but only a small number are really cut out to be opera stars. You may be part of that select number, but if you're not, and your main goal is to be an opera singer, you can be setting yourself up for a great deal of frustration. In formulating your goals, you should come up with a realistic assessment of your capabilities and then dedicate yourself to stretching them to the limit, or even a bit beyond. That's certainly a challenge, but it's an attainable one.

Fifth: *How can progress toward this goal be measured?* Measuring improvement is easy for someone competing in a decathlon. It's as simple as looking at the dial of a stopwatch. But what if your goal is more abstract? Suppose you have a hot temper, for instance, and you're deeply motivated to bring your temper under control. Here you're dealing with emotions, and those can't be measured with a watch.

You could end up saying to yourself, "Let's see, I think I was angrier today when I spilled the milk than I was yesterday when I stubbed my toe. But wait a minute, my toe really hurt..." To measure your progress toward that kind of inner goal, you should focus on the external, demonstrable evidence. Did you raise your voice today? Did you slam down the telephone? Some of the most worthwhile goals can be the most difficult to measure. The key is to discover how they express themselves objectively.

And sixth: *Does this goal lead me to concrete planning?* Am I making my cognitive map? This is the logical continuation of measuring progress. Once you've formulated your goal in a measurable way, formulate a plan that will lead you to the desired result, a plan that takes into account the setbacks and detours that you're certain to encounter along the way. Suppose you had to measure the distance around your house without using a yardstick or a tape measure. Just saying, "Well, it's bigger than a breadbox" won't do the trick. So you decide how you can objectively express the distance . . . by a certain number of footsteps, for instance. Then you create a cognitive map that puts the measurement into action. You decide to walk in a counter-clockwise direction. If you encounter your neighbor and the two of you talk for twenty minutes about baseball, you'll still have both your method of measurement and your plan for implementing it, and you can start right over from the point at which you left off.

After you have answered these six questions and set your goal, list all the benefits you expect to derive from reaching it. This is a form of visualization, but right now you're focusing not so much on the goal itself as on the results of achieving it. Notice that I am talking about listing the benefits, which are intrinsic, and not about rewards, which are extrinsic. If your goal is to be the top salesperson in your corporation, the benefits might be heightened self-esteem, belief in your sales ability, and the confidence to start your own company. The rewards would be increased commissions and the Salesperson-of-the-Year award.

And now some final questions: Are you willing to pay the price to reach your goal, in terms of time and effort? Is the motivating image strong enough to keep drawing you toward it? If it's a sub-goal, is it clear in your mind exactly how this sub-goal will increase the perceived probability of success of reaching your major objective?

If the answers to any of these final questions is negative, you adjust, restate, or reset. If your answers are positive, release your brakes and start imagining!

All of this has been documented for you by scientific research and psychological fact. Pay no attention to the disbelievers, pessimists, and doomsayers. They have an excuse for their failures.

You, on the other hand, have all the reasons in the world to achieve your grandest dreams. Remember the magic formula: *Imagination + Motivation = Realization!*

Creating Focused Goals

Let me share with you five "powers" that will enable you to create focused goals and achieve your dreams:

The Power of the Positive. Your goals must be stated in a positive manner. Winners dwell on the rewards of success, while losers dwell on the penalties of failure. In other words, instead of focusing on "not being late," "not being fat," "not being in debt," or "not working for the company," winners focus on images of achievement, such as "I'm an on-time person," "I am lean and in great shape," I am financially free," and "I am creating wealth and success in my own business." Remember that your mind cannot concentrate on the reverse of an idea, so keep your goals framed in the positive.

The Power of the Present. Your goals must be stated in the present tense. Your long-term memory stores information in real time, which is present tense. The reason your memory stores information in the present tense is obvious. Can you imagine what would happen if your mind decided to remind your heart to beat tomorrow? Or what if it put the command for breathing, eating, or calorie burning on next week's agenda?

If you say, "I want to weigh 165 pounds by next summer," your long-term memory won't even consider working on the goal because it is so far away. It will simply dismiss it as something that might come up later in the distant future. So by combining the first two powers, you will have your goals framed in the present and in the positive. Some examples: "I weigh a lean, trim, healthy 165 pounds." "I am financially free and spending time with my family." "My business generates $1.5 million in annual sales." "I have a high degree of achievement motivation."

The Power of the Personal. I cannot stress this enough. Your images of achievement must be *yours*. They cannot be your spouse's goals, your company's goals, your friend's goals, or your significant other's goals. They also can't be the goals that the media or the filmmakers are placing in front of you. Goals that are created by others for you have very little staying power. If it is your boss's goal, for instance, and you hit a major obstacle or challenge, it is easy to throw up your hands and say, "I knew it wasn't going to work, anyway. The boss's goals never work!" No goal set for you by others will ever be sought with the same passion, effort, commitment, or motivation as the one you set for yourself.

As you set your goals, I would caution you to share them

Stating your personal goals positively, precisely, and in the present tense can spur you into any action, from business success to losing weight. Facing your goals with with anticipation rather than apprehension can make all the difference in the world.

only with those individuals who will take the time to give you positive feedback and input. Never share a personal image of achievement with a cynic, a jealous relative, or an acquaintance who is likely to rain on your parade and try to shoot holes in your goals and ideas. Share your goals only with winners who have similar goals, who have achieved your goals, or who really are interested in helping you accomplish your goals.

The Power of Precision. Your mind does not relate or respond to vague ideas. Make your images of achievement specific and precise. Remember that when you talk about goals in generalities, you will very rarely succeed, but when you talk about your goals in the specific, you will very rarely fail. A good way for you to determine if your images of achievement are specific enough is to simply ask yourself, "Can this goal be timed, checked, or measured?" If you cannot time, check, or measure your performance in some way, there is a good chance that you are not getting specific enough.

One of the major reasons so few people reach their goals is that most people don't set specific goals, and the mind just dismisses them as irrelevant. Most people want financial security but have never considered how much money it will take. The mind cannot begin to formulate the strategies and actions required without specific information. Your mind will simply not respond to a request to get rich, have more, do better, or make money. You must act like a bank loan officer with your goals. The reason a loan officer wants to see a detailed business plan is that they know the entrepreneurs who are precise and specific are the ones who will succeed and pay off their loan. Get specific in your "goal mind," and you will soon have a gold mine of motivation with which to create your success and happiness.

The Power of the Possible. My philosophy has always been that your goals should be just out of reach but not out of sight. Another way to say that is that your goals should be realistic, yet not achievable by ordinary means. You do not want the daydreaming, pie-in-the-sky kind of goal. Your mind will dismiss this type of goal as impossible and not worthy of future thought or consideration.

At the same time, your goals must be challenging. You should not be able to accomplish your goals by doing what you have always been doing. The challenge is what engages your mind and gets your adrenaline flowing. Your goals should also be broken down into small action steps. Remember that the best way to eat an elephant is one bite at a time. Too often, we set these big, wonderful goals but they are just that: too *big*. They quickly seem impossible, or we fall behind or get discouraged and then throw up our hands and say, "I didn't really want that goal, anyway!" So set challenging, realistic goals with small doable action steps.

Resource Allocation

Douglas Mook has pointed out that all goals come down to the question of resource allocation. These life resources fall into four basic groups: money, time, energy, and cognition. Only one of the four, money, is a physical, material resource. There's a worn-out old saying, "Time is money," as if the major reason time exists is that we can use it to make money. Money itself should not be the focus. Money should free us from the need to toil constantly to meet our survival needs without being able to achieve true satisfaction in our work.

I had a call from a young life insurance salesman recently who told me he was thinking of leaving the business because he wasn't making enough money. He said, "I try to sell it, but nobody wants to buy it!"

I suggested that maybe his problem was related to his motivation. He was trying to sell something to make money rather than trying to do something worthwhile to help people solve a problem. The fact is that the average family, and business executives especially, are grossly underinsured. If he saw his work as solving this problem, he would probably find himself quite successful in providing life insurance.

Money itself is a neutral element. A great deal of it is not necessarily a blessing, nor is the lack of it necessarily a curse. Certainly it's easier to have a wholesome abundance of money than not. It better for everyone in the world to have enough for daily needs plus a little extra for comfort, culture, hospitality, education, and charity.

Compared to the three other resources—time, energy, and cognition—money is the least important in most of our lives. Our time, energy, and ability to think have a much greater value than any material resource—that is, as long as we have the minimum needed to live with dignity. I'm not against money; in fact, I enjoy having enough of it to educate my six children, explore the natural and cultural wonders of the world, and help others who are less fortunate than we are. But I view money like a train or plane ticket. It will be of no use unless we validate it. A ticket does us no good unless we employ it as a way of travelling. Actually, money and knowledge are very much alike: They mean nothing when we simply collect them; they mean everything when we employ them, share them, and put them to work.

Putting Your Goals in Writing

Commit your goals to writing, whether it be on paper or on a computer. Ideally, you should keep a goal journal, which will be discussed in a later chapter, but the most important thing is that you write your goals down and keep that list somewhere safe where you can always refer to it, modify it, or add to it.

Attorneys know the wisdom of a written contract. It requires that a commitment be put in very clear, concise terms, with all conditions, dollar amounts, responsibilities, and time frames carefully detailed. Make a contract with yourself, and you will enter into a successful relationship with yourself.

Make your list of goals as long and as ambitious as possible. Enjoy doing it! Pull out all the stops! Aim high, and be specific in stating your goals.

After over twenty years of goal-achievement seminars,

I've found that goals easily cluster in eight major areas of life. I'll provide a few key goal-starting ideas and words for you to consider in each of the eight areas, which aren't necessarily in the order of importance to you:

1. *Physical goals.* Write down your wellness and fitness goals. Include your nutrition plans, new sports skills, exercise schedule, physical exams, dental and eye exams, stress test, hair and facial care, and wardrobe improvement.

2. *Family goals.* This includes your relationship with your significant partner or spouse, your parents, your children, and your other relatives. These goals can concern family priorities, family activities, and changes in family routine or habits.

3. *Professional goals.* Write down your career goals. Include promotion and advancement objectives and professional-development activities, such as continuing education, developing new skills, and acquiring licenses or meeting certification needs. Also included should be participation in professional societies, networking with colleagues or mentors, building a relationship with supervisors, other employees, clients, vendors, and suppliers, plus meeting facility and equipment needs.

4. *Mental goals.* Here, I put down my nonfiction and fiction reading objectives, self-education study goals, plans to enroll in seminars and writing skills courses, and titles to acquire in my audio and video cassette library.

5. *Financial goals*. These include budgeting current income, goals for increasing income, a plan to save some of every paycheck for the future, investment and retirement strategies, entertainment, vacation and education funds, and charitable giving.

6. *Community goals*. These include volunteer work, civic clubs, political involvement, relationship with neighbors, environmental issues, and community improvement programs.

7. *Social goals*. These are goals for enriching current friendships, making new friends, club activities, and developing new recreational pursuits.

8. *Spiritual goals*. This category is for planning church or synagogue attendance, inspirational reading and study, prayer, mediation, communion with nature, service to the needy, and relationship with clergy.

Take the time to write down your own goals in each of the eight areas. Study the list. Ponder each item. What does it mean to you personally? Clearly imagine achieving each goal. How will it affect the quality of your life?

Don't consider recording these goals an assignment like you were given in school. View it as an adventure you really relish, like learning to fly, ski, or scuba dive. When I entered flight training, I had to go through a lot of writing and studying during ground school before I ever sat in the cockpit of my Navy jet fighter on the steam catapult of an aircraft carrier. The thrill of anticipation of supersonic flying made ground-school reading, writing, and study interesting and motivating. After all, these were my goals, and it was my life at stake.

Finally, remember that a dream is what you would like for your life to become; a goal is what you are truly willing to do to achieve what you really want. A dream is a vision; a goal is a promise. You can help yourself keep the promises you've made by writing down all of your goals as you develop them.

Setting Goals so Everyone Wins

When I served as Chairman of Psychology on the U.S. Olympic Sports Medicine Council, we spent long hours with athletes of all kinds seeking ways to enhance their performance.

The Olympics seem like a "winner-take-all" enterprise, in which one contestant takes home the gold. The original intention of the Olympic Games, however, was more complex. In addition to developing individual ability and giving it proper recognition, there was a focus on collective accomplishment. The Olympics were intended to build an *esprit de corps* through which an athlete would feel joint responsibility for all the other members of the team. It's important to make this shared effort a part of your approach to goal setting and achievement. In fact, I suggest that one of your personal goals should be achieving personal success within the context of group accomplishment.

Your group may be your family, your friends from your work or place of worship, or even your entire community. No matter how you define your group, I urge you to evaluate your individual achievements within the group context.

You may be already doing this, perhaps without ever really thinking about it. I have a dream of making a positive difference for other people. I want my life to count in some way in the lives of others, and I'm sure you feel the same. Make sure that you take the time to assess how the accomplishment of your goal will effect the people who mean the most to you.

A Life of Creative Goal Setting

Many people resist goal setting because they assume it leads to a formula-driven, highly uncreative life. Actually, the exact opposite is true. People who passively assume that everything will somehow work out in the end can hardly be termed creative. They're not creating their lives, they're just hoping that something good will happen to them.

Setting worthwhile goals is a much more imaginative approach. It's fashioning and molding the life of your choice. It's approaching your life the way an artist might stand before a new canvas on which a beautiful painting can be crafted. There are other useful metaphors for creativity in goal setting. The rudder of a ship, for example, is small and rigid, like a short-term goal you might accomplish in just one day. But the rudder can turn the ship in any direction the captain chooses. In that, there's a great deal of freedom and flexibility.

Once you set a goal, you can adjust and fine-tune it any way you wish. That's creativity. And achievement motivation is what allows you to keep progressing toward the goal no matter how many adjustments are required and no matter how long they may take to work.

MOTIVATIONAL SKILLS

Twenty Ways to Live in Prime Time • Creating Focus by Planning Your Time • The Rules of Decision Making • Crisis Decision Making • Framing for Decision Making • Becoming an Innovator • Taking Smart Risks • Steps for Smart Risk Taking

"Make minor decisions quickly and live with those decisions. Don't engage in what I call 'majoring in minors.' Don't waffle or change your mind about choices that lack serious consequences."

"One problem facing millions of us is that of dieting and weight control. I believe we frequently experience failure in this area because of the way we frame our thinking. We usually go into the program with the wrong concept from the start. We view dieting as a short-term solution to a long-term condition."

"This new era is often called the 'Information Age' because most people today are responsible for handling information as part of their jobs. I prefer to call it the 'Innovation Age,' since it is what we do with the information that counts."

"Life is inherently risky. Driving at night is a risk. Entering a relationship is a risk. Beginning a new job is a risk. Even putting your money in the bank is a risk. The one risk to avoid is the risk of letting fear overwhelm your initiative and your dreams."

Twenty Ways to Live in Prime Time

One of the characteristics of good time management is maximum return on energy and effort. I call this "living in prime time." On the East Coast, prime-time television is from 8:00 PM to 11:00 PM. For the rest of the nation, prime time is from 7:00 PM to 10:00 PM. Surveys have shown that the most viewers are available between those hours.

Likewise, you should start thinking of your days and weeks in terms of these prime-time categories. When is the best time of day or night for you? Are you a morning person or a night person? When do you rate yourself as sharpest and most cost-effective in terms of performance? Your peak hours will vary with your age, physical condition, and your biological clock.

Television networks match their programming schedule to their audience. It's no coincidence that Saturday morning—sleep-in time for exhausted adults—is slotted with cartoons and sugar cereal and toy commercials. Take your cue from the networks. Put your peak performance projects into prime time. Save your low-level, routine tasks for low-energy periods.

My friend and colleague Lyle Sussman is one of the best time-management consultants in the nation. He and I have toured the country, addressing business leaders and employee groups in seminars sponsored by major universities. His action steps on how to make all of your time into prime time have helped thousands of executives, me included, to manage their resources of money, time, energy, and cognition. Here's a check-off list from his outstanding guidebook *Smart Moves,* which he coauthored with Sam Deep. I call this list "Twenty Ways to Live in Prime Time."

1. Commit yourself to yearly goals for personal development and professional accomplishment. Translate yearly goals into quarterly goals, and quarterly goals into "to-do" lists that are revised weekly and daily.

2. Buy or construct your own comprehensive calendar planning system. Record in this planner all the people and projects you manage and all pertinent addresses and phone numbers. In this calender, write down every commitment you make at the time that you make it.

3. Create a time-analysis chart of your activities. Break your day into fifteen-minute blocks. Note your chief activities for each block. After logging your activities for

a week or so, you'll have a representative sample of how your time is spent. Study the results. Decide what you will do to make better use of your time.

4. Stop wasting the first hour of your workday. The first cup of coffee, reading the newspaper, and socializing are three costly opening exercises that lower productivity.

5. Get enough rest, nutrition, and exercise. If you don't feel good, you can't do good. Maintain your health and build your stamina. Treat your own body the way you would if it were a space shuttle in which you were being launched or a one-of-a-kind Rolls Royce in which you had invested, as if it belonged to your only child, or as if it belonged to a beloved pet. Treat yourself as if you were worth any effort or expense to nurture.

6. Recognize when your prime time occurs during the day. Allocate the most difficult projects to that period. Work on easy projects at low-energy times.

7. When you realize that your energy level is dropping, take a break. For many people, this occurs around 3:00 or 4:00 PM. For you, it may be in the early morning or evening, or right after lunch.

8. Do one thing at a time. It takes time to start and stop work on each activity. Stay with a task until it's completed.

9. Don't open unimportant mail. At least twenty-five

percent of the mail you receive can be safely thrown away without opening it.

10. Try to handle each piece of paper only once—and never more than twice. Don't set anything aside without taking some action.

11. Carry work, audio tapes, or reading material with you everywhere you go. Convert "downtime" into "uplink" time.

12. Spend twenty minutes at the beginning of each week and ten minutes at the beginning of each day planning your "to-do" list. Ask yourself, "What do I need to accomplish this week and this day."

13. Set aside personal relaxation time during the day. Don't work during lunch. It's neither noble nor nutritional to skip important energy-input and stress-relieving times.

14. Periodically each day, focus on your long-term vision. This will keep your cognitive map vivid and strong.

15. Establish time limits for meetings and conversations in advance. Look at your watch as the deadline approaches. End the conversation when it arrives.

16. Write answers in the margins of letters you receive, and mail the original back to the sender.

17. Take vacations and leave your work at home. The harder

you work, the more you need to balance your exercise and leisure time.

18. When possible, plan your work so your tasks end when your day does. Take work home as an exception, not a rule. Your professional life requires a whole human being with a satisfying personal life.

19. Throughout the day, ask yourself, "What's the best use of my time right now?" As the day grows short, focus on those projects you can least afford to leave undone.

20. End the day by listing all of the next day's important tasks. In the morning, incorporate these projects into your daily "to-do" list.

Highly motivated achievers learn from the past, set vivid, detailed goals for the future, and live in the only moment of time over which they have any control: *now*. They have a sense of "now-ness," a sense of positive urgency for living in the prime time of this day.

Creating Focus by Planning Your Time

Let me share with you a strategy that may seem like simple time management, yet as you apply this principle, you will discover the impact it can have on your ability to deal with the unexpected challenges you are sure to encounter on your road to success.

The strategy is planning each week the week before and planning each day the day before. This simple formula is a powerful process for creating focus. Let's start by looking at planning your week the week before.

To create your weekly focus, I suggest that, each Friday, you schedule a "one-percent" meeting with yourself. Block out one percent of your twenty-four hour day for a meeting with yourself. One percent of twenty-four hours is approximately fourteen-and-a-half minutes; you can round it up to fifteen if you like. During this fifteen minutes, you should not take any calls or interruptions of any kind. You must consider this meeting as if it is a meeting with your boss or your most important client. Remember that the most important meetings you will ever attend are the meetings you have with yourself.

During your one-percent meeting, you should review that past seven days. What went right? What went wrong? What could have been done better or more effectively? After you have reviewed the past seven days, take a look at where you are on your seasonal or long-term goals and projects. Then focus on the next seven days. What do you need to accomplish before next Friday? Write these things down, and this will become your weekly focus.

I like to do my one-percent meeting just before I am ready to leave work on Friday. One of the nice benefits of planning your week the week before is that it will actually allow you to enjoy your weekend more. How many times are you at home on the weekend, trying to enjoy family or personal relaxation time, when your mind starts firing away: "Remember to call Mary on Monday," "Don't forget to get the report to Dave by Tuesday," or "I have to get going on that presentation for the sales meeting."

Many people are more tired and stressed out on Sunday afternoon then they were on Friday afternoon when they left work! They have not been able to truly relax and renew because their mind was busy thinking about work when it should have been thinking about fun, family, and friends. By planning your week the week before, your mind will let go of all those tasks and to-dos, and you will really start to enjoy your weekend for a change. So plan your week the week before.

The second half of this strategy is to plan your day the

day before. Planning your day the day before should only take three or four minutes. If you have created your weekly focus, your daily focus is easy. I like to plan my tomorrow right before I leave my office each day. I just quickly review my performance for the day, looking at what kinds of activities I engaged in, then I look at my goals, projects, and appointments and determine what needs to be done the next day. It works great for me, and I am sure it will for you too.

By planning your day the day before, you will gain two benefits. First, it will allow you to enjoy your evenings more because you won't be worrying about what you have to do the next day. Second, and more importantly, planning your day the day before gives you more control of your life. More control empowers you to make focused choices. You will be acting on purpose rather than reacting to pressures.

Many people tell me that it doesn't do them any good to plan because their day changes so rapidly. I want to emphasize that you do not have to be scripted and rigid in your planning and use of time. In fact, if you are overly rigid, you may lose your motivation. I believe that one of the main reasons you should plan is not just to have a plan, because you know that it will change. But to have continuing achievement motivation, you need something to change *from.*

The Rules of Decision Making

Henry Ford, the auto magnate, was once asked how he handled the pressures of decision making. Ford replied, "I go out and trot around the yard. While I'm running off the excess energy that wants to do too much, my mind clears and I see what should be done first."

This is still sound advice, but we have come a long way toward understanding effective decision-making concepts since the days of the old Model-A. Following are some rules for making the best decision possible in any situation:

Make minor decisions quickly and live with those decisions. Don't engage in what I call "majoring in minors." Don't waffle or change your mind about choices that lack serious consequences.

For shared goals, teamwork is vital. But when it comes to

decisions involving your own individual dreams and success, avoid choosing projects that depend extensively on another person's efforts. This doesn't mean you should operate a large business all by yourself. I'm referring here to your independent, personal goals. Remember, motivation is an inner force that compels behavior. If you're going to depend upon someone else to help you achieve your personal dreams, you're going to have to motivate that person to your level of excitement and dedication. Researchers believe it's better to invest your energy in maintaining your own motivation.

Behavioral scientists have identified three major decision-making strategies: maximizing, "satisficing," and bettering.

Maximizing means laying out all of your choices and then selecting the best alternative. Obviously, when it comes to picking an important collaborator, this is the right strategy to follow. What architect wouldn't want the best builder to execute his designs? And what prospective patient wouldn't want the finest medical specialist reviewing his or her case? It is worth a great deal of time and effort to find the best.

Suppose, however, you have a client or friend visiting you from out of town and you want to have dinner at a good restaurant. You wouldn't devote the same kind of resources to investigating the hundreds of possible eating establishments in your city.

In this case, you may decide to follow the second major decision strategy, which is "satisficing." Satisficing is decision making by establishing criteria and then selecting the first available option that meets the requirements. In the restaurant example, you could decide you want a four-star establishment, quiet enough so you can talk comfortably, an Italian menu with some seafood and pasta specialties, moderate prices, not to exceed twelve to fifteen dollars per person, within fifteen minutes of your guest's hotel.

Once these requirements are set, you take the first option that satisfies each of them. By establishing the criteria, you refine the choices. You also set an acceptable standard by which you can make a decision. By taking the first option that meets your standards, you minimize the time and cognitive effort required to accomplish your objective.

You also can combine these two strategies of satisficing and maximizing. You can establish the criteria for the restaurant selection and then maximize your choice by picking three alternatives, checking them out, and deciding on the best of the three.

The third strategy, bettering, is the most passive of the decision-making strategies. Instead of actively investigating the best choice, the decision maker takes the easiest available course of action until something apparently better comes along. This strategy would be appropriate in the case of things that don't mean much to you or in which you do not want to invest much time and energy.

Suppose your savings account at your local bank was earning six percent interest, and you noticed during your lunch hour that another bank was offering seven percent on short-term deposits. You immediately move the account because the seven-percent opportunity is better.

We all want to improve our situation when an obvious advantage presents itself. However, bettering might not be best in the long run. By maximizing and satisficing, you may discover that the bank is dangerously undercapitalized, so it's offering the higher rates in order to attract deposits. Or your relationships with the personnel at your former bank may be stronger and more important to you when you want to apply for a line of credit or home equity loan.

Motivational researchers warn that individuals who make decisions solely by bettering have trouble achieving their long-term goals. The advantage of bettering—that is, limiting your options to the first apparently better one—is also a disadvantage in that it narrows your vision and your field of perspective.

Recently, I glanced at an article that made me chuckle and shake my head in disbelief. It was about a man in Atlanta who was cheated in a cocaine transaction. He made the decision to report the matter to the Atlanta police, who were dumfounded when he told them, "I paid good money for bad stuff." He wanted the police to arrest the dealer who had sold him the bad drugs. Obviously, he didn't consult his cognitive map, and he made an impulsive decision that he thought was bettering. Now that he's in prison, he has a lot more time to consider his past and future choices.

Researchers also caution that bettering does not serve us very well when we are in a rut, when we lack energy and our motivation level is low. Bettering involves deciding on the run, making quick decisions without interrupting the daily flow of life. It doesn't allow for stepping back from the canvas and thinking about how your day-to-day decisions relate to your major, lifetime goals. Decision making by bettering is like an airline pilot who always heads in the direction of the best weather. The sky is clearer, the flight smoother, and he appears better off in every new minute of travel than he was the minute before. But he will probably end up at a destination where he never intended to go.

Many people approach their entire professional careers in just this manner. They look for greener pastures, with a slightly higher salary and what they perceive to be a few more perks. With no long-term strategy, they are the first to go and last to know in a downsizing company during challenging economic times.

Why is there so much emphasis on bettering, when maximizing and satisficing are by far the superior strategies for decision making? The fact is, most people use bettering to make all their important decisions in life. They see new as better, without even considering the long-range impact and consequences. It reminds me of the song lyrics: "Oh, it's sad to belong to someone else when the right one comes along." Although a lot of people identify with these lyrics, they are probably basing these feelings on impulse rather than the cognitive map of a highly motivated achiever.

Crisis Decision Making

Two psychologists, Irving Janis and Leon Mann, have studied carefully how we approach the decision-making process. They learned that, basically, most human beings would rather not make any major decisions. To force them to do so, there needs to be either a crisis or the presentation of an obviously preferable alternative.

Calling human beings "reluctant decision makers," Janis and Mann went on to define the condition that moves us to make active decisions as a "crisis." A crisis is anything serious enough to bring a person to the realization that some action has to be taken. A crisis is reached when one concludes that serious consequences will result if the present course of action is not changed.

I read an incredible story about a woman named RaNelle Wallace who saved three people from a fire. What made the incident so unusual was that this woman who rescued the others was a burn victim herself and deathly afraid of fire. She had been burned so badly by a fireball in a plane crash that she had to wear a stocking mask to protect her burned face. Not only had she suffered terribly from the burns, but she had $300,000 in medical bills and no insurance. She needed ten operations for facial reconstruction.

She had been asked to leave places of business several times because she made the other customers feel uncomfortable. Once, in a fast-food restaurant, she was handcuffed and detained until the police arrived because the manager thought she was a robber wearing a stocking mask.

Wallace says she is grateful for the house fire that forced her to confront her greatest fear. Prior to that time, she no longer had the strength to deal with flames. "I couldn't even put a fire in my fireplace this winter," she said. "Every time I looked at flames, I'd get sick."

But the urgency of the house fire forced her to act. She made a brave decision in a crisis situation, hoping to spare others from the terror and excruciating pain she had experienced.

"Something happened inside me," she said. "It was like reliving the plane crash all over again. This was a choice I made. Somehow, making the decision to risk my own life helped me. Now it's not like every time I see flames I'm going to get sick," Wallace said. "When I lost my face, my mom felt that I probably would die from that alone. But I've dealt with it."

In a time of crisis, RaNelle Wallace made a decision by quickly maximizing. What an amazing testimony to the human spirit.

* * *

The social and political decisions of our country always have been crisis driven. We see this in our dealings with pollution, energy shortages, disease, crime, and other social injustices. There are many pressing problems that we have not decided to solve directly yet because they have not reached the crisis point, or at least they are not yet perceived as crises by the majority of our leaders.

I saw a list of sixteen ways to dodge decisions that I'm sure must be framed on many politicians' office walls:

1. Take flight into detail.
2. Counsel infinite delay of action.
3. Delegate the problem to a committee.
4. Look for the answer in a book.
5. Induce the other political party to commit itself on how to handle the problem.
6. Give an answer in doubletalk.
7. Delegate the problem to a subordinate.
8. Indicate that all problems must be considered in chronological order.
9. Have a "study" commissioned to "get all the facts."
10. Arrange to be called out of town.
11. Call in an expert to make sure "we're on solid ground."
12. Deny that any problem exists.
13. Take sick leave.
14. Check into a substance-abuse rehabilitation center.
15. State that the problem belongs in someone else's province.
16. Simply put on your hat and go home.

Janis and Mann found that it is in a perceived crisis that we

Despite being a burn victim herself and deathly afraid of fire, RaNelle Wallace made a crisis decision and rescued three people from a burning building. Compare this reaction to the self-serving decision-dodging techniques of many politicians!

finally take control of our decision-making process. If we have time for rational decision-making, we will go into a maximizing mode, vigilantly seeking the best alternative. If there's no time for rationally considering our alternatives, we tend to make our snap decision in a satisficing manner, quickly setting up the criteria of what we need and selecting the first alternative that fits the parameters. Unfortunately, they found that this approach does not always work out well. In a study of people who survived or who died in tornadoes, it was discovered that people who had plenty of warning were the most likely to survive, obviously having the most planning options. Strangely enough, the people who had no warning at all were more likely to survive the twister than those who had a few minutes warning.

Under the pressure of the oncoming crisis, people with the short warning period behaved in the worst possible manner and made the wrong decisions. Janis and Mann point out that the key to using satisficing correctly is the establishment of a useful set of requirements. In pressure situations, many individuals tend to follow the example of others or act on primitive "fight-or-flight" impulses without any thought in setting up their criteria. We have witnessed this in soccer stadiums where the fans stampede for the exits and crush each other; we witness it during building fires, where people jump from upper-story windows.

When employing a satisficing strategy—that is, choosing the first acceptable option—you must be certain the criteria you have established are reasonable and useful. Your decision is really made when you set those standards.

Framing for Decision Making

A crucial aspect of our decision-making process is the framing of a problem or challenge. I touched on this in an earlier chapter regarding goal setting, when I said that goals should be positively stated.

To illustrate the significance of framing, let's look at an experiment conducted by researchers Tversky and Kahnemann in the 1980s. Imagine that you have decided to see a play for which admission is ten dollars, and tickets are available at the box office. As you enter the theater, you discover that you have lost a ten-dollar bill. Would you still pay another ten dollars for a ticket to attend that play?

Suppose instead that you had decided to see the play and had already bought your ticket for the ten-dollar admission price. As you go to enter the theater, you discover that the ticket has been lost. Would you pay ten dollars more to buy another ticket?

In the study, eighty-eight percent of the individuals responding to the first case said that the loss of a ten-dollar bill would not stop them from spending another ten dollars to go to the show. However, in the group where the ten-dollar ticket had been lost, a majority said, "No, I wouldn't go."

That's interesting isn't it? Something one wouldn't generally have expected. Objectively, both cases are the same. Each individual is already out the original ten dollars and must spend another ten dollars to see the play. In the first case, however, the lost ten-dollar bill is not directly framed as the ten dollars spent for the ticket. You've lost ten dollars, but not the ten dollars allocated for the show. In the second case, you've lost the ticket you already paid ten dollars for. That is, you've lost the money allocated for entertainment.

Of course, in both cases, the researchers framed the problem for the subjects. But it's important to realize the role that your own framing of situations plays in the decision-making process.

In the 1920s, when he was working hard to perfect his craft, writer Ernest Hemingway lost a suitcase containing all his manuscripts—all of his stories, polished to a jewel-like perfection—that he'd been planning to turn into a book. Hemingway was devastated and couldn't conceive of redoing his work. All he could think about was the months he'd devoted to his task . . . all wasted. But when he told the poet Ezra Pound about the loss, Pound said that it was a actually a stroke of luck. In rewriting the stories, Pound assured Hemingway, the weak parts would be forgotten, and only the best material would reappear. Instead of framing the event in disappointment and loss, Pound cast it in the light of opportunity. Hemingway rewrote the stories and became one of the major figures in American literature.

One problem facing millions of us is that of dieting and weight control. I believe we frequently experience failure in this area because of the way we frame our thinking. We usually go into the program with the wrong concept from the start. We view dieting as a short-term solution to a long-term condition. We are led to believe that we will lose all the weight we need to, and keep it off, if we follow the advertised regimen. Our focus is on losing weight quickly, with the bathroom scale as our feedback mechanism. We go into each diet program with positive expectations, but when we slip up, we berate ourselves and give in easily to negative framing: "Well, I knew I couldn't do it anyway," or "I guess I don't have the willpower," or "Being fat runs in the family . . . it's genetic!"

I'm reminded of a letter I received from a woman in Arizona named Alina. She wrote: "Your *Psychology of Winning* [audio] program was the catalyst for me to shed twenty-five pounds of excess weight permanently." Since I had never mentioned dieting in any of my works, I was interested in her story.

The letter continued: "I had tried many diets before—with a negative attitude, and almost expecting to fail. The worst feeling I remember during those half-hearted attempts came when I would pig out, which was inevitable, and the contempt I had for myself the next morning. Your concepts helped me realize that we only have one pass through life, with no replays . . . that we have to concentrate on the desired result, not the penalty of failure . . . and that we must start today, not five days or five years later."

The next day, Alina began a personal program for lifelong nutrition. When she'd lost five pounds, positive comments from friends and family spurred her on. She became an expert on calories, fat content, and nutritional values in food groups. If she faltered, she simply adjusted with lower fat and fewer calories at the next meal instead of degrading herself with negative thoughts.

It took Alina two years to reach her desired weight and stay there. She says she is a size four, weighs 105 pounds, and feels this is ideal for her height of five feet, two inches. She concluded her letter with: "I still love to eat good food at fine restaurants, and when I do, I diligently go back to my sensible eating plan the next day. Being at this weight and feeling this good is a dream I thought was unattainable. The resulting self-esteem and positive outlook on life is beyond measure."

That's really what it's all about: winning and succeeding, not failing. If positive framing can help Alina reach her dream, it also can help you and I to make the decision our goals. When you face a difficult decision, frame the problem to yourself in a way that concentrates on the solution and how you'll achieve it.

Becoming an Innovator

This new era is often called the "Information Age" because most people today are responsible for handling information as part of their jobs. I prefer to call it the "Innovation Age," since it is what we *do* with the information that counts. Innovators create ideas that help people cope with the information explosion. This is what the independent college financial-aid advisor does, or the "knowledge merchant" who develops expertise in a given subject and then distills it in the form of seminars, books, and consultations.

Because they are dealing effectively with change, innovators are in demand. Major companies may be cutting costs, but they are not cutting innovators from their ranks. Nor are nonprofit organizations and the government. Whether or not they have defined it as such, they are searching for individuals who can create new opportunities.

Following are ten characteristics of innovators. As you

will see, many of them correspond with traits we've already identified with highly motivated achievers.

First, innovators are opportunity oriented. They look for hidden opportunities in problems and trends they encounter. Innovators search for the unsolved problems, the market inefficiencies, and the unmet needs and wants of existing customer groups; they also search for unmet needs and wants and build new customer groups. To become opportunity oriented, read business and trade journals to spot trends, and attend as many trade and entrepreneurial shows as possible.

Second, innovators are strategists. They attempt to anticipate the future for the purpose of maximizing their ability to thrive and prosper in that future. They continually define and redefine their goals and have well-developed but flexible plans to reach them.

Third, innovators "unhook" their prejudices. In their approach to problem solving and opportunity creation, they constantly attempt to rid their thinking of preconceived beliefs, biases, thinking ruts, and unchallenged assumptions. You must abandon your assumptions but hold on to your core values and moral convictions.

Fourth, innovators are trend spotters. Innovators monitor change—social, attitudinal, technological, and so on—to spot new opportunities before everyone else. But what passes for "vision" is really just a unique way of deciphering where things are headed. Innovators do this by concerning themselves with the "big picture"; they utilize every available moment to keep abreast of changing situations.

Fifth, innovators are idea oriented. Innovators gain an edge through the way they work with ideas. They are constantly generating and experimenting with ideas and are always on the lookout for concepts they can borrow and apply from other fields.

Sixth, innovators rely upon intuition. In a world that is growing ever more complex and fast paced, innovators use their intuition to help assess risks, "read" people, spot emerging patterns of change, and make complex decisions.

Seventh, innovators are extraordinarily persistent. They are willing to "face the heat" in pursuit of their dreams. Their passion for ideas helps them overcome what might otherwise be roadblocks. Again, they are long-term thinkers.

Eighth, innovators are resourceful. They see no walls to implementing new ideas because of their skill and persistence at gathering strategic information, specialized, state-of-the-art knowledge, and insight. They understand the role of information in the Innovation Age.

Ninth, innovators are feedback oriented. They constantly poll their customer group to determine how their product or service can be improved. Feedback acts as their "checks-and-balances" mechanism. It guides their decisions and helps them avoid prejudices and blind spots.

And finally, innovators are superior team builders. They realize they cannot succeed alone. They either need teams to help them implement their ideas, or if they work alone, they require support networks of fellow professionals, mentors, friends, and advisors.

Taking Smart Risks

What happens to people who always play it safe, whose first priority is their own security, who never take risks? First, their paths seem to become narrower as they grow older. As they take fewer and fewer risks, they limit their opportunities and reduce the flow of fresh viewpoints and new ideas into their lives. Security-oriented people stop learning whenever school ends and stop looking for new career opportunities as soon as a basic minimum level of job status has been achieved. People like this form a small number of friendships and then consider their circle of friends to be closed. They seek out a comfort zone and prefer not to move unless they absolutely must. If change is required for some reason, it should be the smallest amount possible.

When faced with challenges or opportunities, the play-it-safers will avoid them at all cost. If confronted, they will take the easy way out. If given choices, they will chose the path of least resistance.

These people rarely test their potential. They are seldom concerned about personal or career growth. They tend to see their career as a job, and they define *free time* as a means of escaping that job. They hate taking chances. They prefer not to know if something goes wrong. They may not know what it takes to succeed, but they know everything about avoiding the possibility of failure.

In my opinion, the percentage of people who aspire to this no-risk, belt-and-suspenders approach is growing. This represents a major change in the American viewpoint. I am not suggesting that we all spend our time trying to think up the next Intel, Microsoft, or Netscape. But it is interesting to visit the Smithsonian in Washington and see the thousands of inventions and assorted contraptions that people were building and patenting a hundred years ago. Most of them came to naught, most of them represented someone's wrong-headed dream, but there was also a kind of energy and optimism that has largely been supplanted by caution and fear.

The truth is that security is never possible with a hundred-percent money-back guarantee. The only totally secure person is one lying horizontally, lily in hand, six feet underground.

Life is inherently risky. Driving at night is a risk. Entering a relationship is a risk. Beginning a new job is a risk. Even putting your money in the bank is a risk. The one risk to avoid is the risk of letting fear overwhelm your initiative and your dreams. When that happens, you don't do the wrong things, you simply do nothing at all. Risk taking is part of life, and people who seek to live risk free are simply wasting their energy. That same energy could just as easily have been channeled into taking the calculated risks that bring greater success, less frustration, and genuine satisfaction in life.

Steps for Smart Risk Taking

Here are some action steps you can consider in taking risks to achieve your goals.

1. *Check the source of your motivation to reach your goals.* What are the real benefits of achievement? Make certain you are not considering risking your future out of fear of some penalty or so you won't disappoint someone else. Also, be careful not to use money alone as a primary motivator. The best motivation is an inner force that inspires you to solve a problem, fill a need, or do something truly excellent. Money is the by-product of accomplishment. If you make it the prime motivator, you may take risk without doing your homework.

2. *Incorporate yourself mentally.* Begin to think of yourself as "You, Inc.," a company with one employee: you!

Today, You, Inc. may contract its services to XYZ Corporation; tomorrow it is likely to sell its services to a different organization. Incorporating yourself mentally doesn't mean you are any less loyal to your present employer. Loyalty and integrity are at the top of the list in importance. It does mean, however, that you never confuse your personal long-term interests with your employer's.

By deciding not to suffer the fate of those who are being bounced out of jobs to find that their skills were obsolete, you begin the process of protecting yourself against this possibility. Ask yourself: How vulnerable am I, and what can I do about it? What conditions must I watch? In this way, you are being proactive instead of reactive.

Just as companies must "reinvent" themselves to meet the demands of the future, so it is with You, Inc. Establish your own strategic planning department. Set up your own training department, and make sure your prized employee is updating his or her skills and techniques. Start your own pension plan.

Of course, this is not only to benefit you in the case that you are dislocated by your company. The flip side of this coin is that you may choose to dislocate yourself. Today, the person who puts up with a tyrannical boss or a dead-end job does so as a matter of choice. Once crucial only to the self-employed, the mind-set of acting self-employed is now essential to all of us. Today's typical American will have five separate careers in his or her lifetime. If you are not already planning for an eventful career change, you should be.

3. *As you risk, prepare to be criticized and second-guessed.* It may come from members of your own profession. It may come from your own company. It may come from the media. It may even come from your own family and friends. Expect it, but don't let it stop you.

   If you can't stand the heat, you'll never be able to take a risk. Size up the resistance to your achieving your goals. Anticipate where the heat will come from. And be flexible enough to overcome objections to your approach.

4. *Be prepared to sell your goals to an indifferent world.* Don't expect other people to be excited and motivated about your goals and ideas. They won't, unless the idea solves their problem or creates an opportunity for them. Even then, they still won't, unless you sell them on the benefits.

5. *Challenge your assumptions about risk taking.* Interview risk takers about how they approach the issue. Learn how they measure the benefits and drawbacks and how they make the decision to move forward.

6. *You don't have to take the full risk all at once.* You can turn an avocation into a vocation gradually, after you have gotten all the bugs out of it. You can test market your goals on a limited basis. Take baby steps until you become sure-footed.

7. *You don't have to assume all the risk yourself.* Partners or lenders can share risk. And the people you attract to share your dream can also.

8. *Realize that you'll never feel completely prepared to take a big risk.* But remember: Nothing ventured, nothing gained!

MOTIVATIONAL ATTITUDES

The Power of Belief • Money vs. Personal Satisfaction • Self-Esteem: The Four-Legged Chair • Self-Confidence and Self-Efficacy • Developing Self-Efficacy • Four Factors in Increasing Self-Efficacy • Six Behaviors that Increase Self-Esteem • Living Life Hopefully • Making Your Hard Work Enjoyable

"Like a two-edged sword, belief cuts both ways. Positive belief, in the form of a goal, is the key to unlocking the door of success for every human being. Conversely, as a negative obsession, it's the lock that imprisons and keeps that human being from ever experiencing success."

"The problem is, money alone does not stimulate intrinsic motivation and therefore is a means, not an end. Money is fuel for your car. It is not the destination. It is not the journey. It is only part of the transportation system."

"As with every other feeling and motivation, learning to like yourself takes practice. And just as practicing any skill needs to be carefully structured, the same is true for the process of building self-esteem."

"In general, hopeful people are more likely to find ways, try methods, and formulate plans of action that lead to beneficial outcomes. In short, hopeful people have more achievement motivation."

The Power of Belief

In all of my studies of highly motivated and happy individuals, I have found several common denominators that make the critical difference between those who are successful achievers and those who are part of the vast, unsuccessful majority. Here is the most important of them: Successful people believe in the validity of their own dreams and goals, even if dreams are all they have to go on.

They understand that although we, as individuals, are not born with equal physical and mental attributes, and that many of us must come from behind as far as our early family environments are concerned, we do have equal rights to feel the excitement and motivation in believing that we deserve the very best in life if we devote the time and energy to achieve it.

But like a two-edged sword, belief cuts both ways. Positive belief, in the form of a goal, is the key to unlocking the door of success for every human being. Conversely, as a negative obsession, it's the lock that imprisons and keeps that human being from ever experiencing success.

As positive energy, belief is the promise of the realization of goals hoped for and unseen except in the imagination. As negative energy, it is the premonition of our deepest fears and unseen feelings of inadequacy. As children, we had fantasies about what we wanted to be when we grew up. As we grew older, we began to narrow the possibilities. Some careers and aspirations seemed beyond our reach. We were advised—or ill-advised, as the case might be—by teachers, parents, peers, and other adults that we couldn't be, shouldn't be, or wouldn't be an expert, leader, or success in this field or that. Over time, many of our targets seemed inaccessible or out of range to us, even in our imaginations.

I'll never forget how this was dramatically illustrated during a goal-setting seminar I conducted in 1980. I had asked the participants to write down and discuss the answers to several questions that centered around their goals. I asked them what they would be doing five years and twenty years in the future, how good their health might be, and what their assets would be. As you can imagine, they all looked stunned when asked to get that specific about their future . . . all but one person who was too young to have given up on his dreams!

That young person was a red-haired, freckle-faced ten-year-old boy named Eric, whose father had brought him to the program to get some positive input. Instead of getting input, he provided us all output that put our adult fears and insecurities to shame. While all the grown-ups struggled for answers they had never really focused on before, young Eric volunteered to come up to the podium to share his answers to the series of goal-setting questions.

He said his greatest talents were building model airplanes, doing well in video games, and operating a personal computer. He said he needed improvement in cleaning his room and being nice to his sister. His personal goal for 1980 was to build a model of the space shuttle, and his professional goal was to earn four hundred dollars doing yard work for neighbors. For 1981, he said his personal goal was to take a trip to Hawaii, and his professional goal was to earn seven hundred dollars for the super-saver airfare and room package offered by the airlines. He said the hardest part of that goal was to get his mom and dad to save enough money for their own tickets so they could take him!

When asked about his five-year goals, he said, "I'll be fifteen in 1985, in the tenth grade, and I'll be taking a lot of math, science, and computer classes."

Eric had to think for a moment, when I asked him about his twenty-year life goals. He said, "In the year 2000—I'll be thirty years old then, right?—I'll be living in Cape Canaveral, Florida. I'll be a space shuttle astronaut working for NASA or a communications company putting satellites into orbit. And I'll be in great physical shape. You have to be in good shape to be an astronaut," he finished proudly.

Where is Eric today? The ten-year-old boy who dared to dream so specifically and vividly about the future back in 1980 graduated from the Air Force Academy in the Class of 1992, entered flight training, and has his sights firmly set on performing well enough as a pilot and officer to become a candidate for the astronaut program before June 2 of the year 2000, which will be his thirtieth birthday!

The critical point to recognize, of course, is that both the unlimited potential of childhood and the tight constraints of adulthood originate and reside primarily in the imagination.

If you believe you can, you probably can. If you believe you won't, you most assuredly won't! Belief is the ignition switch that gets you off the launching pad.

Money vs. Personal Satisfaction

For the highly motivated achiever, it's natural to seek out challenging goals because he or she has an inner, intrinsic drive to succeed. And success doesn't mean pet rocks, get-rich-quick schemes, lotto jackpots, or pyramid fads. Highly motivated achievers are looking not to receive, but to contribute, to give. They're looking for problems that are personally satisfying to solve.

Since the accomplishment of a difficult task means more to the highly motivated achiever than any extrinsic motivation, it means that his motivation will remain strong throughout his career. Think of how much stronger and more permanent such a motivation is compared to a motivation that is extrinsic.

Suppose you choose a particular career because of the money. What happens when there's more money in doing something else? You're likely to abandon one path as soon as another possibility opens up, and eventually you'll find yourself wondering what you're really doing . . . maybe even who you really *are*. Since there is no intrinsic motivation to stay on any particular path, the journey will be arduous, and motivation will tend to weaken whenever the external reward seems remote or out of sight. Some people spend their entire lives wandering from one path to another, always looking for an easier way to find that pot of gold, never achieving a significant goal worthy of their inner potential.

I've met many people who fit this description. If they're in sales, they move from company to company, from industry to industry, from one product or service to another. They are very hard to keep in your address book because they are always either coming or going or starting a new business of their own. When that doesn't work, they get involved in sketchy enterprises, such as a new diet company where you can lose all the weight you want by wearing a plastic patch on your arm. They go from one Roman candle to another, from one "exciting opportunity" to another disappointment.

The problem is, money alone does not stimulate intrinsic motivation and therefore is a means, not an end. Money is fuel for your car. It is not the destination. It is not the journey. It is only part of the transportation system.

Self-Esteem: The Four-Legged Chair

Self-esteem is at the root of all positive and negative motivation, yet no one is born with self-esteem. As with every other feeling and motivation, learning to like yourself takes practice. And just as practicing any skill needs to be carefully structured, the same is true for the process of building self-esteem.

Think of self-esteem as a four-legged chair that you're sitting on while looking in the mirror in judgment of yourself. To some, the chair is a throne; to others, it's a seat at a marvelous banquet table; and to many others, it is a chair to which we have been assigned as punishment, to sit in the corner of life feeling guilty or inadequate.

When you sit on your four-legged chair of self-esteem, looking in the mirror, what do you see?

Are you looking at someone you respect? Do you see someone you really want to be? Are you going where you want to go in life? Are you doing what you want to do in life? Are you becoming who you want to become in life? Are you in charge of what happens to you?

If you can answer an unhesitating "yes" to a majority of these questions, your self-esteem ought to be in pretty good shape. If you gave negative answers to most of the questions, the rest of this chapter will be especially beneficial and important.

Returning to the image of the chair, the four legs of self-esteem are: (1) a sense of belonging, (2) a sense of identity, (3) a sense of worthiness, and (4) a sense of control and competency

Each of us has a deep-seated need to belong something larger than ourselves. This is the first leg of the self-esteem chair. Psychologists call it an "affiliation drive." This is our instinct for belonging—of being wanted, accepted, enjoyed, and loved by those close to us. This need encompasses people, places, and things. It leads to some of the motivations I've mentioned, such as Status with Peers, Status with the Experts, and Acquisitiveness with an emphasis on material things.

The second leg of the self-esteem chair is complementary to the sense of belonging: our sense of individual identity. Even among identical twins, no two human beings are exactly alike. We all have unique combinations of talents and traits that have never existed before in the same package and will never exist in quite the same way again.

Highly motivated achievers know who they are, have confidence in what they believe, and feel respect for their present role in life as well as for their personal potential.

What do you see when you sit in the four-legged chair of self-esteem and look in the mirror? Is your chair a throne or a stepping stool? Can you gaze proudly at your reflection, or do you hide your face?

The third leg of self-esteem is a sense of worthiness— the intrinsic belief that, given your body, your background, and your genes, you're glad you're you. Others may accept you and make you feel you belong, others may praise who and what you are, but if you've violated your own conscience or sense of values, you won't feel very worthy.

This principle isn't limited to individuals. The sense of feeling worthy of quality, worthy of success, worthy of excellence, is one of the basic corporate missions across America. In a global market, with increasing competition from Asia, Europe, and other developing regions, it is imperative that each member of the workforce believes that he or she is a high-quality individual and expresses that quality in excellent production and service. With increasing pressure on profits and the need to do more with fewer workers, it is important that we "raise the value" of the employees' stock in *themselves,* since in a volatile economy we can't give them more stock in the company or more money as an incentive to do their best.

What society desperately needs is the fourth leg of self-esteem, which is self-efficacy, a functional belief in your own ability to positively and effectively control what happens to you in an uncertain world.

A sense of worthiness may give you permission to try to succeed, but self-efficacy, that sense of competency and control, lets you truly believe "I am able to do it!"

When you sit in the four-legged chair of self-esteem and look in the mirror, what do you see? Do you see someone who is happy and content with his or her life? Or do you see someone who feels alone, confused, unworthy, and out of control? If you are unhappy with yourself for any reason, ask yourself if the problem is real or only perceived. If the problem is perceived, you must concentrate on reframing the issue in a positive light. If the problem is real, the best time to begin to change it is right this minute. Our time is too short and precious to waste it feeling bad about ourselves or our place in the world.

Self-Confidence and Self-Efficacy

The foundation of real inner confidence is knowing you can cope with whatever comes up. Writing in the *Psychological Review,* Dr. Albert Bandura of Stanford University expressed it like this: "The strength of people's conviction in their own effectiveness is likely to affect whether they will even try to cope with the given situation."

Dr. Bandura, who has made some of the most important contributions to motivational psychology, was influenced by the work of Robert White, who found that the desire to feel competent was always a strong motivation in an emotionally healthy person. Bandura brought greater precision to White's work and formulated the concept of "self-efficacy," which he defined as the "feeling that one can perform any particular task successfully." This may very well be the strongest of all intrinsic motivations.

Self-efficacy is essentially a feeling of personal power—

not with the petty connotation of controlling or dominating others, but in the richly creative sense of empowerment, of being able to project one's will effectively into the world. The desire for this type of creative power has been proven to be one of the strongest motivations known to human beings.

When the drive for power is aroused, it also has a noticeable physical impact on our bodies. For example, psychologists have found that, by listening to speakers who inspire a mental image of this creative power, individuals not only perceived heightened motivation, but also experienced significantly increased levels of adrenaline released in their bodies. Once a sense of self-efficacy is aroused, both your mind and your body respond to help you achieve your goal, whether it's as an inventor, artist, executive, or nurturing parent.

In theory, once a motivation is satisfied, you should no longer be motivated to satisfy it. If hunger motivates you, you stop eating after you are full. If you need venture capital to launch your business, you don't keep looking for new investors after you have sufficient capital. But self-efficacy is the exception. Like the mythical Excalibur, a marvelous two-edged sword, self-efficacy not only empowers you to strive for your goals, it continues to motivate you even after you've reached your initial objective. Once a person feels that he can perform any task successfully, he will actually find that his motivation to achieve has been strengthened by this feeling rather than lessened, and his performance will continue to improve, reaching and surpassing excellence.

How can people keep on performing at higher and higher levels of excellence? Because the term *self-efficacy* actually means "self-perceived competency." It all depends upon your own perception of your own ability to successfully achieve your goals, not on your actual ability level. Henry Ford, the automobile pioneer, put it this way: "Whether you think you can or think you can't do something . . . either way you're right!"

The young administrator who sees himself as a poor communicator will invariably find he has trouble motivating others. He then has "proof." An executive assistant who believes she will have difficulty breaking into the male-dominated ranks of top management in her company will indeed find that the "glass ceiling" is real. She becomes defensive and frustrated, and her resentment gets in the way of her performance, thus completing the self-fulfilling prophesy that advancement is limited.

This is equally true for any professional with marginal feelings of self-efficacy. Actual experiences tend to prove that their self-image is correct. Because of this environmental and external proof, it very seldom occurs to these individuals that their trouble lies in a faulty, pre-conceived evaluation of themselves.

Of course, the greatest tragedy in human development is what happens to children between the primary grades and high school. Students who are treated as though they are mentally slow by teachers and parents will assume they are indeed inferior to normal children—and act accordingly. Between the age of six and sixteen, eighty percent of the younger generation abandons its feeling of creativity and ability and settles in for a life of mediocrity because of perceived incompetency and learned helplessness.

One of the best ways to foster a sense of positive self-efficacy in your children today is to help them view the problems of the world as normal ingredients in the process of change. Don't preach about the good old days when you were growing up. Don't fill their ears with gripes about the government and the economy and all the disasters that are taking place today. In order for kids to go out and contribute creatively, they need to know that adversity is the mother of invention.

Above all, let them experiment . . . and fail . . . and succeed. Don't do anything for your children that they can do for themselves. The more you do for them, the more dependent they will become on you, and the more habits of "learned helplessness" they will develop. Give them lots of early responsibilities and let them feel the pride of competency and control. Encourage their dreams, and support them through their awkward struggles to test and experience new methods, new actions, new people, and new places.

Developing Self-Efficacy

Follow-up studies confirmed Dr. Albert Bandura's insights into the benefits of self-efficacy on performance and the maintenance of high motivation levels. They also confirmed that self-efficacy is not strongly linked to personality type or intangible character traits like "drive" or "willpower." Almost anyone can develop his or her own sense of self-efficacy, as illustrated by my friend Nelie Gray.

As a young adult during the Great Depression in the early 1930s, Nelie Gray grew up totally self-sufficiently and learned to clothe and feed her family of four young children without relying on outside help. Her "victory" garden and small orchard provided fresh foods during the summer, and during the winter they survived on what she had canned. A small chicken coop in the backyard produced eggs and poultry. She made her own lye soap, did her laundry on a washboard, and sewed the family's clothes out of printed fifty-pound flour sacks. Of course, with that as an environmental backdrop, Nelie believed she could perform any task successfully and modeled the same attitude in her children. After all, they had never seen her fail in anything she attempted.

That is, not until she tried to develop her artistic talents.

Nelie loved music, and she loved to sing. Each Sunday at church, a travelling group of musicians would perform during the service in exchange for an offering of food. On one particular Sunday, a man performed an incredible concert with a bow from a violin and an ordinary-looking hand saw. He steadied the saw by putting his foot through the hole in the handle, and then bent the saw into various positions, running the violin bow across it. Like magic, he was creating beautiful music from an ordinary, quivering hand saw.

Nelie was spellbound. Having devoted her whole life to her family, making beautiful music was a new, exciting, and motivating goal. Money for something as frivolous as a musical instrument was out of the question, so she decided to learn to play the musical saw. Borrowing a neighbor's violin bow, she proceeded to create sounds reminiscent of two cats on a hot tin roof.

The children were aggravated, and Nelie was frustrated. "But I've always been able to do everything I've tried. Well, there must have been a trick to it," she asserted. "That man in church had a finer, more expensive saw. After all, he's no different than I am. If he can do it, so can I!"

But much to the children's relief, she couldn't.

However, the following week, there was a man deftly rubbing his fingers around the rims of ordinary drinking glasses filled with various amounts of water. The result was heavenly music. Nelie thought it resembled sounds from an angel's harp.

"That's what I'm going to play," she announced to the kids. "We have lots of glasses and canning jars." But the outcome was again disappointing. In fact, this time there was no sound at all. All she got was sore fingers and bored children.

Although psychologists Albert Bandura and Robert White probably hadn't been born when Nelie Gray was testing their theories, she is a perfect example of an emotionally healthy person with a strong motivation to feel competent. It was beyond her comprehension that any ordinary person could do something she couldn't do.

"I know why I can't make the glasses sing like a harp," Nelie informed the children. "He must have used fine crystal glasses, and all I have are cheap jelly glasses and heavy canning jars." The next week, there was a bell choir, with people ringing bells of all sizes and shapes in harmony, playing hymns and old favorites. Nelie's bells sounded more like a herd of cows coming home from the pasture.

The experiments continued, and Nelie's continuing failures never led to a feeling of "learned helplessness." She confirmed Bandura's later findings that failure does not seriously impair self-efficacy until the point that failure is admitted and the subject gives up.

Nelie refused to give up. While she was waiting for her children at a church party, she sat down at the church piano and began probing around, trying to find notes to match some of the songs she continually sang. Soon, with one finger, she could play the melody of the song as she was

Almost anyone can develop his or her own sense of self-efficacy. Ask Nelie Gray, whose strong motivation to express the music in her soul led her to teach herself how to play the piano.

singing. Over and over, she played the tune and sang. Each time she repeated it, she added a few more notes with other fingers. Amazingly, it sounded pretty good. Her feeling of self-efficacy was pumping in the adrenaline. Her belief in her ability actually lifted her ability level. Soon she began to improvise with chords, teaching herself to play with both hands. The entire process took a little over two hours. Her kids watched and listened in complete disbelief.

From that day forward, her family would arrive at church each Sunday a couple of hours early or stay an hour or so after the service so Mom could practice on the piano. Each week, she added new songs to her repertoire and new chords to the songs she had worked on earlier. Nelie Gray never learned to read notes and she never really tried. Although she never gave a concert, except for her own family, she became highly proficient as a pianist playing by ear. All she ever wanted to do was learn to embellish the music that continually played in her mind, and at this she was a complete success.

Four Factors in Increasing Self-Efficacy

Dr. Albert Bandura's studies revealed that there are four major factors that increase self-efficacy. The first is called "enactive mastery." This is the experience of feeling that you are doing well during a performance. For example, it would describe an basketball player in the midst of a game in which he feels he is performing well. The longer he hits his jump shot, the more he will believe in a strong, successful outcome of the contest.

Another form of enactive mastery comes from the knowledge that we have succeeded at this task, or a similar one, before. When most people get behind the steering wheel of their car, they give little thought to whether or not they can actually drive the car safely to their destination. Their previous experience has given them enough faith in their own ability to avoid accidents. Their self-efficacy is high and, in the majority of cases, they get where they want to go.

Dr. Bandura discovered that, as accomplishments mount, the individual's self-efficacy grows in other areas beyond his specific field of achievement. The more we accomplish, the more we see that we have been endowed with an enormous capacity for creative growth. Too often, we don't appreciate the remarkable strides we have made. When we were born, we didn't know a single word—we had no idea what language was. Yet in less than five years, we mastered almost the whole structure of human communication. No psychologist has been able to explain how we can digest and master such an incredible amount of data with almost no reference base upon which to build.

The second factor that increases self-efficacy is role modeling. We learn by observation and imitation. Self-efficacy rises as we see role models succeeding, and it diminishes if we habitually see our role models failing.

Look for role models who have succeeded in achieving goals similar to your own, individuals with whom you can personally identify. You can discover them among your colleagues or by reading biographies of achievers. Many prominent and historical individuals have found themselves in the same position that you're in now. If you have been subjected to negative role models in the past, don't give it too much concern. In a study published in the late 1980s, Weiss and Rakestraw, two respected psychologists, found that negative role models could be countered by proceeding ahead and achieving self-efficacy through direct enactive mastery. Your own success will be more vivid to you than the failure of a role model in your life. I know of many highly motivated achievers who have gone from ghettos into lives of great contribution.

The third factor that increases self-efficacy is verbal persuasion, which we have come to know as "self-affirmation" or "self-talk." This process will only be effective if it is combined with enactive mastery, which is actual perceived success.

Many of my colleagues in the Olympic Sports Psychology program have used the technique of mental rehearsal and guided imagery to bolster their athletes' self-efficacy. Dr. Herb Fensterheim of Cornell University worked with the U.S. Olympic Fencing team and wrote that one of his fencers had always been beaten by a certain rival at previous international meets. His fencer's problem was that he was in awe of his competitor and couldn't see himself standing up to him. With Dr. Fensterheim's guidance, the fencer made a two-minute audio tape saying positive things about himself that should make the opposing fencer stand in awe of him. He listened to it daily, once in the morning and once at night. This form of positive reinforcement worked effectively, and the fencer won his next important bout.

The final factor that increases your self-efficacy is control of emotional arousal. Elite athletes generally do better in competitive situations where their emotional arousal is higher than in more relaxed conditions of practice. However, they rarely press, try too hard, or force their actions. Many high-pressure situations call for complete concentration and a relaxed, reflexive performance. Heightened arousal should be confined to a level that will enhance your awareness, tune in all your senses, and generate the optimum amount of adrenaline for power and energy.

The crux of this message is that belief in your ability to succeed dramatically enhances the mental and physiological factors involved in your actual success. The more you perceive your competence, the more success you will experience. For the highly motivated achiever, failure does not necessarily breed failure, but success definitely breeds success.

Six Behaviors that Increase Self-Esteem

Following are six behaviors that increase self-esteem, enhance your self-confidence, and spur your motivation. You may recognize some of them as things you naturally do in your interactions with other people. But if you don't, I suggest you motivate yourself to take some of these important steps immediately.

First, greet others with a smile and look them directly in the eye. A smile and direct eye contact convey confidence born of self-respect. In the same way, answer the phone pleasantly whether at work or at home, and when placing a call, give your name before asking to speak to the party you want to reach. Leading with your name underscores that a person with self-respect is making the call.

Second, always show real appreciation for a gift or complement. Don't downplay or sidestep expressions of affection or honor from others. The ability to accept or receive is a universal mark of an individual with solid self-esteem.

Third, don't brag. It's almost a paradox that genuine modesty is actually part of the capacity to gracefully receive complements. People who brag about their own exploits or demand special attention are simply trying to build themselves up in the eyes of others—and that's because they don't perceive themselves as already worthy of respect.

Fourth, don't make your problems the centerpiece of your conversation. Talk positively about your life and the progress you're trying to make. Be aware of any negative thinking, and take notice of how often you complain. When you hear yourself criticize someone—and this includes self-criticism—find a way to be helpful instead of critical.

Fifth, respond to difficult times or depressing moments by increasing your level of productive activity. When your self-esteem is being challenged, don't sit around and fall victim to "paralysis by analysis." The late Malcolm Forbes said, "Vehicles in motion use their generators to charge their own batteries. Unless you happen to be a golf cart, you can't recharge your battery when you're parked in the garage!"

Sixth, choose to see mistakes and rejections as opportunities to learn. View a failure as the conclusion of one performance, not the end of your entire career. Own up to your shortcomings, but refuse to see yourself as a failure. A failure may be something you have done—and it may even be something you'll have to do again on the way to success—but a failure is definitely not something you are.

Even if you're at a point where you're feeling very negatively about yourself, be aware that you're now ideally positioned to make rapid and dramatic improvement. A negative self-evaluation, if it's honest and insightful, takes much more courage and character than the self-delusions that underlie arrogance and conceit. I've seen the truth of this proven many times in my work with athletes. After an extremely poor performance, a team or an individual athlete often does much better the next time out, especially when the poor performance was so bad that there was simply no way to shirk responsibility for it. Disappointment, defeat, and even apparent failure are in no way permanent conditions unless we choose to make them so. On the contrary, these undeniably painful experiences can be the solid foundation on which to build future success.

Living Life Hopefully

One of the most important distinctions between hopeful and hopeless people is referred to by psychologists as "explanatory style." More specifically, a person's explanatory style is the way he or she understands and explains the bad things that happen in life. If two people both miss the bus that takes them to work in the morning, the hopeful person will most likely find some consolation in the fact that another bus will soon be coming along. The hopeless person, on the other hand, will feel fundamentally inadequate and diminished. "I'm an inadequate human being," he will conclude. "I can't even do something as simple as catching a bus!"

What are the building blocks of these two different explanations? First, the hopeful person sees disappointments as originating from some cause outside himself. When something goes wrong, he doesn't feel it's because he's essentially repulsive in the sight of the universe; he just thinks that it didn't work out this time, but maybe it will next time. In contrast, the hopeless person has an internal explanation for misfortune. When things go wrong, it's not because of chance, and it's not just a one-time thing. For a hopeless person, every negative experience springs from the very core of his or her being.

The second distinction between optimistic and pessimistic people has to do with time. Hopeless people see misfortune as long lasting or even as a permanent condition of their lives. There's a certain internal logic to this: Since bad things happen because of an internal condition of one's being, and since this internal condition can't be changed, bad things will continue to happen forever. As the old blues song puts it, a hopeless person feels that if he didn't have bad luck, he wouldn't have any luck at all. But the hopeful individual is confident that bad luck won't last forever.

The third difference between these two kinds of people is a kind of spatial distinction. To a hopeless person, every negative event is what psychologists refer to as global. If something goes wrong in one area of life, it means that everything is going to go wrong in every other area as well. But if a hopeful person has a bad day at work, she doesn't assume it means she's going to have a fight with her husband or that her car insurance will be canceled.

Dr. Martin Seligman found specific evidence for the practical effects of explanatory style in a study of collegiate swimmers. At the outset of the study, the athletes were given a psychological test to determine their levels of hopefulness or pessimism. Following the test, they were timed in some practice laps, but when the times were told to the swimmers, they were deliberately reported as being a second or two slower than they actually were. Since one second can mean the difference between winning or coming in last in a competition, all the athletes took the disappointing news very seriously. But they also responded in very different ways. When the pessimists were timed again, they were consistently slower than their usual performances. It was as if they somehow felt they had to confirm the negative results they'd received earlier. The hopeful athletes, however, either maintained the level of their times or in some cases got even faster.

Let me emphasize again that hopefulness is an essentially internal element of the personality, but it clearly leads to very tangible positive results. In general, hopeful people are more likely to find ways, try methods, and formulate plans of action that lead to beneficial outcomes. In short, hopeful people have more achievement motivation.

The research we've mentioned has some very important implications for how we experience the world every day. So many of negative feelings—boredom, irritation, a sense of having to hurry all the time—are really a function of whether we feel hopeful and motivated in our lives or negative and pessimistic.

Making Your Hard Work Enjoyable

As you are pursuing your goals, here are seven motivating ways to make your hard work satisfying and enjoyable:

First, view the work you are engaged in as a challenge. If it's something you already know how to do well and just seems like tedium or drudgery, then try to think of new ways to do it better or quicker. Make sure that, no matter what it is or what you would rather be doing, your work is *always* of the highest quality. In his book *Excellence,* which is one of my favorites, John W. Gardner reminds us: "An excellent plumber is infinitely more admirable than an incompetent philosopher. The society which scorns excellence in plumbing because plumbing is a humble activity and tolerates shoddiness in philosophy because it is an exalted activity will have neither good plumbing nor good philosophy. Neither its pipes nor its theories will hold water."

There is not job too unworthy to do well. As they say in show business, "There are no small parts, only small actors." My friend Lisa is an example of employing great talent in a small part. She went to New York City fresh out of college looking for a job in publishing. No one was hiring. Finally, economic necessity made her take a job as a waitress in a coffee shop.

Undaunted, she did her best. She acted professionally and always greeted each person with courtesy and a smile. Several months later, a regular customer said to her, "I'll bet you aren't a waitress all the time. What else do you do?"

"Well," she said, "I'd like to become an editor, so I'm working evenings here and going out on job interviews during the day." As it turned out, the customer was a prominent literary agent who needed a bright assistant. An interview was arranged, and she got the job. Lisa put into practice the principle of doing your best and bringing something fresh and new to whatever you are doing, every day.

Second, approach what you are doing as if it were the first time doing it. When faced with a routine—prospecting for customers, making a number of phone calls, typing letters, filling out forms, chairing a meeting—challenge yourself to attack it from a fresh angle. Each letter, each form, and each meeting is, after all, different. So rather than see the individual assignments as a lump of indistinguishable work, handle each one with a fresh mind. The same applies to a sales presentation. Even if you've promoted the benefits of the product or service hundreds of times before, it is the first time for your customer in front of you. Make it fresh and interesting, as if it were the first time.

I've had a long career of giving keynote speeches four days a week, in cities all over the world. The only way I can maintain my enthusiasm and motivation is to tell myself as I walk out on the stage: "This is brand new for them, and the first time for you to speak in front of them. So keep it crisp and upbeat, Denis, whatever you do!" And it works for me. I sure hope it works as well for my audiences!

Third, follow the "as if" principle. When you must do work that is dull and repetitious, do it *as if* it were interesting. Make a game of your work: Try to surpass a self-imposed quota, discover what personal creativity you can add to the job at hand, attempt to do each portion of the task perfectly. Do your work *as if* you really enjoy it. An immediate benefit is the ease and rapidity with which you'll accomplish your work. Besides which, you'll have a lot more energy at the end of the day.

Fourth, write down your accomplishments along the way to your goal and take pride in them. The satisfaction of doing your job well and efficiently, of always moving toward your goals, will go a long way to making hard work enjoyable. Remember, as children, when our parents posted a picture we painted, or a test we passed with flying colors, or a story we wrote on the refrigerator door or bulletin board? Those tangible reminders of our accomplishments did a lot to build our self-esteem and keep us motivated to do our best. As adults, our small accomplishments are rarely noticed or featured by others. That's why it's so important to note your own accomplishments as you achieve them.

Be willing to say to yourself, "I'm on the right road. I'm

doing okay. I'm succeeding." We too frequently become adept at pointing out our flaws and identifying failures. Become equally adept at citing your achievements. Identify things you are doing now that you weren't doing one month ago, six months ago, a year ago, five years ago. What habits have changed? What progress has been made? Chart your progress. Use the same type of charts that we make in business to forecast or report trends. Note areas of growth. List the goals you have reached. Put a star by them.

Doing well once or twice is relatively easy. Continuing to move upward is tough, in part because we so easily revert to old habits and former lifestyles. Over the long run, you need to give yourself regular feedback to monitor your performance and reinforce yourself positively. If you note that you are starting to experience a downward trend, these feedback notes can help you recognize it and take steps to revert its course. If you can learn to give yourself positive feedback, you will find it much easier to turn goal achievement into habit.

Dante Gabriel Rossetti, the famous nineteenth-century poet and artist, was once approached by an elderly man. The old fellow had some sketches and drawings he wanted Rossetti to look at and tell him if they were any good, or if they at least showed potential talent.

Rossetti looked over the batch of sketches and immediately became enthusiastic over the talent they revealed. "Oh, these are good!" he said. "This young student has great talent. He or she should be given every help and encouragement in his career as an artist. He has a great future if he will work hard and stick to it."

Rossetti could see that the old fellow was deeply moved.

"Who is this fine young artist?" he asked. "Your son or daughter?"

"No," said the old man sadly. "It is me—forty years ago. If only I had your praise of my work then! For you see, I got discouraged and gave up too soon."

Don't wait for an employer, friend, or mentor to show appreciation for your work. Take pride in your own efforts on a daily basis.

Fifth, keep the end result in sight. Always see the big picture of the ultimate goal you're working for and the benefits that come with it. An insurance agent should see every stack of forms as representing a family with needs, aspirations, and dreams. An auto worker should know each car he or she helps build is taking someone on a safe and productive journey. A cellular phone salesperson should feel he or she is contributing to the growth of a global communication network. A bank executive should understand each customer is working and saving, as he or she is, toward personal and professional goals. These are the visions that drive us through tedious details to the top.

Sixth, set up a dynamic daily routine. Getting into a positive routine or groove instead of a negative rut will help you become more effective. Why are the railroad and subway still the most energy-efficient means of transportation? Because they run on a track.

That's what the daily application of goals can do for you. That's why writing and checking your goals each day is important. But there are other important points in getting the most out of your energy each day. The more healthy habits and positive routines that can be worked into your day, the more energy you save that would have been expended with trivial decisions such as what to wear, when and where to eat, and how to use your break time.

You can learn a lot by studying our top Olympic athletes. I observed the American Olympians preparing for the last Summer Olympics of the twentieth century in Atlanta, Georgia. They were up and showered by 5:30 in the morning. They ate a nutritional breakfast. They reflected on their progress from the day before and studied their goals for the day. They did a specific regimen of activities in the morning. They ate a light, nutritious lunch high in complex, fiber-based carbohydrates. They reserved a certain part of the early afternoon for phone calls, media interviews, and study. Then they went back to their training routine. They took a short, creative break in the afternoon. They continued training until just before supper time. They had a debriefing session with their coach and trainer in the early evening. They listened to music, relaxed, and socialized with other champions until bedtime. Prior to getting a good night's sleep, they planned the next day and called or wrote friends or relatives. They did this six days a week for 1,200 days just for the privilege of *competing* in the Olympics. They must do much more to *win.*

Now, it's true that you and I are not on a single track that affords us specialization in just one area, like Olympic athletes are. But when we stop to consider that they also have relationships, coaches, trainers, sponsors, equipment, weather, injury, travel, sickness, trial meets, and competitive considerations, we realize that one of the secrets to their success may be in the channeling of their energy into achieving their primary goals, tolerating little or no distraction.

When most people think of a daily routine, they think of a military regimen or doing the same thing over and over again. The important thing is not to do the same things every day, but to have a schedule that minimizes interruptions, trivial activity, and downtime.

Think of the order in your day instead of the routine. Order is not sameness, neatness, or "everything in its place." Order is not taking on more than you can manage without still being able to do what you really choose.

Order is the opposite of complication; it's *simplification.* Order is not wasting a lot of time trying to find new things. Order is avoiding a lot of recriminations by doing the things you've promised you'll do.

Order is setting an effective agenda with others so neither of you is disappointed. Order is doing in a day what you set out to do. Order frees you up. Get into the swing of a healthy, daily routine, and discover how much more control you gain in your life!

Seventh, schedule time for relaxation and exercise into your daily routine. Relaxation and exercise are primary ingredients in creativity and inspiration. Before you can use your imagination effectively, you need to relax your mind and body. Mental relaxation allows the right hemisphere of your brain more freedom because the verbal, judgmental, and analytical left hemisphere is quiet. Physical exercise and relaxation improves circulation, releases tension, and puts you in touch with your body's internal environment without distraction.

I was sharing a plane ride with a CEO of a very successful company who has been in the corporate fast lane for over forty years. When he told me he was celebrating his seventieth birthday, I nearly dropped my pretzels into my Diet Coke. He was trim and unwrinkled with natural dark hair (I can tell Grecian Formula or a professional dye job when I see one!). He had piercing, clear eyes and a completely relaxed manner. He showed me his daily planner and proudly revealed that he had taken a one-hour swim in a swimming pool five days a week for thirty years without missing a single day.

When he was thirty-nine, he had been diagnosed with chronic high blood pressure and hypoglycemia. Every weekday thereafter, he had his secretary schedule him for one hour at his local health club to swim laps during the noon hour. When I inquired about luncheon meetings, he said his policy was to have after-lunch meetings instead. "All people do is eat too much, drink too much, and make small talk too much at lunch," he said. He said he never missed anything or anyone important by swimming during lunch.

He taught me that if you take time out to relax and exercise every day, you'll rarely have to take time away from your goals or your life because your energy level is running low.

Find an exercise that you really enjoy. For me, it's taking a brisk, long walk every day, hiking and swimming as often as possible, and tennis when my travel schedule permits.

You should also take frequent thinking and stretch breaks during the day. The brain retains more and functions most efficiently at the beginning and ending of a work period. That means periodic breaks actually increase the amount you learn and accomplish in one day. Breaks also make the work you do more satisfying because they divide your work into chunks, which makes it easier to see what you've done and when.

I hope this helps you to see that rest, relaxation, and exercise are not time-wasting interruptions in a busy day. They are actually the key to getting more energy to accomplish more of what you need to do.

SUSTAINING MOTIVATION

Cognitive Dissonance • Defensiveness in Times of Low Motivation • Failing to Justify Your Actions • Avoiding the Blame-the-Victim Syndrome • Staying Motivated during Tough Times • Finding the Right Search Image • Are You Chasing the Right Goals? • Doing What You Love • Helping Yourself by Helping Others • No One Is an Island

"Every human being wants to think that he or she acts in a manner consistent with his or her own beliefs. When our actions conflict with the way we think we should act, we experience what scientists call 'cognitive dissonance,' which can cause depression and procrastination in our daily lives."

"So great is the human need for love and approval that we will even deceive ourselves rather than face the fact that we might not deserve approval. Actually, all of us sometimes do things that are unkind, irrational, and inconsiderate. But rather than view ourselves in an unfavorable light, we unconsciously protect our self-image."

"To maintain a high level of motivation when the going gets tough, we need a challenging level of aspiration—a goal with real pulling power—and we also need the flexibility to create a number of sub-goals or search images, which are short-term reasons for staying in whatever race we are running."

"Balancing individual goals with goals for the good of the group is the only way to serve your own long-term interests. The longer I live, the more I realize that the individuals who want to help themselves can only do so by helping others."

Cognitive Dissonance

We all experience times when it is tough to stay motivated. Our goals can appear hopelessly remote or not worth the effort needed to achieve them, and it is hard to know what seems right in life. Even the little matters can confound us in their own subtle ways.

Beginning early in life, we are confronted by a barrage of confusing messages. Parents spend five years teaching children how to stand up and speak for themselves and another twelve years teaching them to sit down and be quiet.

Life is filled with contradictions, and we don't always resolve them in the most effective way. Many times, the decisions we make in our lifestyles and professional careers conflict with our values and beliefs. Somehow, we manage to rationalize and justify behaviors that are harmful, even to ourselves and our associates.

Most of the time when we evaluate a situation, we

believe we are basing it on three factors: (1) the truth as we see it, (2) the best course of action, and (3) something that is compatible with our sincere personal beliefs.

However, this is not really the way it works deep down inside of ourselves.

In the play *The Man of La Mancha,* Don Quixote makes a telling remark in an attempt to hide from the fact that his beloved "Dolcinea" is actually a common barmaid, and the dragon he's fighting is only a windmill.

Confronted with these facts, Don Quixote retorts, "Facts? Facts are enemies of the truth."

My friend and fellow researcher Dr. Robert C. Larson observes: "If facts can be enemies of the truth, then it should come as no surprise to you and me that good intentions can be the enemies of integrity."

Nevertheless, every human being wants to think that he or she acts in a manner consistent with his or her own beliefs. When our actions conflict with the way we think we should act, we experience what scientists call "cognitive dissonance," which can cause depression and procrastination in our daily lives.

Suppose, for example, you believe that you should get into a fitness regimen and develop a healthy lifestyle. That's a decision many of us make at one time or another, but for some people, it's much easier than for others.

If you smoke, for instance, and you want to stop smoking, you're very likely to experience substantial mental discomfort, because you'll realize that you're not living up to your own rational plan of action.

The idea of cognitive dissonance was first proposed by Leon Festinger. While studying this phenomenon, he found that it causes considerable stress, and that we all react instinctively to relieve this stress whenever we're subjected to it. For example, in order to bring his actions in line with his stated beliefs, this smoker might actually kick the habit. But there are also two other options available to him.

He could give up his desire to lead a healthy life, rationalizing, "Ah, well, it's all genetic in the long run. I could just as easily get hit by a bus. Then what will be the point have been in losing all the pleasure while really gaining no additional years?" We've all heard people make this excuse.

The other alternative is no less destructive. He can lie to himself and convince himself that smoking isn't really dangerous. Dangerous for other people, possibly, but not to him. This may seem outlandish, but the human mind has an almost limitless capacity to lie to itself, especially during times of emotional pressure caused by cognitive dissonance.

Defensiveness in Times of Low Motivation

Psychologist Mortimer Feinberg says that one of the hardest things we can do is to look at ourselves objectively, realistically, without self-glorification, deception, or despair.

All of us are born into this world helpless and dependent. To survive, we need to lean on others. The child growing up looks to its mother not only for the comforts of physical help, but for the more rewarding comfort of approval.

As we grow older, we continue this search. We want friends and business associates to like us and to approve of what we do. In their approval, we find reassurance of our own worth.

So great is the human need for love and approval that we will even deceive ourselves rather than face the fact that we might not deserve approval. Actually, all of us sometimes do things that are unkind, irrational, and inconsiderate. But rather than view ourselves in an unfavorable light, we unconsciously protect our self-image.

Then we tell ourselves, "I did it because..." providing supposedly good and substantial reasons for our behavior. We disown responsibility and project it as another person's problem. We displace by blaming someone else for our own faults. We compensate by stretching ourselves in one area when we have failed in another.

Our defenses serve two purposes. First, they prove to others that we're really fine people, and if we did something wrong, at least we did it for the right reasons. Second, our defenses help us deceive ourselves.

This is why periods in which it is difficult to maintain motivation can be so harmful to our quest for high-level achievement. We suffer from cognitive dissonance caused by the contradiction between our belief that we should be highly motivated and the great difficulty we find in doing just that.

We face the same options that the smoker in the previous chapter faced. We can bring our actions back in line with our belief in our own goals and the value of achieving them. Or we can engage in destructive behavior to reconcile two contradictory emotions. This involves losing motivation and giving into feelings of low self-esteem. And unfortunately, this is the path of least resistance.

Failing to Justify Your Actions

Psychologist Leon Festinger conducted several studies that demonstrate clearly how humans tend to deal with cognitive dissonance. In one study, the subjects were given an extremely dull, tedious task to perform for a long period of time. At the end of the experiment, they were asked to try to convince the next person in the waiting room that the project was interesting and enjoyable. (Rather like adults telling their children that doing their homework or cleaning their rooms will be interesting and enjoyable!)

Half the test subjects were offered twenty dollars to tell this lie, and the other half were offered only one dollar to do the same. Although the test subjects thought they would be trying to convince an actual member of their group, the would-be candidates for the task were actually research assistants posing as test subjects.

Festinger's hypothesis was that the subjects who were

paid twenty dollars would not feel a great deal of cognitive dissonance. Although they had told a lie about the work being interesting, they did not normally consider themselves to be liars, and therefore could think it was altogether rational for them to tell a harmless lie in return for twenty dollars.

Conversely, he forecasted that the subjects who were paid only one dollar for telling the lie would experience quite a bit of cognitive dissonance. They also would not normally think of themselves as liars, and yet they each would be lying with virtually no reward in return. Festinger predicted that the subjects who had lied for one dollar would look back in retrospect and actually convince themselves that the task was more interesting and enjoyable than it had been. And, of course, the scientist was correct in his predictions.

When you can't justify your own actions, do you change your belief system? Or do you keep your perspective and your poise in the face of temporary stress?

Think about it. When you are tired and your motivation is low, it is no time to make fundamental decisions or changes. On the contrary, it's a time for calm reflection and for a positive assessment of the inner riches still in your "BAG."

B is for *Blessings*. What do you consider your blessings? Being alive, your family, your friends, your career, your love of nature, music, art, children, or your spiritual dimension?

A is for *Accomplishments*. What have you done so far that you're proud of? You've accomplished a great deal in your life, whether you realize it or not. When I work with sports teams who are suffering through a slump in their season, I go back and get film highlights from their greatest games. I also show clips of each player doing a great job in helping the team or making an outstanding individual effort. This reinforcement of past accomplishments during a tough motivational period really makes a positive difference.

And finally, *G* is for *Goals*. When you get stuck in a rut of boredom, routine, and monotony, always keep your long-range goals in mind. Think of the people who sew parachutes. If you're sewing pieces of silk together day after day, there's not much variety to your job. But remember what I wrote earlier about framing. If you keep in mind that the parachute you're sewing is one that will open and save a person's life, your daily drudgery will take on a whole new meaning. When you're in a valley, keep the goal firmly in view and you'll get the renewed energy to continue the climb.

Avoiding the Blame-the-Victim Syndrome

Psychologists see a connection between cognitive dissonance and a condition known as the "blame-the-victim syndrome." During the last century in the United States, the relationship between masters and slaves was a classic example of this syndrome.

Most slave owners thought of themselves as good and humane people. At the same time, they also accepted the fact that they had bought other human beings and kept them in service against their will. From our perspective in history, we can see that their actions were in contradiction to their belief in themselves as fine, upstanding citizens. In their own minds, they reconciled this dissonance by telling themselves that their slaves were inferior and were better off in captivity than they would be as free citizens.

This is an extreme example of how the blame-the-victim syndrome functions. Psychologists have found that we tend to harbor anger and resentment toward, and lower our opinion of, anyone whom we mistreat. In a confirming experiment, subjects were given the assignment of listening to another student being interviewed and then telling the interviewee, to his face, that he was a dull and untrustworthy person. Afterward, the critical listener would then privately rate the worthiness and likability of the interviewee on a form shared only with the researchers. As the researchers had thought, the critical listener tended to give the interviewees very low ratings in areas of worthiness and likability, much lower than those subjects they had not been asked to insult.

The key lesson here for all of us is that we tend to mistreat and think less of those people whom we have hurt. Clearly, this is a way of justifying our behavior. But what if the one you've hurt is yourself? Will you then begin to think less of yourself to rationalize your actions? As a matter of fact, this is exactly what happens. The psychological reflex of blaming the victim will still be in force even if the victim is you!

It is typical during tough motivational periods to get down on ourselves, hurling self-directed insults and invectives, and lowering our opinion of ourselves and what we can achieve. The studies on self-efficacy that I outlined in earlier chapters illustrated how devastating lowered self-esteem and self-expectancy are to the possibility of reaching our long-term goals.

I devoted some of my graduate studies to the prisoners of war in Viet Nam, the Korean War, and World War Two. I also had the privilege of sitting in on lectures by Dr. Viktor Frankl, who was a visiting professor at United States International University in San Diego, California. As you are probably aware, Dr. Frankl led the resistance movement in the Nazi death camps during the Holocaust. After months and years of torture, when the prisoners were finally freed by the Allied forces, many did not rejoice or express emotion. They had developed the ultimate in passive resistance to an undesirable situation. They were victims of learned helplessness and low self-efficacy.

We should be acutely aware of the effect that punishment can have on behavior. Children who are continually punished for unacceptable behavior may acquire learned helplessness because they quickly learn there is no escape from their parents or their adult supervisors. As a general rule, you should reward positive behavior and let "punishment," if that's the right word, take care of itself as much as possible. Allow children and subordinates to experience the logical consequences of their actions, as long as there is no threat to their physical or emotional safety. If inappropriate behavior is rewarded with punishment, either the behavior will continue as a means to attract further attention, or the subject will passively learn to accept the pain and develop learned helplessness. For this reason, we should be positive caretakers for our associates and loved ones when motivation is lacking or misplaced. And we should be positive caretakers for ourselves during those times when we are most vulnerable to lowered self-esteem.

Staying Motivated during Tough Times

Here are some reminders to help you stay motivated during tough times.

1. *Don't blame yourself when you're feeling down.* You're not a robot. Accept yourself as a changing, growing, vulnerable human being.

2. *Remember the line from that old Olivia Newton-John song: "Listen to your body talk."* Depression or lack of energy may be a physiological problem, not a motivational one. Review your eating, resting, and exercise habits. The leading cause of depression among American males is lack of exercise, and the leading cause of depression among American females is fatigue, possibly from trying to act out a "superwoman syndrome" of professional and personal responsibilities. Try to eliminate

physical causes by consulting a doctor and getting a physical check-up.

3. *Check the pulling power of your goals.* You may have outgrown your current targets and present lifestyle. It may be time for motivation by elevation. Raise your sights and challenge yourself with some goals farther out on the horizon. This may require more knowledge, new skills, or a new lifestyle. If so, that's great! When I worked in the Apollo program at NASA, we knew that when the rockets experienced first-stage burnout, a new second-stage ignition was needed to send the spacecraft into higher orbit. You may be ready for a new staging to a new orbit in your life.

4. *Check your motivating images.* Status with peers, for instance, may have worked during adolescence, but it doesn't have as much power in mature adults. Focus more on intrinsic motivators. Examine your deepest desires and their relationships to your goals. Go back to the list of benefits you attached to your goals. Do these benefits still attract you?

5. *Tell yourself, "This is where I am now, fairly or unfairly. Where do I really want to go now? What are my first steps? And what is the process to get from here to where I want to be?"* This is according to my friend Dr. Herbert Fensterheim, who in his book *Making Life Right When It Feels All Wrong,* says that you don't have to live with the heartache of remaining an emotional victim.

6. *Know that only you can change yourself.* Regardless of what has happened in the past, you are in control of the present. You may have been your own enemy before, but starting today, you are your strongest ally. You can and will change your future.

Finding the Right Search Image

What if, even though your goals match your deepest desires and your level of aspiration seems right for your ability and available time, you still have difficulty motivating yourself? What should you do?

Psychologists stress that during periods like these, your motivating image lacks sufficient driving or compelling power. It seems remote and not worth the effort instead of clear, real, and exciting. Maybe it even seems unreachable. Deep down, this is not your true opinion, but at the day-to-day level, you have real difficulty combatting the idea that what you want is out of reach.

Researchers have found that, in difficult times, one of the most stressful strategies is replacing your final motivating image with a less-remote search image.

A "search image" is the image of something we already have identified as what we want. A hungry person knows he is looking for food. There is not much doubt in his mind or conflict among his different motivational drives.

When we're feeling good about ourselves and our ability to achieve our major goals, we use those actual goals as our motivating search images. A marathon runner just starting to race feels good. He is rested and confident that he can cross the finish line. This is his search image. When he starts the race, he knows what he wants. He wants to finish. There are no conflicting motivations.

But when he hits the "wall of fatigue" at the eighteen-mile mark, he's no longer focused on his final goal. He's suddenly so tired that his legs feel like they can't take him forward another mile, much less another eight miles. Now he's no longer certain that crossing the finish line is worth the struggle to get there. The image of himself crossing the finish line has lost its power to motivate him past the exhaustion and physical pain.

At this moment in time, the runner should start looking for a new search image that can keep him moving ahead. Where would such an image come from? Most likely, it will appear from a very surprising source: from the same conflicting desires that have begun to convince him to drop out of the race.

For example, the runner might be thinking, "My legs are tired. What can I do to rest them that will help me finish the race?"

Unfortunately, he can't come up with an answer. Anything he tries to do to rest his legs will put him out of the competition. Too bad. That finish line is looking a long way off, but he's still unwilling to give up without a spartan effort. So he continues to search through his desires of the moment, to the images of things he knows he wants.

The next image he may bring up from his desire inventory could be thirst. As well as being tired, he is very thirsty. His parched throat is one of the reasons he's thinking of quitting. But then he remembers that there's an aid station at the twentieth mile. Two miles further doesn't seem as impossible as seven miles to the finish line, and in two miles he can get a cool, thirst-quenching drink. At this point, the new search image keeps him running on his path toward his major goal.

It's quite possible that, by the time he reaches the aid station, he'll have renewed his belief in himself and his ability to endure. At least his final motivating image will be two miles closer than before, and he might get that elusive second wind. If worse comes to worse, he can try to generate another interim search image to keep himself going another increment further.

To maintain a high level of motivation when the going gets tough, we need a challenging level of aspiration—a goal with real pulling power—and we also need the flexibility to create a number of sub-goals or search images, which are short-term reasons for staying in whatever race we are running.

Are You Chasing the Right Goals?

The race we are running may be a "rat race." We may be running in circles in search of the wrong goal. We may be clawing our way to the top, trying to stay motivated, when we don't know what the top really is.

In her charming book *Hope for the Flowers,* Trina Paulus tells a parable that accurately exposes the futility of trying to claw your way to the top of the success ladder just because you believe it's the competitive thing to do.

When the caterpillar Stripe finds his normal routine unrewarding, he crawls off to discover life in the fast lane. He comes across other caterpillars who don't seem to know any more about life than he does, but he joins a group who all seem to be wiggling in the same direction.

Soon, they come to a towering column of squirming caterpillars—a literal caterpillar pillar—that seems to rise forever into the clouds high above. All the caterpillars seem to be desperately trying to crawl over each other to reach the top of the pillar. Stripe gets excited. This must be the right place!

"What's at the top?" Stripe asks, his motivation running high.

"We're not sure," respond the other caterpillars, "But it must be awfully good, because everyone's rushing up there."

With ruthless discipline, Stripe keeps stepping on others to reach the summit. He realizes he can't get to the absolute peak of the pile unless he gets rid of those who are above him. Already, he can hear the screams of falling bodies that have been displaced by the ones next in line. He is only a few wiggles from the top when he hears someone whisper, "There's nothing up here after all."

Stripe stops crawling and looks around over the edge of the pillar. As he gazes out beyond his own wriggling mass of competitors, he can't believe his eyes! All around him, as far as he can see, the world is full of thousands of giant pillars like his own, with countless caterpillars trying to reach the tops of them!

I once saw an article about Japan by Jeff Shear in *Reader's Digest*. It's not unlike the parable of Stripe and his caterpillar colleagues. Japan is the undisputed world leader in consumer electronics, automobile quality, and many areas of high technology, with a per-capita income among the highest in the world. But there's another side to their economic miracle. An eight-hundred-square-foot apartment in Tokyo sells for about $440,000. Jammed commuter trains are filled to 250 percent of capacity. The average workday is from 8:30 AM until 8:00 PM, with after-hour company functions making it a common practice for executives to arrive home near midnight during the week. A popular Japanese song recites the days of the week as "Monday, Monday, Tuesday, Wednesday, Thursday, Friday, Friday." With nearly thirty-three million automobiles in Japan, rush-hour traffic makes Los Angeles seem like the open road. Many who commute by car leave home at 5:00 AM and park in front of their offices, sleeping for an hour or so in their autos, so they will have a parking space during the workday.

To compensate for all this stress, the Japanese have a new pep-up beverage to combat fatigue. Called Regain, its ingredients include caffeine, a nicotine derivative, and vitamin B1. It's like a cup of coffee, a cigarette, and a dose of vitamins all in one bottle.

The Japanese refer to their living conditions as *manuke,* which means "we lack three things: time, space, and private lives." Like the fictional Stripe, they are beginning to reevaluate their goals and motivations.

We can learn a lot from these two different accounts of high motivation. Before setting your sights on a lofty goal and focusing all of your energy on it to the exclusion of everything else, it's best to ask yourself if attaining the goal is worth the trouble. Sometimes, you might be surprised at the answer.

The Japanese refer to their hectic and expensive living conditions as manuke, *which means "we lack three things: time, space, and private lives."*

Doing What You Love

The late Roy Kroc, founder of McDonald's restaurants, stressed the importance of people doing a good job, not just for the money, but for the inner satisfaction it brings.

He said that the first thing a business executive needs is an idea that he or she loves. If you don't love it, drop it. If you're going to prostitute yourself at an early age and look for a job where the money is, you'll be working for money all your life. To love your work is very important, particularly for young people. If they lose that love, they'll never be able to recapture it.

In her study of highly motivated achievers, as reported in her book *Megatraits,* Doris Lee McCoy notes that the number one cause of lost motivation is a career that's unsuited to one's talents. Too many people choose a "convenient" career, one in which they merely put in their hours and then go home to do what they really enjoy. The real achievers choose a different course of action. First, to use their full potential, they find out what career is most rewarding and interesting to pursue. Second, they realize they may find it necessary to go through several job changes, testing and discovering new talents in the process. And finally, they use their jobs as opportunities for developing their talents to the maximum. What does this mean for you? It means that you should carefully assess the areas in your life that are most enjoyable and in which you are most talented. This is where you'll do your best and feel rewarded.

Although a competitive nature may be of help in pushing an individual toward doing an outstanding job, it can also hold him or her back from enjoying the success once it's been attained. It's better to set your own internal standards for success rather than living by competition or comparison. When you compare yourself with others less successful than yourself, you run the risk of an overly inflated ego, which requires a lot of time and energy to maintain. But if you compare yourself unfavorably with others, you may become frustrated. Both of these emotions make it difficult to maintain a highly motivated state.

To maintain your motivation to win, consider the following actions:

1. *If you feel locked into your present job, recognize that other options exist.* See a career counselor. If you haven't read the classic book *What Color Is Your Parachute?*, I highly recommend it.

2. *Take time to analyze your interests and talents.* During this process, totally forget any thoughts about making

money. Think only about what gives you the most satisfaction. What activities excite you? What do you get the most praise for?

3. *Get rid of the idea that your career and work should not be enjoyable.* The more you like your career, the more productive you'll be—and, chances are, the more money you'll make in the long run as a result.

4. *Make a list of every talent you have, however small, and every goal you have accomplished that has been important to you.* Go back even to your childhood and teen years. It has been discovered that some of your greatest gifts and aspirations can be buried in past experiences.

5. *Surround yourself with positive, supportive people.* Remember that one of the ways to feel good about yourself is to help and be supportive of others while, at the same time, they are encouraging you.

6. *Start becoming aware of your negative thinking.* Notice how often you complain. When you hear yourself criticize something or someone, say to yourself: "Bad seeds! That's not like me." And find a way to be helpful instead of critical.

7. *Increase your productive activity level.* During times of weakened motivation, there's a tendency for us to sit around and engage in "analysis to paralysis." Get out of bed or the chair and get into an activity that, at least, requires physical activity. Forget about television or the

daily newspaper. Take on a specific project, do it well, complete it, and get the accompanying reward—even if it's not a tangible reward, but an feeling of satisfaction—for having been successful.

Helping Yourself by Helping Others

Beware of "utility traps," situations in which following your own self-interest in the short run hurts everyone's long-term interest. Industrial companies, oil companies, and lumber companies come to mind when we think of short-term versus long-term global consequences . . . or the farmer or rancher who lets too many cattle out to graze on a range of land used by many others. Initially, he gets ahead. Eventually, though, the other ranchers do the same thing out of self-defense, the land is ruined, and everybody loses.

Balancing individual goals with goals for the good of the group is the only way to serve your own long-term interests. The longer I live, the more I realize that the individuals who want to help themselves can only do so by helping others.

I came across a little-known story about just such an individual that really moved me. It's the true account of a blind boy whose team effort changed the lives of millions of people in future generations. It is a story of sacrifice, courage, and frustration, filled with obstacles caused by jealous, self-serving adults who felt that allowing a young boy to succeed would threaten and diminish their own efforts.

Although he had perfect vision as a baby and a toddler, Louis Braille lost his eyesight as a young child playing with a sharp tool in his father's workshop. During the time he lived, in the early 1800s, blind children rarely were allowed to go to school. When they did, they didn't have an opportunity to learn to read or write, but simply went to develop a skill or two. Most blind people at that time became beggars.

Louis's parents were determined to help him make something of his life, and although their friends thought they were unreasonably strict, his parents loved him enough to treat him as a normal child with plenty of responsibilities along with caring guidance. He was required to clean his room, help with the yard work, and dress himself, all of which he finally mastered after stumbling and falling during months of trial and error.

A priest named Father Palluy took special interest in Louis and taught him history, science, and astrology in lessons at church. When the priest could no longer answer his questions, he made a special effort to arrange for Louis, age ten, to be sent to a boarding school for the blind, where he would have an opportunity to learn to read.

Although conditions at the school were harsh and primitive, Louis soon proved to be a gifted student and taught himself to play the piano. Reading, however, proved to be more difficult. In the books the school provided, each letter of the alphabet was raised three inches so it could be traced with the fingers; but the letters were extremely complex, and often it took several months to read a single book. Reading with this system was so slow that Louis and the other students forget the words at the beginning of a sentence before they got to the end. The entire school library had only fourteen specially made books. Because each one had to be created by hand, they were so difficult and expensive to produce.

Louis's teacher told him that people had tried for many years to find a better way for the blind to read and study to become professional people like lawyers, doctors, scientists, and educators. At the age of ten, Louis Braille made it his life's goal to find a better way. He had heard his teacher talk about "night writing," used by soldiers to send messages in the dark. Each word was broken into sounds, which were represented by a different pattern of raised dots punched into paper by a stylus. Its inventor, Captain Barbier, worked with the school for the blind to help them learn to use it.

Captain Barbier's night-writing system was far too complicated for the blind students to use, however, because it took almost a hundred dots to write a simple word. Using an awl, the same tool that had blinded him, Louis spent two years punching out of paper an improved reading system.

Word soon spread outside of the school that a better way to read was being improvised. Captain Barbier rushed to the school to meet the teacher who had streamlined his method and was outraged to discover that it was a boy of twelve! He wanted no part of the research and left the school in a huff, suggesting that the blind had diminished mental capabilities, anyway, and he wasn't going to waste his valuable time observing the efforts of a demented child!

For three more years, Louis worked every night after school and every free day—including spring, summer, and winter breaks at home—trying to simplify his system. Everyone told him to give it up. For hundreds of years, brilliant scientists and scholars older than he was had failed. Why not face the facts that handicapped people are destined to stay that way?

At the age of fifteen, Louis worked out a six-dot pattern, which he called a "cell," and then he numbered each dot in the cell, creating a different, simple pattern for each letter. Excited and motivated, he taught all the boys in his dormitory so they could take notes in class. When the headmaster called Louis in for a demonstration, he read back the principal's dictation word for word.

Although the headmaster was astounded, no one would contribute any funds to produce new books with Louis's system: The school patrons were insulted by the implication that the previous books they had paid for were now obsolete. They weren't about to invest in a boy's dream. One wrote, "I have been giving you money to print books, and now you tell me they are not good enough. You'll never get another cent from me!"

Louis graduated from the school at nineteen and was asked to stay on as a teacher. He was only offered a meager salary despite the fact that he was an expert in grammar, history, geography, math, and music. Since no one would help finance the creation of a library for the blind, Louis taught classes by day and worked through the night punching dots to make books, one at a time, for the blind students. Sacrificing his health for his glorious cause, his resistance to disease was lowered by his grueling schedule, and he contracted tuberculosis at the age of twenty-six.

During his convalescence and subsequent relapses, a new headmaster took over the leadership of the school and was shocked by the unorthodox methods and disquieting progress being made by the blind students with their classwork. As has happened so often throughout history, all of the books were burned, the tools destroyed, and the students forbidden to continue this nontraditional method.

Louis Braille and the students soon formed an underground network. Late at night, the boys would use darning needles or nails to punch out the dots and use Braille's method to study from. When they were caught, they were beaten severely on the hands with wooden rulers and deprived of food.

They continued steadfastly until a new teacher approached the headmaster, Dr. Dufau, and advised him that the beatings and starvings were not holding back progress. He could forbid the students to do what they were doing, but one day all blind people would be using this alphabet, and his school would be left behind. Appealing to the headmaster's pride, the teacher said, "Wouldn't you like to be known as the man who helped launch this unique method?"

This new slant on the problem flattered Dr. Dufau's competitive instinct. He loved being on the winning side of issues, and he decided he could use Louis's dot system to attract attention, prestige, and money for himself and the school. Louis was put on stage in front of scientists, teachers, and government officials. Most of them thought it was a trick until he called two blind children up on the stage, sent one out of the room, and asked for a member of the audience to pick any book from the stack and read one page aloud.

The blind child on the stage wrote down what was presented using Louis's dot system, and then the other blind child was led back into the room and asked to read it. Brushing his fingers quickly and smoothly across the page of dots, he read it confidently and clearly verbatim. The audience stood and cheered. This was truly a miracle in the making! Louis smiled and walked out of the auditorium with a procession of joyous students behind him.

People from all the world began asking for information on this new raised-dot alphabet for the blind, which they called the Braille system. A Braille printing press was designed and put into operation. Schools for the blind soon opened everywhere.

With his health continuing to deteriorate, Louis continued punching out his books by hand for the students at his school. When he died at age thirty-five, he was still virtually unknown to the public. Not a single newspaper printed even a one-line obituary mentioning his passing. Yet today, he is known worldwide as the deliverer of one of the greatest gifts a nonsighted person can ever receive: the ability to read and learn through his raised-dot alphabet, which was fashioned by a crude tool like the one in his father's workshop that had blinded him at the age of three.

Louis Braille had the marvelous goal of improving a complex reading system for individuals like himself. It was not a competitive goal. He was competing with himself to find a better way to enjoy his passion for reading so it didn't take several months to complete just one book. He sacrificed his own pleasures and even his health to perfect a system that would help his students have this privilege, one that most people take for granted.

Each nearly insurmountable obstacle in his path was caused by short-sighted individuals caught in their own selfish motives. Louis Braille, like the Roeblings who built the Brooklyn Bridge, is the kind of hero that our society needs to embrace and that our young people need to emulate. He had better vision than all the sighted people in his life. He saw the big picture in his mind—a picture that was able to sustain his motivation to devote his entire life, his every waking moment, to a cause that helped the greater need of the team.

No One Is an Island

When you're overwhelmed by a situation or decision that you can't figure out, ask for answers from a source other than your analytical mind. For some, this may mean going to a church or a synagogue. For others, it may mean meditating in a quiet room. It may mean sitting in the woods or park, or walking by a beach or lake to attain peace of mind and communion with your spiritual dimension. Use whatever method works to allow you to hear the answers that your wonderfully busy—yet often fearful—rational mind sometimes just won't acknowledge.

When my motivations are questioning me, I always "Let go, and let God" enter the picture. I have never failed to find renewal.

No man or woman is an island. To exist, to work just for yourself, is meaningless. You can achieve the most satisfaction when you feel related to some greater purpose in life, something greater than yourself.

What you achieve externally will never have the sustaining power as from that which you inwardly feel. Ask, and you will receive.

Believe, and you will find new strength to go on and achieve your aspirations.

OVERCOMING FAILURE

Accepting Failure • Dealing with Failure Creatively • Overcoming Learned Helplessness • The Fear of Failure • High Achievers vs. Failure Avoiders • Risking Failure • Using Failure as a Teacher • Attributional Analysis • Paradigms of Attribution • Preparing to Combat Fear • Facing the Truth • Turning Failure and Hardship into Success • Allowing Setbacks to Spur You On • Keeping Problems in Perspective

"Remember that true achievers can taste success because they imagine their goals in such vivid detail. Setbacks, especially those that are overcome by creative means, only seem to add spice and savor to the final taste of victory."

"If you ever feel you're trying your hardest but just getting nowhere, take a moment and ask yourself whether you really believe you can succeed. If you're not really convinced of the possibility of success, make a conscious effort to clear your mind of that feeling of learned helplessness."

"If you're a prisoner of fear, you don't—you can't*—attain your goals because you aren't really attempting to reach them. The fact is, until you do make that attempt, you don't really know the limits of what you can accomplish. By trying, you may discover that the limits never even existed at all."*

"Contemporary psychologists agree that setbacks and failures mean little or nothing in themselves. The whole meaning of any setback—or any success, for that matter—is in how we take it and what we make of it."

Accepting Failure

Highly motivated achievers are willing to accept a certain amount of failure in their lives. They aren't afraid of it, and it doesn't destroy their self-image when they experience it. Failure and mistakes are merely the dues we pay to understand the value of our successes.

My favorite lines about failure were written by Teddy Roosevelt, and I can recite them from memory: "The credit belongs to the man or woman who is actually in the arena, whose face is marred by dust and sweat and blood; who strives valiantly; who errs and comes up short again and again; who knows the great enthusiasms, the great devotions, and spends himself or herself in a worthy cause; who at the best, knows the triumph of high achievement; and who, at the worst, if he or she fails, at least fails while daring greatly, so that his or her place shall never be with those cold and timid souls who know neither victory nor defeat."

Stirring words aren't they? And appropriate for this section.

Ted Williams, the great baseball professional, grew up very close to my old house in San Diego, California. As I was growing up, my father and I kept a diary on his batting average as we listened to the games he played for the Boston Red Sox. My father would always remind me not to worry about striking out because, in his finest year as the greatest hitter in the game, Ted Williams would come away from the plate a failure nearly sixty percent of the time, without even getting to first base. I never forgot that as I have stepped up to take my swings in the batting average of life, and you should never forget that either.

Dealing with Failure Creatively

Every time I think I have seen it all in terms of someone dealing with failure in a creative way, another true story comes along. Did you read about this in the paper? It was carried by UPI wire service.

When the transmission in Jack Azevedo's pickup got stuck in reverse, he couldn't afford to have it fixed at the time, so he started driving from Nevada home to Sacramento the only way he could: backwards. He made it fifty miles on Interstate 80, driving backwards at seven miles per hour, before the California Highway Patrol gave him a ticket and arranged for alternate transportation the rest of the way. "It wasn't that dangerous," Azevedo said. "I rode the shoulder the whole way. I had to drive with my head out the window, and I got a kink in my neck."

He had gone to Reno with his wife and two children to pick up a used clothes dryer from a friend, and when the transmission went out, getting stuck in reverse, he considered the alternatives. Not enough money to fix it. Not enough for food and a motel. "What was I going to do?" he asked. "If I'd been alone, I might have hitchhiked home, but I had my family, and I just decided to go ahead and drive home backward."

Well, I don't know whether you could really call Jack an achiever, but he was definitely highly motivated. He wasn't going to let a little transmission failure stop him.

The next time you experience a setback, exercise your creativity and imagination and brainstorm some solutions to your difficulty. You may not end up driving backward down the Interstate, and you may not come up with any useful ideas at all, but even the process of brainstorming will keep you from becoming mired in inaction and focused on problem solving.

Remember that true achievers can taste success because they imagine their goals in such vivid detail. Setbacks, especially those that are overcome by creative means, only seem to add spice and savor to the final taste of victory.

Overcoming Learned Helplessness

My friends have an English bulldog named Spike, who looks so ferocious that he scares everyone who comes to visit his owners. Actually, Spike is quite gregarious and fun loving. He wants to welcome the guests by jumping up on them, giving them a big hug and kiss, and tatooing his friendly paw and claw marks on their clothes and skin. Much to his dismay, Spike usually gets locked out of the room when visitors are present.

To make him socially acceptable, Spike gets a weekly bath. His owner fastens his thick, leather leash on his choke chain and says enthusiastically, "Let's go take our nice bath!" Spike puts on his brakes by digging all four paws into the carpet and refuses to budge one muscle of his sixty-pound, solid, Arnold Schwarzenegger-like, physique. His owner has to use all her strength to literally drag him outside and across the patio to the designated post where she gives him—and much of the time herself, as well—a bath. Witnessing this struggle gives you an idea of Spike's strength and ingenuity.

Recently, Spike's family had a group of about twenty people over. Several wanted Spike to be allowed in the house so they could play with him, but most were afraid of what he might do. Spike's owner put on his leash and brought him in the house. Much to the delight of most of the guests, he jumped and ran from guest to guest, checking them out and dragging his owner with him at the end of the leash. He grabbed his ball and indicated that he wanted to play his favorite ball game: keep away. Nothing could hold Spike down . . . except his leash.

His owner took him over to a small antique chair weighing about five pounds, lifted one of the legs, put the loop of his leash around the leg, and walked away. Spike looked forlorn and helpless. Everyone said, "That chair won't hold him. He's going to get loose and jump on us and get revenge because we won't play ball with him!"

"*I* know the chair won't restrain him," said the owner, "but *Spike* doesn't know it."

Totally put down, submissive, and disappointed—we might even say depressed—Spike sat through the duration of the party with his leather leash held down by a five-pound chair with no one sitting on it.

No one told Spike to stay and that he couldn't move. He hadn't been to obedience school. He simply assumed he couldn't move because when he has his bath, that leash is fastened to a post, and he can't get away. So he doesn't even try to move the chair for fear of the same results.

* * *

Are you trapped by learned helplessness? Like the bulldog Spike, are you held back by nonexistent limitations? Ask yourself if your obstacles are real or only perceived. You might be surprised at the answer!

Unfortunately, too many of us are like Spike. We find ourselves in a situation in which we assume we're helpless and we give up. Some past experience tells us we can't move ahead, and we give up without even trying. Sometimes, it's only a five-pound weight that is holding us back, but it weighs five hundred tons as far as we're concerned, and we can't do anything but sit down like Spike and work our way into a state of depression.

Martin Seligman, a psychologist at the University of Pennsylvania, has made a very detailed study of the effects of "learned helplessness," which is what Spike the bulldog was suffering from. Learned helplessness is the belief that we are at the mercy of external forces, that we no longer have control over what is happening to us. Psychologists emphasize that this feeling of helplessness is *learned.* We are not born feeling helpless; it is a trait we acquire.

There is a telling experiment in which two groups of college students were subjected to a very unpleasant and loud noise. In the first group, the students could shut off the noise by pressing the button in plain sight before them. In the second group, pushing the button had no effect, and the students had to endure the experiment listening to the obnoxious noise. The students in both groups were then moved into another room in which the unpleasant noise could be turned off by manipulating some buttons hidden in a small box.

The students who had been able to turn off the noise previously by pressing the plainly visible button in the other room immediately began looking in the box for a way to turn off the noise, and they quickly found the right way to do it.

The second group of students, who in the other room had not been able to turn off the sound by pressing the button, didn't even look for a way to stop the noise in the second room. They probably said to themselves, "Why bother? It didn't work before!" Instead, they sat helplessly listening to a loud, shrill noise while the experiment continued, although they had the power to easily stop the assault upon their ears.

The students who had been able to turn off the noise in the first room hadn't actually learned how to turn off the noise in the second room. The experimenters made sure that the precise means of shutting off the noise was significantly different in each room. But the students *had* learned one thing, and they only needed to learn one thing to be able to turn off the noise in the second room. They learned they could do it. They learned they could successfully turn off the noise in the room.

The second group, the ones who did not turn off the noise, had also learned something very important in the first room. They learned that they were helpless. So they didn't even try the second time around.

In a related study, researchers found that depressed college students had much more trouble solving anagram problems than other students did. This is very important because much depression is a physical reaction to a sense of helplessness.

Some years ago, I presented a seminar on the psychology of winning to a champion NFL team trying to repeat its near-perfect season. A clinical hypnotist was on the program with me, and he demonstrated to all of us how easy it is to become trapped into the "learned helplessness" type of thinking. After relaxing a huge fullback, who seemed like he could bench-press the Brooklyn Bridge, the hypnotist suggested to the player that a three-ounce glass paperweight weighed five hundred pounds and placed the paperweight on the locker room floor. When he asked the burly fullback to pick it up, the player replied: "If it weighs five hundred pounds, I don't think I can lift it." His face turned purple, the veins on his arms and neck popped out and he strained and puffed, but couldn't lift the three-ounce paperweight off the floor.

We all thought it was a set-up or some kind of comedy act the two had worked out before. However, when the full-back's bicep muscles were monitored with biofeedback instruments, they indicated that he was pulling up with a force that would have brought a four-hundred-pound barbell off the floor. Why couldn't he lift a three-ounce paperweight?

Interestingly, when his tricep muscles were measured with the same biofeedback instruments, it was revealed that they were pushing down to keep the paperweight where he *knew* it belonged, with more force than he was using to try to pick it up. His mind was forcing him to work against himself in order for him to fulfill the currently dominant suggestion of an immovable five-hundred-pound object.

Think about what this means. Because of an idea that he'd accepted, this powerful man had become his own worst enemy.

How often we hypnotize ourselves, our employees, and our children into believing we are the helpless victims of external circumstance when the helplessness is really just something we've chosen to believe in.

If you ever feel you're trying your hardest but just getting nowhere, take a moment and ask yourself whether you really believe you can succeed. If you're not really convinced of the possibility of success, make a conscious effort to clear your mind of that feeling of learned helplessness. Think of that football player trying to lift the paperweight, fighting against himself, when in fact he could easily have thrown that thing right through the roof of the Superdome.

The Fear of Failure

Perhaps the most destructive type of motivation—and, sadly, one of the most pervasive—is the fear of failure. This desire to avoid failure is a strong motivator and can make us do things we normally would not do. Famous British essayist and critic Charles Lamb had his first play hissed off the stage. Lamb was seated in the audience but was so afraid that someone would recognize him and identify him as the author that he hissed the play along with everyone else.

We learn from early experiences of rejection that failure is something to avoid at all costs. It begins in childhood when we encounter the first "No!" It grows like a weed as we face criticism from our parents, our other family members, in some cases our teachers, and most definitely our peers. It leads to the association of ourselves with our mistakes, in which our personhood becomes a mirror of our clumsiness and awkwardness in performance.

As we continue to live in a world of "put downs," where problems are magnified by the media and success is often viewed as selfishness, manipulation, or just plain luck, we tend to seek security by simply going with the system and not rocking the boat.

Despite inspiring biographies, documentaries, and audio programs about "rags-to-riches" success achieved by common individuals, most people can't imagine it happening to themselves. So they're resigned to mediocrity and even failure, wishing and envying away their lives. They develop the habits of looking back at past problems (which is failure reinforcement) and of imagining similar performances in the future (which is failure forecasting).

They either set their sights too high, thus ensuring failure and reinforcing their fears, or so low that they're only certain of reaching an unworthy goal, thus avoiding failure with a sure thing. Their inner dialogue usually falls somewhere in between the two extremes: "Something bad will spoil this! Things are going too well." And, "I knew it was too good to be true. With my luck, it was bound to go sour."

Fear of failure can be a built-in, intrinsic motivation. Just as high achievers like to succeed and feel good about themselves, people who fear failure work not to fail in order to avoid feeling bad about themselves. Or they concentrate on failure avoidance by refusing to try in the first place.

Fear of failure also can occur as an extrinsic motivation. For example, a factory worker who has performed well, without experiencing much fear, for a long period of time will suddenly begin to fear failure if half his division must be laid off. A few years ago, I presented an employee productivity program to a large division of a Fortune 500 company that manufactured integrated circuit boards in competition with the Japanese. After I finished my talk on the psychology of positive human motivation and the mind-set of champions, the general manager of the huge facility came up on stage and gave his 2,000 salaried and hourly workers a parting motivational message: "What we have to have from all of you is a seventeen-percent increase in quality production in six months, or we're closing down the plant! Have a good weekend!"

The impact of his words on their cognitive maps was as you would expect. The highly motivated achievers increased their performance about twenty percent, but the failure avoiders quit within a few weeks after finding more secure jobs. And of course, the plant was shut down after about six months.

John Atkinson, who has studied the fear of failure extensively, says that both the highly motivated achiever and the failure avoider are motivated by their desire to feel good about themselves. They simply use entirely different approaches to the same intrinsic motivation.

The high achiever frames the task through what Atkinson calls the "positive utility of success." The failure avoider frames the task by concentrating on the negative cost of failure. This is why it is so important to list all the positive benefits of your goals. Highly motivated achievers focus on the benefits that come with success, while those motivated by fear concentrate on the painful consequences of failure.

A negative framer once said, "If at first you don't succeed, destroy all the evidence that you have tried." We all know people who do this, don't we?

Some bosses and managers might argue that fear-motivated employees will work just as hard or harder than their positively motivated peers. Unfortunately, they are deluding themselves. Fear motivation is simply not an effective leadership tool. It's as obsolete as Communism or spankings in Sunday school.

Research proves that people who fear failure are more likely to fail in assignments of medium difficulty—that is, those involving approximately equal opportunity for success or failure—than those lacking such fears. And this is true even in situations where the failure avoiders are better qualified for the assignments than their more positively motivated associates. Anxiety about failure not only reduces performance, it also stifles the motivation to succeed in the first place.

A new prison was completed not too long ago in British Columbia with much of the labor done by the prisoners themselves. The new structure replaced the old Fort Alcan prison that for hundreds of years had housed many convicted felons. After the prisoners were moved into their new quarters, they spent long and physically tiring days stripping the old prison of lumber, appliances, and plumbing to be used for the needy miners nearby. Under the supervision of the prison guards, the inmates then proceeded to tear down the old prison walls.

While dismantling the walls, they were shocked and infuriated to find that, although huge locks were attached to the heavy doors and two-inch steel bars covered the windows, the walls had been constructed of paperboard and clay, painted to resemble iron. It was obvious to all the prisoners that a hard kick could have easily knocked out a wall, allowing them to escape. For years, they had huddled in their locked cells, believing they were in an impregnable fortress. Nobody had ever tried to escape because they all thought it was impossible.

If you're a prisoner of fear, you don't—you *can't*—attain your goals because you aren't really attempting to reach them. The fact is, until you do make that attempt, you don't really know the limits of what you can accomplish. By trying, you may discover that the limits never even existed at all.

High Achievers vs. Failure Avoiders

I recently came across an experiment that illuminates the differences between high achievers and failure avoiders. It involved playing a game of ring toss in a large room.

The key element in the experiment was that the researchers did not tell the subjects how far to stand from the stake, nor did they suggest what level of success the players should expect. All these measurements and decisions were left to the individual players themselves.

The results were that the players who had been identified as highly motivated achievers stood at a moderate distance from the stake, making each toss a challenge, but with the possibility of a significant percentage of successful ringers. Those who feared failure, however, stood either extraordinarily close to the stake in order to assure success, or they stood so far away that successful throws were virtually impossible. Therefore, failure carried no stigma or guilt.

This is significant isn't it? Those who fear failure find little or no motivation to succeed because of their fear; instead, they are motivated to not really try.

It strikes me as strange that the failure avoider does not consider this unwillingness to try as a significant failure in itself. Perhaps thinking the same thing, scientist Douglas Mook points out that in choosing the easy task, the failure avoider learns nothing about himself. It means nothing that he can successfully accomplish such an easy objective. Everybody else can do it, too. Nor does he learn anything about himself by choosing the impossibly difficult task.

Continuing with the findings of the ring-toss experiment, the subjects were free to move after each toss. The highly motivated achievers tended to change their targets realistically, based on experience. If they missed several tosses at one distance, they moved a little closer in range. When they hit several ringers in a row or group, they tended to move away from the target. They were constantly trying to keep the game meaningful to themselves by selecting levels of competency that would challenge them realistically.

Failure avoiders had a different strategy. They would move even closer after hitting the target and move even farther away after missing. This is almost inconceivable, isn't it? . . . and very sad to consider. The failure avoider doesn't even enjoy his achievements. On the other hand, when he fails, he simply takes himself out of the game.

You can see this same mechanism at work in sports, business, personal relationships, and, in a most devastating way, in health and physical well-being.

There's a true story I share with many of my live audiences about a man named Nick Sitzman, a strong, healthy man who worked as a yardman for a railroad company. Nick was a good worker who got along fine with his fellow workers and was reliable on the job. He had one noticeable fault, however. He was a notorious worrier. He was cynical about everything and usually feared the worst.

One summer day, the train crews were informed that they could quit an hour early in honor of the foreman's birthday. Accidentally, Nick was locked in an empty, isolated refrigerator boxcar that was in the yard for repairs, and the rest of the workmen left the site.

Nick panicked. He banged and shouted until his fists were bloody and his voice hoarse. No one paid any attention. If they heard him, they associated the sound with a playground nearby or with the noise of other trains backing in and out of the yard. "It must be zero degrees in here," he must have thought. "If I can't get out, I'll freeze to death." He found a cardboard box and, shivering uncontrollably, he scrawled this message to his wife and family: "So cold, body is getting numb. If I could just go to sleep. These may be my last words."

The next morning, the crew slid open the heavy doors of the boxcar and found Nick dead. An autopsy revealed that every physical sign in his body indicated he had frozen to death. But the irony was that the refrigeration unit was inoperative, there was plenty of fresh air in the boxcar, and the temperature inside was about sixty-one degrees. His intrinsic fear motivation became a self-fulfilling prophecy.

Here are some action ideas that will help you avoid negative motivation by framing your expectations in a healthy, positive way:

1. *Visualize, think, and speak well of your health.* Don't dwell on your ailments, or they will reward you by staying with you longer and visiting your house more often. Focus on your own well-being and that of your family, and you will be blessed with greater health.

2. *Don't become emotionally involved needlessly with the stories of people you don't know.* Read and listen to the news for professional and personal growth, and practice compassion for those who truly need it, but resist the temptation to waste time and pollute your mind with the sordid details of someone else's tragedies. You'll become jaded and cynical if you get hooked on tabloid exposés.

3. *Select more friends and associates who are optimists and highly motivated achievers.* The mutual attraction should not be the sharing of problems so much as the sharing of solutions and goals.

4. *Find a positive lesson in and a positive reason for all of your personal relationships.* Accentuate the blessings and knowledge gained from each.

5. *Learn to stay relaxed and friendly no matter how much pressure you're under.* Instead of being unhelpfully critical, be constructively helpful.

6. *Make a list of your most current wants and desires.* Right next to each, put down what benefit or payoff there is to achieving them. Look at this list often throughout the day and before retiring at night.

7. *Instead of comparing yourself to others, set your own internal standards for achievement.* Accept yourself as you are right now, but keep upgrading your goals, professional skills, and personal desires so they are challenging and include real effort and commitment to achieve. Don't treat life like a ring-toss game with the stakes too close to be testing or too impossible to be plausible.

8. *Above all, frame your desires and goals in positive terms.* Don't live your life by failure avoidance. Live by success encounters.

Risking Failure

As Vice-President of Software Development at Data General Corporation, Bill Foster had an enviable position. In his early thirties, Foster was already earning a hundred thousand dollars a year. In a few more years, his invested stock options would be worth nearly a million dollars. Yet he left behind the stock options and the cushy job to take a very big risk.

"I'd been hemming and hawing about quitting for a couple of years," Foster said. His desire to start a business began in the late 1970s. On a family vacation, Foster took along a notebook, planning to spend the week working up some ideas. He returned with a tan and a blank notebook. "I got home and said to myself, 'Ah, you're too old. Just forget it . . . just be happy doing what you're doing.'"

A year later, on a business trip, the idea suddenly reinvented itself at two in the morning. He awoke with the thought that he was going to quit his job and start his own company. Foster pulled out his notebook and started writing down ideas. He started to formulate a business plan. He began thinking about where he could get financial backing. The next morning, he called his wife and said, "Honey, when I get back, I'm going to quit." The response was more one of disbelief than of distress.

Two weeks later, Foster was no longer an employee of Data General. His former colleagues thought he was crazy. A friend took him sailing to tell him how many people were convinced he'd been fired. They could not believe he would quit.

Foster said he left because trying to build his own company while still working for his current employer would have been unethical and too complicated. He had a year's salary saved up. He had only the barest outline for his new proposed business. But he had the dream, and he was willing to risk his present security to pursue it.

He had decided to enter the field of "fault-tolerant" computers, which do not lose data even during power outages, and which use software as the basis for their fail-safe operation.

What he didn't fully realize is that having the idea and selling the idea are like night and day. He had naively presumed that since there was a lot of money out there, someone would invest in him.

By Christmas of his first year of going it alone, Foster didn't want to attend any parties. He said, "I didn't want to see all those people who were still working, who still had money coming in. For the first time in my life, I was withdrawing money from my savings every week. It was a strange feeling. Having been conditioned to save and put money away, I never realized how I would react to taking it out. It was a very depressing thing to do. I actually started to believe some of the people who told me I had made a big mistake."

Desperate for funding, Foster arranged for an appointment with a bank. When he arrived, he was informed that his appointment had been canceled. In need of positive reinforcement, he stopped by to visit Robert Freiburghouse, who owned a small software company nearby. Toward the end of their conversation, Foster gave him a copy of the business plan he had brought along for his bank appointment.

"He called me that evening," Foster said, "and told me that this was better than what he was doing, then asked, 'How would you like to have a partner?' "

Freiburghouse came on board to take charge of software development. Venture capital was arranged. In mid-1980, the new company, Stratus, opened for business. By 1985, the company was generating revenues of over eighty million dollars.

Foster said that the most important attribute in his success was the willingness to take risk without worrying about the fear of failing. He said, "I guess I finally woke up to the fact that it didn't matter if I failed—that was the worst reason in the world not to try. I don't consider myself a special person. When I was a kid, I was an underachiever. No one really had very big expectations for me. I'm not smarter than other people. I don't have very clever ideas. But when you say, 'Why don't people act on their dreams?', my answer is that most people avoid risk and success because they don't like to take chances.

"I view risk not as a life-or-death matter . . . it is more of an ego risk. Can your ego accept failure, and can your mind stay focused on your dream? These are the questions that you must ask yourself."

If you can answer yes to these questions, if you are willing to risk failure in the face of greater rewards, then you have what it takes to be a motivated high achiever.

Using Failure as a Teacher

It has been said that failure should be our teacher, not our undertaker. Failure is delay, not defeat. It is a temporary detour, not a dead-end. Failure is something we can avoid only by saying nothing, doing nothing, and being nothing.

Thomas Edison's father called him a "dunce." His headmaster in school told Edison he would never make a success of anything.

Henry Ford barely made it through high school.

The machines of the world's greatest inventor, Leonardo Da Vinci, were never built, and many wouldn't have worked, anyway.

Edwin Land, the inventor of the Polaroid Land camera, failed absolutely at developing instant movies. He described his attempts as trying to use an impossible chemistry and a nonexistent technology to make an unmanufacturable product for which there was no discernable demand. This, in his opinion, created the optimum working conditions for the creative mind.

Testifying before a House subcommittee, violinist Isaac Stern said, "The most important thing the National Council on the Arts can do is give the creative mind the right to fail. It is only through failure and experiment that we learn and grow."

Joe Paterno, head coach of the Penn State University football team, was asked by the media how he felt when his team lost a game. He replied that losing was probably good for the team, since that was how the players learned what they were doing wrong.

My former mentor, Dr. Jonas Salk, who developed the polio vaccine and who is now engaged in research to find a vaccine for the AIDS virus, said he spent ninety-eight percent of his time documenting the things that didn't work until he found the things that did.

The board game called "Monopoly" was created by Charles Darrow, an unemployed heating engineer. Darrow brought his first version of the game to a toy company in 1935. That company originally rejected the game for containing fifty-two fundamental errors. Today, the game is so successful that its publisher, Parker Brothers, prints more than forty billion dollars in "Monopoly" money every year. That's twice the amount of real money printed annually by the U.S. Mint!

Contemporary psychologists agree that setbacks and failures mean little or nothing in themselves. The whole meaning of any setback—or any success, for that matter—is in how we take it and what we make of it. James Joyce, the Irish novelist who wrote *Ulysses,* one of the greatest novels of this century, had one of his characters say, "The genius makes no mistakes . . . his errors are portals of discovery." According to the most recent research in behavioral science, Joyce is essentially correct.

Let's go back, for a moment, to a famous illustration of this concept from the American Civil War. It had been raging almost three years before Ulysses Grant was called to Virginia from the western theater of the conflict to confront General Lee. Historians consider this an important turning point in the war because none of the Union generals who had previously faced Lee had been particularly effective or successful. Most had crossed the Potomac River, fought one battle on Lee's home turf, and hightailed it back home licking their wounds. George McClellan, Ambrose Burnside, John Pope, and Joe Hooker all had crossed south into Virginia only to return in haste, under the most intense pressure, a few days later.

By the time Grant came East, the Union army forces were very skeptical that any Union general could beat "Bobby Lee," as they called the enemy commander. General Grant remarked to his staff that his men were so frightened of Lee, they seemed to think he could jump up into the air, turn a somersault, and land, with his entire army, in their rear. It was a light-hearted remark by Grant, but his staff didn't laugh. They thought Grant would change his tune after one battle.

Lee and Grant first met in the battle known as "The Wilderness." In a dense woods in Virginia, Lee inflicted heavy losses, with over seventeen thousand Northern casualties in just two days. As the cover of darkness brought the second day of fighting to a close, Grant's staff and men knew they had been whipped and humiliated. Lee had lost only a third of the men Grant had, and he held the battlefield at all points.

As the Northern army prepared to move, the Union soldiers may have felt a grim satisfaction in knowing that Grant had learned the same painful lesson experienced by all the previous commanders: that there was no beating the brilliant Bobby Lee. What they didn't know what that Grant had learned no such lesson.

As the men assembled in formation, they found to their utter astonishment that they were not retreating. Instead, they were given the order to advance! They were not headed north with their backs to the rebels. They were marching south, looking resolutely ahead.

Any of the previous generals would have considered the Wilderness Battle a defeat and a failure. Not Grant. He adjusted his plan, slid to the right, and set out on a foot race with Lee toward the major Rebel base of supply.

Grant's men came to understand an idea that you should also take to heart: The difference between a victory and a defeat is not as great as you may think. The big difference is in deciding what the difference means to you and to your future success.

Attributional Analysis

The branch of motivational psychology that deals with human reaction to successes or setbacks is called "Attributional Analysis," and some of the most important work in the field has been done by psychologist Bernard Weiner. Utilizing John Atkinson's insights into the similarity between achievement motivation and motivation by fear of failure, Weiner went a bit further. He began with the assumption that what highly motivated achievers really desired was the pride or self-esteem that came with success, and that the failure avoider is less concerned with the failure itself than with the shame he would feel as a result.

You remember that old saying that it's not whether you win or lose that really counts, it's how you play the game? Weiner found that it's not whether you succeed or fail that counts, it's how you explain it to yourself and others. Psychologists refer to our explanations as "attributions," or the act of making inferences as to the cause of the success or failure.

Consider a gambler who has a lucky streak one night. If he's rational about the run of good luck, he won't say what a brilliant and clever person he is. He won't attribute the success to himself. He'll attribute any success or failure he has in gambling to luck. If he lost a small sum of money the following evening, he also would be able to accept it without considering himself a failure. He may feel bad about losing the money, but he wouldn't attribute the loss to his own lack of ability.

In a similar way, Weiner felt that our actual success or failure should have less impact on our future expectations than would our attribution of what had caused the particular result. For example, he guessed that the confidence of a baseball player in a hitting slump would not be diminished if he discovered that he had a minor eye infection that impaired his vision. Once the infection cleared up, he would go back to the plate with confidence.

However, a superstitious baseball player may have a lucky bat that has taken him through the current season with a .300 batting average. If he breaks his bat, he may be less confident because he's given the credit for his hitting more to his bat than to his own ability.

To test his theories, Weiner studied the different ways in which highly motivated achievers and failure avoiders attribute both their successes and their failures.

When it comes to success, highly motivated achievers tend to attribute their success to a combination of ability and effort. Failure avoiders attribute their success to a combination of luck and ability. I'm sure you see how important this difference is. It means, quite simply, that achievers feel much more in control of their destinies than do failure avoiders.

Both groups feel that ability plays a role in success, but then a crucial attributional split occurs. Highly motivated achievers feel that their effort plays a large part in any success they have. Think about it. Since ability is a given, we can only control what we do with that ability. We can develop skills, gain knowledge, and take action toward our goals.

To failure avoiders, it comes down to being at the right place at the right time—by chance, not by choice. The failure avoider tends to attribute his failure to his own inherent low level of ability. Using this line of reasoning, he sees failure as an inevitable result in the long run.

The difference in the two attributions of failure is that the highly motivated achiever is not shaken in confidence by a setback. It was either a lack of the proper effort or external events that caused the failure. He still has the drive and ability to succeed, and with a greater, more prudent application of effort and a little bit of luck, he will succeed the next time around.

Paradigms of Attribution

Psychologists in attributional analysis point out that our attributions of success or failure can be assigned to three different paradigms or modes: (1) stable or unstable causes, (2) internal or external causes, and (3) local or global causes.

Let's look at the first paradigm. Do we attribute our success or failure to stable or unstable causes? A stable cause is one that won't change, and an unstable cause is one that might change. For instance, attributing success or failure to ability level is to make a stable attribution, because talent or ability level probably won't change.

Highly motivated achievers almost always make unstable attributions of their success or failure. While they believe in their ability to succeed, they also believe that their ability won't mean much without real effort to back it up.

For the achiever, both success and failure result from factors that can change or be changed. People who give up easily believe the causes of the bad things that happen to them are permanent or stable. They will always be there to influence and even govern their lives.

For example, a failure avoider would explain his unsuccessful dieting with the statement: "Diets never work." The achiever would say, "Diets don't work when you eat out." The failure avoider attributed permanence; the achiever attributed the setback to temporary factors.

If you think about setbacks and disappointments in terms of "always" and "never," you have what Dr. Martin Seligman, author of *Learned Optimism,* calls a "permanent, pessimistic style." But if you think in terms of "sometimes" and "lately"—that is, if you use qualifiers and attribute events to transient conditions—then you have an optimistic style.

In an interesting experiment, psychologists took a group of highly motivated achievers and divided them into two groups. They did the same with failure avoiders. The first group of each motivational type were then given an assignment to perform that was too difficult for almost anyone to accomplish. After the initial failure, the subjects were allowed to keep trying for as long as they desired. As expected, the highly motivated achievers persisted for a long period of time. Some of them actually performed the task successfully. The failure avoiders gave up quickly and easily.

The second group of subjects in each motivational type were given a harmless placebo, a pill that they were told would impair their ability to undertake the task successfully. As you know, placebos are substances, like glucose and water, that are substituted for pharmaceuticals in blind studies to determine the effects of certain drugs on test subjects.

It turned out that the achievers soon gave in to the difficult task because, for once in their lives, they had a stable or unchangeable attribution for failing. Their failure to perform the complicated assignment was due, they thought, to the drug they had taken. They reasoned that since their individual ability and effort would not be able to play a full and meaningful role in the outcome, why continue? Why waste the energy?

But why do you suppose the failure avoiders, who under normal circumstances would quit right away, suddenly developed persistence and even continued long enough to achieve some measure of success in the assignment?

Because, perhaps for the first time, failure carried no shame. They could attribute it to something out of their control. There was no risk to their self-esteem to keep on trying.

There's another distinction in the attribution of failure in this experiment. It's the second attributional paradigm: internal versus external causes. In the placebo test, for example, where the subjects thought a drug had been used to impair their performance, both the achievers and failure avoiders attributed the failure in the experiment to an external cause.

For the failure avoiders, however, attribution of failure is almost always internal. They tend to explain their failure in terms of lack of ability, but in this experiment they were able to attribute the failure safely to the external cause, the drug. This gave them enough mental justification to stick with the task.

High achievers usually attribute their failures to external causes. This would include the temporary or unstable reasons, such as bad timing or an unexpected outside event.

Interestingly enough, achievers almost never attribute their *successes* to external factors. No matter how much luck would have come their way in life, they believe they would not have been successful had they not been prepared and willing to make the right decisions with the opportunity.

So failure avoiders attribute their success to externals and their failures to internals. The self-talk might be: "I just got lucky. I was at the right place at the right time. I just happened to be on the right team." In attributing their failures, their self-talk might be: "I'm stupid. I don't have the talent to succeed at this." People who blame themselves when they fail and credit externals for their success have low self-esteem as a consequence.

People who blame external events when they fail and accept the credit honestly and graciously when they succeed don't lose self-esteem during a setback and are positively reinforced by their achievements. Their self-talk during a failure might be: "The market turned up a few surprises we hadn't figured on, but we'll be better prepared for the future." Their self-talk as a result of a success might be: "I'm proud of my own contribution to the team success. I worked very hard, and it was all worth the effort."

The third paradigm is local versus global causes. Failure avoiders tend to globalize their failures. A failure in one area of their life brings about a catastrophic response across the board. If a failure avoider was turned down for a date, for example, his response would be: "I'm ugly or repulsive to other people." If he's fired, he's an incompetent human being and no good. The failure avoider believes that bad events or setbacks have global consequences and a totally destructive impact on his or her life, but the positive events or successes have only a specific or local impact. In this way, they maximize the impact of any mistake or problem and minimize the effect of any success on their self-esteem.

These three attributional paradigms are related and function in concert with each other. Stable versus unstable causes seem to relate also to internal versus external causes. Ability tends to be a stable, internal cause. Timing in the market tends to be an unstable, external cause, as is luck or an unexpected event.

To sum up, highly motivated achievers tend to focus on causes they can control. When they're looking for what went wrong or right with their plans, they look for what they can change specifically to turn a setback into an advantage, and they focus on what they did internally to succeed, so they can do more of it.

So get to know how you explain your successes and failures to yourself! Do you focus on what you can change about yourself? Do you focus on the forces that are lined up against you? Is failure stable and permanent for you, or is it unstable and temporary? Be honest, and be very aware. This self-knowledge may do more to raise your level of personal and professional achievement than any other insight you could gain.

Do you concentrate on the specific or local things you can change about yourself that aren't working for you? Or do you concentrate on your global, overall faults that you're stuck with for life?

Do your attributions tend to be internal, based upon the amount of creativity and effort you put into success? Or do you attribute your success to the luck of the draw, market conditions, or geography? Are your failures external events or part of your internal design?

Highly motivated achievers are made, not born. As the novelist James Michener put it: "Character is what you do on the third or fourth try." Genius may be innate, but the world is full of failed geniuses and talented losers. Optimism, self-esteem, and self-efficacy can be learned. You can learn to be an motivated lifetime achiever.

Preparing to Combat Fear

The Canadian psychologist S.J. Rachman undertook a study of fear involving first-time parachute jumpers.

Although I ejected safely from a military aircraft during my flying days, I'm not certain that I would deliberately leap out of an airplane on a Sunday afternoon for relaxation, renewal, and recreation. One thing I've always wanted to ask a skydiving fanatic is whether he or she would ever buy a parachute at a discount store or a swap meet. How do they know it will open, even if they pack it themselves? I've always been afraid that if I were to try to skydive, I would pull the D-ring, and either an American Flag would unfurl as some kind of sick patriotic joke, or a note would flutter out as I tumbled to earth that read, "This 'chute packed by worker number twenty-two, who has been out sick with the flu!"

In his study, Rachman found that over sixty-six percent

of the jumpers admitted significant feelings of fear prior to the jump, but they went ahead and successfully completed it. Another twenty-six percent said they were not afraid, and they also made the jump successfully.

That left seven percent who said they experienced no significant feelings of fear, but when push came to shove (so to speak), and the jump leader yelled "Geronimo!" or whatever they yell these days, this seven percent had serious doubts about what would happen when they pulled the D-ring. In fact, a significant number could not muster up the courage to actually jump.

There are two important issues resulting from the parachute-jumper research. One is that self-perception of confidence can be misleading. An individual may be less fearless than he believes himself to be. He may be lying to himself and others about his real feelings. Although most people who say they have no fear go ahead and jump successfully, as you would expect, there is that seven percent who say they feel no fear but don't have the courage to follow through.

The second issue is that, with or without confidence, preparation is once again very important. The overconfident jumpers who had trouble actually making the jump may well have gone ahead with no hesitation if they'd had proper training. The advance preparation definitely was the key factor in the majority of courageous jumpers who parachuted successfully, although they did experience a significant degree of fear. The overconfident jumpers underestimated the stress and difficulty of the event. They had not prepared themselves psychologically and emotionally. As a result, they weren't ready to face the situational demands.

Would you be afraid jump out of an airplane? Motivated high achievers may feel fear, but they will not be stopped by it. Fear does not hold them back; it spurs them into action.

The fearful-but-determined jumpers no doubt took great care in the briefing and preparation phase of the event. Some probably sought out experienced skydivers to ask them about their first jump. They knew the situation would be stressful, and they took control of preparing themselves for the stress and anticipation of the unknown and unfamiliar. In such instances, a certain amount of fear can be a positive and helpful emotion. Interesting, isn't it? The way to develop courage is to not be too much afraid of fear itself—and my apologies to the late President Franklin D. Roosevelt for the play on his historic words.

Let's look more closely at this paradoxical nature of fear. It's the most devastating emotion in the world when it paralyzes or debilitates you. But fear can be very helpful if it spurs you to action.

The first tinge of fear is actually a positive tool. It is our natural early-warning system that danger may be approaching and that we need to prepare ourselves to take action. It is the secondary impulse that is crucial. If we choose our response by making it positive, we will have used the early warning to undertake effective preparation for a stressful event. It is only when we dwell on fear that it gains control and threatens our ability to stay motivated.

Facing the Truth

In the history of American free enterprise, there's no greater story of resilience than that of our automobile industry over the past several years, and the driving force behind that resilience has been customer satisfaction based on improved product quality. It wasn't so long ago that American cars seemed bloated and wasteful compared to their overseas counterparts, but that's no longer true. Many foreign cars are good, but cars built in the United States are now meeting and even exceeding their standards. Many people have played a part in this comeback, but one of the most interesting stories from the car industry's turnaround involves the achievement motivation of a man whose ideas were well ahead of his time.

In the 1960s, John David Power decided to start a business. He would research the quality of cars from the Big Three automakers and market his findings to the companies to help them improve customer satisfaction. Power had worked for Ford and General Motors, testing the quality of cars, but in-house testing was rarely as accurate or demanding as it should have been. Power knew that an independent researcher would have more credibility, but when he approached Detroit about testing vehicles, he got turned down flat. Ford, GM, and Chrysler executives were in no hurry to pay for independent testing, especially when the results might not be what they wanted to hear.

However, the Big Three's competitors in Japan soon began purchasing J.D. Power's research, and they used it to improve both manufacturing and marketing. When the American automobile industry almost collapsed under the onslaught of well-made Japanese cars, there was new interest in Power's unbiased product evaluations. As Detroit began to incorporate the results of Power's research into improved automobiles, the U.S. car industry began bouncing back from its slump, and Power was soon getting as much as a quarter of a million dollars for the right to use his test results in advertising.

J.D. Power's honest product testing played an important role in the comeback of one this country's most important industries. Power was really selling nothing more complicated than a good hard look in the mirror, but an industry that had become fat and complacent was in no hurry to see what it had turned into.

Of course, finally facing this truth was the first step toward renewed success for the Big Three, just as facing the truth, no matter how unpleasant it may be, is the starting point for success in anybody.

You shouldn't need someone to come along and hit you

on the head with an honest appraisal, although sometimes that doesn't hurt! Simply taking some quiet time to analyze your current goals and motivations—both positive and negative—should suffice.

It is said that the truth shall set you free, and it will, if you accept it and begin working from there.

Turning Failure and Hardship into Success

As I mentioned in an earlier chapter, highly motivated achievers accept a certain amount of failure so that when success came it would be meaningful. If you don't scale the mountain, how can you enjoy the view? Challenge always carries some risk of failure, and if the worst should happen, achievers use setbacks to increase their chances for success in the future.

The patient person accepts a certain amount of failure, knowing that it is as important a thread in the fabric of success. Great individuals make great successes out of failure.

We all know about the failures of Abraham Lincoln. They are quoted in every self-help book. In the famous Lincoln-Douglas debates, he often expressed opinions he knew would hurt, if not ruin, his chances of being the Senator from Illinois, but which would help his chances of one day becoming President of the United States. His genius was in his compassion, his vision, and his patience in accepting temporary failure to attain long-term success. This is both the risk of integrity and its reward.

Today, we do not hold Lincoln's failure to win a senate seat against him. His failure there, if anything, magnifies his greatness later. He was a patient and persistent man. He knew exactly what destiny he would accept, and he would accept nothing less. He was willing to take the time, devote the effort, and learn from the setbacks along the way.

Abraham Lincoln had a lot in common with Golda Meir, the fourth prime minister of Israel and the first woman prime minister of a major country. Speaking broken English as a child, she attended school in the fortress-like school building on Fourth Street near Milwaukee's famous Schlitz beer factory.

From humble beginnings, she was a shopkeeper's daughter whose chores made her late for school every day and truant more times than she liked to recall. Humble, brilliant, patient, persistent, plain, divorced, she became one of the wisest and most respected world leaders of our century. At the age of seventy-one, the prime minister of Israel returned to Milwaukee and her former school fifty-one years after she had left the United States.

She told the inner-city youth at her old school that she had been born into a minority environment and had lived, to put it very mildly, without much extravagance. And her education, she said, was not about book learning. She told the children, "It isn't really important to decide when you are young just exactly what you want to become when you grow up. It is much more important to decide on the way you want to live."

Golda Meir was speaking of the purpose behind the purpose. Of destiny instead of money. Of service instead of external reward. These are the things that can help you overcome any obstacle. These are the things of which greatness is made.

Abraham Lincoln, often considered to be the best of the United States' Presidents, suffered many setbacks in his early career. But his many successes came only after acknowledging and learning from his failures.

Allowing Setbacks to Spur You On

Many times, we look at high achievers and assume they had a string of lucky breaks or made it without much effort. Usually, the opposite is true, and the so-called superstar had an incredibly rough time before he or she attained any lasting success.

It may motivate you more toward your own goals to know that some of the most famous and well-known people in modern times had to overcome as difficult obstacles as anyone before they finally reached the top. It takes persistence and total commitment to your goals, but it's possible!

You may not know the background of a certain laundry worker who earned sixty dollars a week at his job but had the burning desire to be a writer. His wife worked nights, and he spent nights and weekends typing manuscripts to send to publishers and agents. Each one was rejected with a form letter that gave him no assurance that his manuscript had even been read. I've received a few of those special valentines myself through the years, and I can tell you first hand that they're not the greatest self-esteem builders.

But finally, a warm, more personal rejection letter came in the mail to the laundry worker, stating that, although his work was not good enough at this point to warrant publishing, he had promise as a writer, and he should keep trying.

He forwarded two more manuscripts to the same friendly-yet-rejecting publisher over the next eighteen months, and as before, he struck out with both of them, too. Finances got so tight for the young couple that they had to disconnect their telephone to pay for medicine for their baby.

Feeling totally discouraged, he threw his latest manuscript into the garbage. His wife, totally committed to his life goals and believing in his talent, took the manuscript out of the trash and sent it back to Doubleday, the publisher who had sent the friendly rejections. The book, titled *Carrie,* sold over five million copies and, as a movie, became one of the top-grossing films in 1976. The laundry worker, of course, was Stephen King.

One well-known woman broadcaster was fired eighteen times. I think that might make *The Guinness Book of World Records!* But every time she got fired, she went after something bigger and better. She used her obstacles as stepping stones and parlayed her experiences into more responsible positions.

When no radio station would hire her, she learned Spanish and moved to Puerto Rico. When a wire service refused to send her to cover the beginnings of a revolution in another Latin American country, she flew there at her own expense to write and sell her own freelance stories.

She continually was frustrated in trying to sell her ideas for a special-interest show to the television networks because the people to whom she presented her concepts were constantly being replaced. Finally, years later, in 1982, she was able to go on the air, talking about issues that were important to her and inviting callers to express their personal opinions. Since then, Sally Jesse Raphael has won several Emmy awards and has her own TV show reaching eight million viewers a day. She says, "I could have let those eighteen firings prevent me from doing what I wanted. Instead, I let them spur me on."

One of the main messages in this book is to help you believe in your ability to turn obstacles into opportunities. Too often, people try to storm their obstacles as if they are forts that need to be taken. It's better to step back and ask yourself: Did I cause this obstacle by my own actions or lack of them? Did someone else cause this obstacle? Is this obstacle one that grew out of the natural progression of circumstances?

This last question may seem complex, but it holds a secret to the way you can set and reach your goals and achieve your destiny!

Keeping Problems in Perspective

Think back to the time in your life you've found most difficult. It may be unpleasant even to remind yourself of that occasion, but I would like you to go even further. Try to see what you gained that day, what you learned, what strength you found even in this most trying time. Perhaps you will have never even been aware of what you gained until you think about it now. The Chinese have a saying: "Eat bitter to taste sweet." It means that by living through painful times, we can become stronger people. I certainly agree with this, and the transformation depends on our ability to discover something beyond the pain.

There is one thing I'm certain everyone can gain from the memory of a difficult time. I know that that memory can bring you a valuable sense of perspective on your current problems, and this may actually be the most important benefit of all. When you recall a moment of genuine difficulty in your life, how does this make you feel about your present situation? The memory of truly trying times in our lives can help us cope with the challenges of today.

The nineteenth-century Russian novelist Fyodor Dostoevsky is one of the greatest writers in any language, and the events of his life are equal to anything in his fiction. While still a young man, Dostoevsky was arrested by the czarist regime for his political activities. Together with a number of other political activists, he was condemned to death before a firing squad. The execution was to take place in a large, open square. It was a clear, bright day, and in the distance, Dostoevsky could see the sun shining on the gold-painted dome of a church.

A military officer announced that the execution would take place in five minutes. The condemned man was surprised to discover that this suddenly sounded like an extremely long time. In fact, it almost seemed like an eternity. He realized that could stare at the sun on the golden dome for a full two minutes and still have three minutes left to think about something else. At that moment, the idea that someone could have hours or even years left in his or her life seemed almost impossible, because every second was now tremendously meaningful. Then, suddenly, a military officer rode into the square and announced that the prisoners had been pardoned, and an incredible thing happened. Almost at once, the normal sensation of time returned, and the gemlike quality of every second began to fade. "Why can't we experience every day of our lives as if it were a precious gift?" the writer wondered. I've often asked myself the same question.

We've all heard of people who promised they'd make fundamental changes in their lives if they could just get out of their current predicament, but the promise usually disappears along with the problem. Use the experience of coping with real problems to help you through the garden-variety annoyances that are always present. This is really an excellent way to counter the tendency to make a mountain out of a molehill—which for most people is a very strong tendency indeed!

LIVING IN THE NOW

Making the Most of Today • Focusing on Now • Happiness Now, Not Later • Maintaining Your Energy and Motivation • Your Energy Bank Account • Consistency: Staying True to Your Values • Believing in Yourself and the World • Keeping Yourself Healthy • Focusing on Positive Results

"You cannot base happiness on an uncertain event or possible occurrence. Another challenge will always come along just as you find the solution to the previous one. Your whole life is a connecting succession of problems and goals, both large and small, which to happy achievers become no more than opportunities for continued motivation and growth. The only time for happiness is right now, *in the process of living."*

"All of us have an energy 'bank account' deposited in our bodies as our life force. We cannot make more deposits into our energy account. We can only make withdrawals until our life force is spent. The reason many people age at different rates, according to stress scientists, is that we spend this energy at varying rates. Big spenders age more quickly."

"When I refer to belief as a quality of a truly motivated person, I am of course thinking primarily of belief in oneself . . . but it's also something more than that. Belief is a certain positive expectation about what the world has to offer you. Belief is a quality that allows motivated people to face whatever happens with an attitude of 'I can handle it.'"

Making the Most of Today

What each of us is doing this minute is the most important event in history for us. We have decided to invest our resources in *this* opportunity rather than in any other.

It is helpful to remember this when we consider the passage of time. As I write this, my mother is in her eighties and I will never see fifty again. As the years pass, I am acutely aware that the bird of time is on the wing. At my fortieth high school reunion, I saw old people who claimed to be my former classmates. We all had big name tags printed in capital letters so we wouldn't have to squint with our reading glasses on trying to associate the name with each well-travelled face. It was only yesterday that I was really enjoying high school. What had happened to the four decades in between? Where had they flown?

To the side of the bandstand, where the big-band sound of the late 1940s and 50s blared our favorite top-ten hits, there was a poster with a printed verse for all of us to see. I read the words out loud: "There are two days in every week about which we should not worry, two days which should be kept free from fear and apprehension.

"One of these days is *Yesterday,* with its mistakes and cares, its faults and blunders, its aches and pains. Yesterday has passed forever beyond our control. All the money in the world cannot bring back Yesterday. We cannot undo a single act we performed; we cannot erase a single word we said. Yesterday is gone.

"The other day we should not worry about is *Tomorrow,* with its possible adversities, its burdens, its large promise, and poor performance. Tomorrow is also beyond our immediate control.

"Tomorrow's sun will rise, either in splendor or behind a mask of clouds—but it will rise. Until it does, we have no stake in tomorrow, for it is as yet unborn.

"This leaves only one day: Today. Anyone can fight the battles of just one day. It is only when you and I add the burdens of those two awful eternities—Yesterday and Tomorrow—that we break down.

"It is not the experience of Today that drives us mad, it is remorse and bitterness for something which happened Yesterday and the dread of what Tomorrow may bring. Let us therefore, live this one full Today."

Malcolm Forbes believed the important thing is never to say die until you're dead, and he lived that example to the hilt. It is, as we realize when we suddenly attend our fortieth high school reunion, a short journey. But it also is difficult to be depressed and active at the same time. So get active!

Focusing on Now

One of the best ways to motivate other people, especially children, is to take an interest in what they are doing right now. We preach too much about what's going to happen. We say, "As soon as you get your work done, you can go out and play." We say, "You need to study so you can get good grades, so you can get into college, so you can get a degree, so you can get an upwardly mobile job, so you can make money, so you can retire, so you can spend your time when you are over sixty-five doing something you enjoy."

This is a major problem with this extrinsic motivation. It is always future oriented. If a child shows an interest in art, reading, music, sports, animals, or nature, he or she should be helped to investigate that inclination right now. Finding pleasure in what you're doing in the present is the key to motivation. If a child doesn't know what he or she wants to do, don't think for a minute the answer will appear on the flickering screen of a music video or sitcom. It may appear at a County Fair, a library, a museum, a home-improvement show, a job-opportunity convention, an art festival, or doing volunteer work for a local charity. *Motivation* means "motive in action." To stay motivated, you need to keep the aspiration level in motion, on the rise. And paradoxically, the only way to ensure future motivation is to concentrate on bettering yourself—and helping your children to do so—in the present.

Happiness Now, Not Later

One of the problems shared most frequently by unhappy people is that they allow their happiness to be put on "lay away" for the future. They are always waiting for some goal to be achieved or for some problem to be solved before they can be happy.

We've all heard people who say things like: "I'll be happy when I get a better job," or "I'll be happy when I have more savings," or "I'll be happy when I buy a new home . . . when I graduate from college . . . when I get married (or *re*married!) . . . when the kids leave home . . . when I retire."

These people are continually let down and frustrated. If they ever get the thing that they wanted, they discover that there is yet something else—another postponement—standing in the way of their happiness.

What they don't realize is that, if the art of being happy is not experienced and related to the present time, it will never be experienced at all.

You cannot base happiness on an uncertain event or possible occurrence. Another challenge will always come along just as you find the solution to the previous one. Your whole life is a connecting succession of problems and goals, both large and small, which to happy achievers become no more than opportunities for continued motivation and growth. The only time for happiness is right *now,* in the process of living.

The essence of motivation is the flexibility to learn from the past, to set energizing goals just out of reach on the horizon of the future, and to live and thrive in the present, that only moment of time over which we have any control.

Maintaining Your Energy and Motivation

Every healthy human being is born with a truly amazing level of energy. The point has often been made that no adult, not even the most highly conditioned triathlete, could sustain the level of physical activity that a one- or two-year-old maintains throughout the day. There was a time in your life when you displayed almost unlimited physical energy. Not only that, but your mental energy was equally without bounds. You were constantly challenging yourself to learn new things, to try new words, to explore new feelings.

But if that kind of exuberant energy is hard wired into us early in our lives, what happens as we get older? Does nature really intend for us to become less capable of exploring and growing? I don't think so. I think the high-energy wiring remains in place, but for many of us it gets short circuited. The power is still there, but it's blocked. It gets blocked when we start learning phrases like, "What difference does it make?" or "I don't feel like it," or "That takes too much effort," or "I quit." At some point, we start saying those things to ourselves in response to frustration or adversity. It's not that we suddenly lack the unlimited energy we were born with; what takes place is a blockage of the energy current, not a shutting down of the power plant. The challenge is getting that natural current flowing again because energy is the raw material from which high achievement motivation can be built.

One of the greatest boxing trainers in the history of the sport is a man named Angelo Dundee. He was in the corner with Muhammad Ali and many other champions during their toughest fights. When some resin got into Ali's eyes and temporarily blinded him during his fight with Sonny Liston in 1964, it was Dundee who badgered the future champion out into the ring despite the fact that Ali could barely see where he was going. When Sugar Ray Leonard was far behind on the judges' scorecards in his match with Thomas Hearns in 1981—and the twelfth and final round was about to begin, and the temperature under the blazing ring lights was close to a hundred degrees—Dundee convinced Leonard that he had the reserve energy to win the fight. Dundee once said that there was one word he had never spoken to any of his fighters during all his years as a trainer, and that word was "tired." Keep that in mind the next time you feel like your batteries have run dry.

Your Energy Bank Account

All of us have an energy "bank account" deposited in our bodies as our life force. We cannot make more deposits into our energy account. We can only make withdrawals until our life force is spent.

The reason many people age at different rates, according to stress scientists, is that we spend this energy at varying rates. Big spenders age more quickly.

What does it mean to be a big spender of one's energy life force? To a great extent, it means to overreact to petty circumstances as if they were life-or-death matters. Being a big spender means doing battle with and fearing imaginary predators and obstacles. In most cases, we aren't facing real enemies or real problems, only the fear of them or the imagined projection of them. As a result, we frequently choose to stew in our own juices and do battle with ourselves rather than flee the scene or fight the enemy. Emotionally upset individuals literally withdraw all of their energy reserves ahead of schedule and run out of life too soon.

How fast are you spending your life force? On what are you spending it? Is this a good use of your energy? What happens if you do nothing in this circumstance? In other words, will the problem go away or resolve itself without your action? If so, let it!

Will this really matter five years from now, ten years from now, fifty years from now? If not, question how much time and energy you should devote to it.

Is this something that directly affects your value system about which you must take a stand to be true to yourself? If so, fight on. If it's really none of your business, you should let the matter rest.

Will anyone, including yourself, be hurt if you do nothing? You should not stand by and allow yourself to be left out or put down. On the other hand, if there's no real consequence, consider it to be a "no-fault" situation.

Is this a nuisance or an issue? Nuisances can be ignored; issues require action.

By asking yourself these questions about areas where you spend a lot of your life force . . . and answering them honestly and impartially . . . it is possible to save yourself a lot of stress and worry, to conserve more life force, thus ensuring yourself a longer and happier life.

Consistency: Staying True to Your Values

By itself, energy means very little unless it's applied and focused in a consistent way. This doesn't mean that you have to wake up at the same time every morning or work for the same corporation all your life, but it does mean that your values and your aspirations remain in place despite the sudden turns that are sure to occur.

The late physicist Richard Feynman was one of the most interesting people I've ever read about. He was truly an original thinker who was always looking for new ways to look at difficult problems so unexpected solutions would suddenly appear. Feynman was an extremely disciplined thinker who would consistently stay with a project to its completion. At one point in his life, Richard Feynman decided he wanted to learn to draw the human figure, and he hired a model to pose for him so he could practice. Unlike his talent for math and physics, Feynman really didn't have any great inborn ability for art, but he was interested in making a consistent effort at learning to draw. That's why he continued to practice with this model every Wednesday night, not for just a couple of months, but for twenty years! No doubt Feynman brought that same sustained effort to the areas in which he really did have natural talent, and that's probably why he won the Nobel Prize—even if none of his drawings are hanging in museums.

Truly motivated people keep at it and avoid getting too excited or too depressed. They stay off of the roller-coaster approach to life and consistently move onward and upward at a steady pace.

Believing in Yourself and the World

When I refer to belief as a quality of a truly motivated person, I am of course thinking primarily of belief in oneself . . . but it's also something more than that. Belief is a certain positive expectation about what the world has to offer you. Belief is a quality that allows motivated people to face whatever happens with an attitude of "I can handle it."

Seismologists in California who study the subterranean fault lines that cause earthquakes have so far been unable to predict exactly when or where a quake will occur, but they are able to predict how strong an earthquake can be in any specific location. This is called the "maximum possible event," or MPE for short. People who have the kind of belief we've been talking about are confident that the even if a MPE happened in their lives, they would still be able to handle it. They would survive.

How do you survive an MPE? I recommend that for each

goal or project, you take the time to prepare a contingency plan. Certainly you don't want to focus or concentrate on the MPE, but you must have a game plan in case it does occur. I use the philosophy of "Expect the Best, Prepare for the Worst, and Work Like Crazy in Between!"

Recognizing the MPE also gives you more confidence to move forward on your goals. If for instance you find that the MPE of contacting a large firm about handling their account is that they might say no, then you can step back and say, "I don't have the account now, and the worst thing that could happen is that it will say no, and then I still won't have the account." So the MPE for this situation really isn't that bad! By understanding the MPE, you can keep your confidence and belief strong and firm.

Keeping Yourself Healthy

Positive self-expectancy brings positive benefits into being. The advice to whistle while you work, therefore, is more than just fairly-tale talk from a Disney character. It's very sound medical and psychological counsel.

Here are specific principles that you should put into practice every day. By diligently acting on these principles, you can do more for your physical well-being than any number of pills from a bottle . . . and at much lower expense.

First, learn to listen to your body. Learn to distinguish between genuine requirements and mere wants or cravings. If you're out walking on a hot day and your throat is parched, you really need a drink of water, and you should have one. But if you just happen to be passing through the kitchen and your eye falls on the cookie jar, that's something else again. The desire for food, exercise, sleep, or entertainment can all arise from authentic needs or just as substitute forms of gratification. So don't fool yourself. Eat when you're hungry, drink when you're thirsty, sleep when you're tired, and *make those decisions yourself.* Don't let a television commercial or an advertisement in a magazine make the decision for you.

Second, live in the present moment. Seize the day! How many times have we heard athletic coaches talk about playing one game at a time? It may be a cliché, but it's got a solid core of truth. Unless you choose to endow them with importance, events from the past have no reality, and neither do fears or premonitions of the future. Everywhere we look in nature, the trees, the flowers, and the animals are all sharply focused on being exactly what they are in the present moment. If we can just learn that lesson, if we can just let go of regret and fear, we can take a huge step toward physical and emotional health.

Third, learn to manage your energy. That means being alert and focused when it's called for and relaxed and calm when the opportunity presents itself. Jim Brown was certainly one of the greatest running backs in the history of football, and I'm convinced that his success was partly due to his ability to manage his energy so efficiently. After he was tackled, Brown used to get off the ground so slowly that you were sure he must be severely injured. He would shuffle back to the huddle like a man badly in need of a chiropractor. But of course this was all a deception. Brown was resting while he had the chance to rest; when he carried the ball again, he would be like a runaway locomotive. This kind of self-management is characteristic of all peak performers. Learn to practice it in every area of your life.

Fourth, resist the ever-present temptations of anger and

vindictiveness. Everyone has a million good reasons to be angry, but healthy and successful people find equally compelling reasons to be calm and happy. The physiological effects of anger—on the heart, for example—have been well documented, but even if anger weren't dangerous, it's still simply unpleasant for everyone. No one has my respect more than a person who can cultivate personal happiness amid the twists and turns of life's journey. It's a far greater and far rarer attribute than the ability to make money, shoot a basketball, or win an election. Cultivate contentment and let go of anger, and you'll live long. More importantly, you'll live well.

Fifth, find your own values, and live by them. Every day, we absorb scores of messages telling us what to wear, what to eat, what to drive, what to feel, and what to think. The much wiser course is to find your own sources of genuine happiness and satisfaction and mine those sources to the fullest extent. Don't try to live anyone else's dreams but your own.

Sixth, learn to take off your judicial robes. At some level, each of feels we ought to rule the world. As kings or queens of creation, we would quickly straighten out everybody's mistakes and put things into good order. We all feel this way, but the wisest and healthiest of us recognize those feelings for the childish and superficial impulses that they are. We should also notice how those judgmental feelings increase in direct proportion to the dissatisfaction and frustrations that we experience in our own lives. Condemning others is really an attempt to bring the rest of the world down to the level at which we see ourselves. The much more healthy solution is to raise *ourselves* up to the point where we really want to be and let everyone else live their own lives.

Seventh, and last, trust that things work out for the best, or at least they always seem *to.* Do your problems seem overwhelming today? Well, two or three years ago, your problems most likely felt that same way, but you now probably can't even remember what they were. Good health is by far the greatest gift we can receive in life. If you have it now, do everything you can to preserve it, and don't allow minor annoyances to distract you from appreciating it. If your health is less than perfect, take heart in the fact that there's much you can do to improve your situation, and draw inspiration from those who have done it before you and are doing it now.

Each of us is a universe unto ourselves, and each day is an infinity of wonder if we live it completely. You were given life to enjoy this magical opportunity. By becoming as healthy as you possibly can be, in mind as well as in body, you can do that to the fullest extent.

Focusing on Positive Results

True achievers take responsibility for their present actions, but equally importantly, they focus their expectations for the future. I call this the "anticipation of excellence." In other words, they take control of their mind and keep it locked on the positive results they desire.

Once the human mind has locked onto something it doesn't want, it's almost impossible to get the mind away from that idea. This is just a fact of cognitive psychology, and it's a fact that gives rise to many problems and reduces achievement motivation.

Here's a case in point from my own experience. I once had the opportunity to play golf in a foursome with Lee Trevino. It was during the Andy Williams San Diego Open, which I originated as a charity benefit for the Salk Institute. Just before our group teed off, Lee did a little psyche job on us when he asked, "Do you fellas breathe in or out during your backswing?" Well, I tried not to think about it, and of course I accomplished just the opposite. I whipped my drive back with three thousand Trevino groupies watching! We never did find my ball.

An positively motivated person acknowledges the possibility of setbacks but doesn't concentrate on them. He or she doesn't focus on setbacks that have occurred in the past and doesn't anticipate them in the future. If you engage in either of these self-defeating thought processes, you'll be overwhelmed by them. Keep your mind focused on the goal or the desired result.

Have you ever heard how the treasury department teaches its personnel to spot counterfeit money? In training, agents deal exclusively with authentic currency. The trainees learn to recognize genuine bills of the various denominations until recognizing them becomes instinctive. That way, when agents come across counterfeit bills, they immediately recognize them. Their minds aren't cluttered with "what usually is left off," or "mistakes that are commonly made." The agents know what they're looking for because they are specialists in the real thing. Mistakes look glaringly obvious to them.

Those Secret Service agents learn to erase any flawed images from their minds, and there's an important lesson here for all of us. You're not being positively motivated if you allow yourself to think of all the things that have ever gone wrong or that might ever go wrong. You're weighing yourself down with a lot of unnecessary baggage. Rather than thinking about what you shouldn't have done or what not to do, learn to focus continually on what you want to achieve.

The mind has a fascinating capability. What you think about most is generally what you do most readily. If you program your mind with a negative idea, you'll more than likely act upon that idea when the opportunity arises. But if you fill your mind with positive thoughts and images, your actions will reflect that positive orientation.

If I say to you, "Don't think about a big dish of ice cream on the table next to you," what is bound to happen? An image of ice cream pops into your mind, regardless of whether you want it to appear on your mental screen. For this reason, it's very important to focus your aspirations in positive rather than negative terms. If you want to weigh 150 pounds and you currently weight 170, avoid self-talk like "I want to lose twenty pounds." That negative phrasing just reminds you of the problem rather than the solution, which is a fundamental characteristic of unmotivated people. Instead, tell yourself, "I want to reach my desired weight, and I *will* reach it," or "Right now, I weigh a healthy 150 pounds."

In their book titled *My Voice Will Go With You*, Drs. Sydney Rose and Milton Erikson advise golfers to play every hole as if it were the first hole. In other words, don't remember what went wrong the last time. Just swing the club again as if you're just beginning to play. A duffer thinks about the sand trap. He recalls how he hit into it during last Saturday's round. He thinks: *Better play it safe and stay as far away from the sand as possible.*

The true pro, however, keeps his eyes fixed on the flag. He sees nothing but the green, and he thinks about nothing except where he wants to position his ball on that green or in the fairway approaching it. He says to himself, "I can make this," and he swings with that thought confidently in mind. So your strategy for continued motivation is to attack each day, each prospective client, each phone call, each new challenge as a "first."

The true golf pro keeps his eyes on the flag and keeps his mind on where he wants his ball to go. Each swing of the club is like his first.

FORGING YOUR DESTINY

Keeping a Goal Journal • Examining Your Childhood Dreams • Finding a Destiny Worthy of Yourself • The Virtue of Patience • Following through on Ideas • Breaking Out of the Jug • Your Ninety-Day Season of Success • Overcoming Self-Imposed Limitations • Getting Rid of Emotional Baggage • Becoming a Master of Change • The True Nature of Success

"Behind our goals lies the inherent desire to think well of ourselves, to find a destiny of our own approval. Think about it. Doesn't that apply to your deepest desires and most intense dreams? No matter what outer form your desire for achievement or your motivating image takes, aren't you really looking for a destiny worthy of yourself?"

"Patience cautions us to focus our efforts on what we can change while accepting what we cannot. When external circumstance rains on our parade, patience is our umbrella. Rather than blaming what we cannot control, patience gives us pause for reflection so we can dry off and start looking for a new way."

"Our motivation to achieve or goals is dependent upon how strong our need is and whether or not we have the determination, optimism, and toughness to follow through our ideas to fruition."

"Real success comes in small portions, day by day: a smile, a hug, a sunrise or sunset, beach sand between the toes, a satisfied customer, a child's happy squeal, a hand extended, a phone call from a loved one, a tree, a tasty meal eaten without haste."

Keeping a Goal Journal

To help you to shape your future, it's a good idea to go out and buy a journal, a small book filled with blank pages. Your journal, which at the moment you buy it is like an unwritten book or a TV screen waiting for the picture to appear, is actually your own very personal storage vault. It may appear to be like a standard diary to you now, but there is a critically important distinction. A diary is a daily reflection of what *has happened* in your life. Your journal is a projection of what you are *going to make happen* in your life.

In my own journal, the first description I have written down is a personal inventory of the person I visualized when I began my goal-achievement program. And every day since, like an artist painting the future, I have added new ideas, concepts, and suggestions. At first, the changes were subtle, like brush strokes that create shading and light. But over time, the portrait of my life has taken on a vivid new character.

Yesterday's dreams have become today's realities. Before you visualize the person you really want to become, you need a baseline of where you are today and what you have to work with. This is accomplished by conducting a personal inventory of your inner assets and writing these notes as your first entries in your journal.

First, identify your personal character strengths. Although your journal is, of course, for your eyes only and should not be shared with anyone, as an example to help you get started, I will share with you a few inventory items that I jotted down regarding my own character strengths. I put down "caring" and "trustworthy." I also added "joyful," "creative," "optimistic," and "a good communicator." Do you see any of these qualities in yourself? In addition to these character strengths, you might have a natural ability, or instance, to lead or motivate others. Or maybe you are very outgoing and are able to put people at ease.

Continue interviewing yourself with more questions. Do people enjoy being around you? Are you inquisitive and curious about the world around you? Do you handle money and possessions in a responsible manner? Are you willing and eager to lend a helping hand? List at least five personal character traits that you perceive as your major strengths.

Second, identify your natural talents and abilities—emphasizing those that you feel you were born with or have exhibited throughout your life. Do you have a strong physical constitution? Do you have the capability to endure hard physical work? Are you artistic? Do you have musical talent? Do you have finger and hand dexterity? Are you good with words? Are you highly intuitive? Are you more audial, visual, or kinesthetic? (In other words, do you learn best by hearing, visualizing, or getting a hands-on demonstration?) Do you have good mechanical reasoning or mathematical ability? Are you highly creative? Everybody has several natural talents and abilities, although they may not utilize or even acknowledge them very often. List as many of your own as you can think of.

Third, list your education and training experiences that have resulted in special knowledge and skills. What degrees do you hold? What special seminars and courses have you taken? What have you read about and studied? Have you worked alongside a parent, other relative, or friend in a business or profession that has given you an apprenticeship in that field? Be sure to include areas of self-study. Remember, this is not like a résumé for a specific job. These journal entries are to help you design your future.

Fourth, name individuals who are your primary personal and professional network. These are friends, associates, and contacts who are mentors, role models, and others I classify as "sounding boards" and "springboards." A mentor is someone who teaches you. A role model is someone who inspires you. A "sounding board" is someone with sound judgment you can bounce ideas off of and get practical, helpful feedback. A "springboard" is a person with influence who can elevate your level of contacts by introduction and referral.

I treat the people I have listed in these categories in my journal very differently from those contacts in my daily planner. I use my daily planner (which I have converted to a software program in my laptop computer) as my time- and priority-management tool for my short-term goals. I keep all the projects, priorities, and people I deal with on a regular basis in that planner. The people I list in my journal, on the other hand, help me focus on and visualize the "big picture" in my life. They are the ones who can boost me toward my long-term goals.

If used properly and regularly, a journal can be your private crystal ball, helping you plan and predict the future and launch yourself toward whatever dreams, goals, and ambitions you aspire to.

Examining Your Childhood Dreams

In the seminars I conduct all over the world, one of the most meaningful exercises I've created for the participants is to have them go for a walk by themselves and answer four basic questions. The first question holds the key to the other three questions. Now I will have you do the same exercise.

First, ask yourself "If it weren't for money, time, and circumstance, what would I really love to do with my life?" In other words, if there were no financial, time, or personal constraints, what would you begin doing tomorrow morning?

To help you answer that big question, here are the other three key questions that will open that door for you:

(1) What did you love to do as a child, and what were you really good at as a child growing up? (2) Are you doing what you enjoy doing now in your personal and professional life, using your talents to achieve your full potential? (3) Are

you making a contribution to the world and to other people that gives you a feeling of self-respect and fulfillment?

You may wonder why I am asking you to go back and revisit your childhood to help you chart your future. A series of remarkable studies conducted by British behavioral scientists over a twenty-eight-year period confirmed that what we love and do well at as children continues to be our latent or real talent as adults. The lives of fifty individuals were tracked. Evaluations began at age seven, and reevaluations took place every seven years until each reached the age of thirty-five.

Incredibly, nearly all of the subjects eventually ended up engaged in a professional pursuit related to the interests they had when they were between seven and fourteen years of age. Although most of them had discarded or strayed from those interests from age fifteen to twenty-one and beyond, virtually all found their way back to recapture their early childhood dreams by the age of thirty-five, even if only as their major hobby or after-work avocation.

Can you remember what you really wanted to be as a child? In my own case, when I was a young boy, I kept having this recurring fantasy that I was standing in a beautiful theater like Lincoln Center or Radio City Music Hall, wearing a tuxedo, and bowing to an appreciative audience after some kind of performance. My mother, father, sister, brother, and grandparents were in the front row smiling. This vision began when I was nine and continued on for many years.

Therefore, it was a dream come true when I found myself a few years ago wearing a tuxedo and speaking to an audience in Carnegie Hall in New York. My parents and family were not in the front row as they had been in my fantasy, but everything else about the setting was nearly identical!

One young boy, only twelve years old, dreamed he would someday be a great aviator. Young Neil Armstrong grew up to be the first man on the moon.

When she was fourteen, this young woman visited the state capitols of several states during her summer vacation and dreamed of being a lawmaker. Young Sandra Day O'Conner grew up to become the first woman Supreme Court Justice.

When he was sixteen, as a representative of his high school student government, he met John F. Kennedy and dreamed of becoming a world leader in international politics. Young Bill Clinton grew up to become President of the United States.

So don't take your childhood dreams lightly! They may contain the seeds of your adult happiness.

Finding a Destiny Worthy of Yourself

Suppose you have a magnificent obsession, an all-consuming dream. For a basketball player, it might be to play in the NBA. For a dancer, to be a prima ballerina. You may want to be a Fortune 500 CEO or a television star. Whatever it is, let's say you make it and have a long and satisfying career. When that's over and you're out of the spotlight, where will you find your motivation?

For many people, the end of something they have lived with for such a long time is a deep let-down. For some, the accomplishment is the end. As long as they were in pursuit of that one big goal, they had a compelling power. But where's the meaning in life now that the motivation that gave it meaning has been removed?

I see it every day. I hear it behind closed boardroom, locker-room, and living-room doors. The former NBA star, the former astronaut, the former actress, or the retired business executive all forgot to ask what was the purpose behind the purpose. "Why did I want to play in the NBA?" "Why did I devote fifteen hours a day to the theater and rehearsals?" "Why as the space program my goal?" "Why did I work so long and hard in the business world?"

Behind our goals lies the inherent desire to think well of ourselves, to find a destiny of our own approval. Think about it. Doesn't that apply to your deepest desires and most intense dreams? No matter what outer form your desire for achievement or your motivating image takes, aren't you really looking for a destiny worthy of yourself?

This brings us back to the NBA player who can no longer compete in the league. To have been a professional basketball player, this individual must surely fit the description of a highly motivated achiever. Walking to school as a kid, he must have dreamed of playing with the pros. In junior high, he watched the games on TV, read books on NBA stars to model their successful habits, and practiced on the playground. In high school and college, he took his training seriously, always seeking the help of his coaches.

His image of playing one day in the NBA was so vivid that, after he made the league, it was impossible for him to imagine himself ever not playing in the NBA. And when it was over, he was lost. His memories became much more important to him than his life after the sport. He had never looked beyond the one goal to the full length and breadth of his life.

The highly motivated achiever can build an image so strong and powerful that in propelling himself forward to his goal, he gives no thought to the person—himself—who created the image.

* * *

A goal behind all of your other goals ultimately should be that of a worthy and lifelong destiny. The challenge and grandeur of this deeper goal is that it can never be fully attained once and forever. It is a process, not a status. It is a way of traveling, not a finish line. Once you stop striving for it, you have definitely lost it.

The NBA player did find a destiny worthy of himself, and he made a great career from it. But when the knees gave out and the reflexes slowed just enough, he was too old to play, and the cheering stopped. There he was, at the starting line or on the playground again. Real persistence is knowing you can never give up on your duty to yourself to find a destiny worthy of yourself.

One of my favorite characters in Greek mythology is Odysseus, the legendary hero who, after fighting ten years in the Trojan War, finally came up with the idea of hiding the soldiers in the Trojan Horse to end the war. He then spent ten years lost at sea trying to make his way back home. Upon arriving, he found his kingdom under siege and used every bit of his ability and cunning to regain his throne and reunite with his wife, Penelope. These parts of the legend are very well known. In case you aren't familiar with the rest of the story, he soon left his throne and went looking for more adventure. Imagining the old monarch's thoughts as he took off again, Tennyson put these words in his mouth, "How dull it is to pause, to make an end. To rust unburnished, not to shine in use."

Consider what a full life Odysseus had lived until that time. He had led his country, fought great battles, seen the world, been reunited with his family, and saved his kingdom.

Many would have said, "I've had the life of ten individuals. Now I can take my ease and rest on my laurels."

The Greeks invented the mythical figure of Odysseus to remind themselves of the importance of the endless quest for a worthy destiny. For you and I, it does not involve fighting wars, ruling over others, or regaining a throne. For us, it is the sheer exhilaration of learning the most, experiencing the most, and sharing the most value with other human beings. To have made one life breathe easier every day because we have lived is a destination that can never be fully achieved. There is always another opportunity to learn, to grow, and to extend our reach to someone groping for our strength.

The Virtue of Patience

While persistence is the determination to strive to achieve your ultimate goal, there is another virtue of equally great value. Persistence keeps us moving inside ourselves to see the purpose behind the purpose, but patience is the wisdom behind persistence.

Patience cautions us to focus our efforts on what we can change while accepting what we cannot. When external circumstance rains on our parade, patience is our umbrella. Rather than blaming what we cannot control, patience gives us pause for reflection so we can dry off and start looking for a new way.

In his book *Time and the Art of Living,* Robert Grudon says that patience harnesses the power of time for our own purposes. What does he mean by "the power of time?"

The answer is change. Time changes everything. No person passes through time unchanged. We grow older. Our relationships either deepen or break up. We achieve our goals, or we abandon them, or we hang in there.

You see, it is when a goal is distant and difficult to reach that patience is our ally. Time changes everything, but with patience we can keep our desires relatively constant. If we can just hang on long enough, we know that time will finally create for us the conditions in which we can succeed.

Imagine you are on a carousel. From the ceiling, the proprietor has hung a ring. Whoever grabs the ring wins another turn, but there's one rule for all: You cannot get off your horse to grab the ring. Suppose the first time your horse passes the ring, as the merry-go-round keeps circling, your horse bobs, and it is physically impossible to reach the prized object.

If you curse your bad luck and the fact that the conditions were not right for you, you will not be doing all you can to prepare yourself for the next time the ring comes around. Suppose you miss again and again. Do you give up and get off? The patient person knows that if he or she can keep the eyes fixed on the ring, on the goal, in time, he or she will catch that ring.

And what of patience in regards to our purpose behind the purpose? How does patience relate to the deep desire to find a destiny worthy of ourselves?

It is absolutely indispensable. No one can attain the fullness of their whole life according to a timetable. No one can find a destiny worthy of a full life without living that life conscientiously, passionately, and organically in the natural order in which it comes. When you plant a flower, you need to have the patience to let it grow, and the same is true of yourself.

As long as we are persistent in our pursuit of our deepest destiny, we will continue to grow. We cannot choose the day or time when we will fully bloom. It happens in its own time.

Following through on Ideas

Years ago, a young mother about go out with her husband prepared to feed their baby before they left. The husband became impatient as she started her daily routine of mashing vegetables through a strainer. Tired of him standing over her with the car keys in one hand and his other hand on the door knob, she turned the task over to him. Within a few minutes, the strainer, peas, carrots, and bowl ended up in his lap.

As he changed clothes, he reasoned that there must be a better way to prepare baby food and that there must be a lot of other frustrated parents who didn't enjoy the monotony of straining fruit and vegetables three times a day. Soon, they began discussing the idea of designing machinery to strain the food in a factory and sell it already prepared.

Fortunately, the young father and his own father owned a small canning plant, but it was difficult to sell the older man on the concept. One mistake that harmed a child would destroy everything it had taken them a lifetime to build. And what about the expense of marketing surveys, developing and financing new machinery, packaging, getting stores to accept the products, and getting parents to buy something totally new at a price that would be both affordable and profitable? The risk was enormous, but in the end, they went forward with their ideas because it filled a need they understood first-hand. They had the skills and experience. And the market was so vast that the positive benefits far outweighed the negative factors.

One year after Dan Gerber dumped the strainer of cooked vegetables into his lap, the Gerber Products Company introduced their first five baby foods to the market. (I, myself, have used their products to feed six stubborn, selective babies. And, still, some of the fruit and vegetables have decorated my shirt, jacket, and tie—not to mention my face and hair! Just because it's preprepared doesn't mean the babies are going to love it!)

The point of the story is that, so often, an idea becomes a goal when we realize it meets a need in our own lives and the lives of others. Our motivation to achieve this goal is dependent upon how strong our need is and whether or not we have the determination, optimism, and toughness to follow through our ideas to fruition.

Breaking Out of the Jug

My favorite mentor, Earl Nightingale, told me a story about a farmer walking through a field where he had planted a crop of pumpkins. He came across a glass jug, which apparently had been thrown into his field by a passing motorist. As an experiment, he poked a very small green pumpkin through the neck of the bottle, taking care not to damage the vine.

Months later, when the field was fully grown and about ready for harvesting, the farmer, making his rounds, again came across the glass jug. This time, it was completely filled with the pumpkin he had put inside. The other pumpkins on the same vine were fully developed, but the pumpkin in the jug had not been able to grow beyond the confines of the glass prison and was shaped to its exact dimensions!

What size and kind of jug are you going to grow into? In enlarging the size and scope of your goals and devising a specific blueprint for achievement, listing the benefits and specific steps to take, your own field of dreams will take any shape you give it. Your success will be as big as you dare to envision it, not constrained in some small, transparent prison.

Your Ninety-Day Season of Success

In my work with Olympic athletes, astronauts, multimillionaires, business executives, and other winners, I discovered that most of them approached their success in ninety-day "seasons."

In many areas of life, ninety days is regarded as an appropriate growing cycle. The business world operates on a quarterly basis, for example: "Earnings are up during the third quarter," "Sales are slightly down in the first-quarter report," "Analysts are expecting a fourth-quarter upturn."

The sports world, to a great extent, operates on a seasonal basis in which the majority of the games are played during a ninety-day cycle, not including the post-season play-offs. The academic world, in many universities and colleges, is set up on a quarterly basis, the fourth quarter usually being summer. Even academic institutions that operate on the semester schedule usually have nine-month terms, or three quarters of the year spent in class.

I personally have found a ninety-day cycle of success to be a wonderful unit of time. It is a time period that is long enough for me to plan for, begin, work hard at, and accomplish certain objectives. At the same time, it isn't forever. It is a short enough time to generate a sense of urgency for me. I can also envision in my mind specific starting and ending dates.

To simply sum up the concept of the ninety-day season of success: It is a long enough period of time to accomplish something significant, yet it is a short enough time that there is urgency to act now.

Your ninety-day season of success will build your motivation because, often, yearly or five-year goals are so distant that it is easy to get discouraged and give up on them in despair. When your goals are proximate and positively pressing, you are more likely to muster the motivation necessary to achieve them.

Let's begin your season of success by creating a seasonal focus. Before you begin your ninety-day success season, take an evening to go through the following exercises. To do this, I recommend you block out some time for yourself when you are alone and can think without being interrupted.

Exercise One: Review your "magnificent obsession" and create a personal mission statement.

Exercise Two: Take ten minutes and write down everything you *must* do professionally and personally in the next ninety days. You can even divide your list into the eight areas of professional, personal, family, financial, physical, spiritual, social, and service. Write down both "to-dos" and commitments, such as appointments, meetings, and events.

Exercise Three: Now review your list from Exercise Two and spend another ten minutes adding things to the list that you *want* to do!

Exercise Four: Take five minutes and record three things that tend to slip through the cracks in your professional life; then do the same for your personal life. These are things that you always mean to accomplish, but somehow never do.

Exercise Five: Create your "Seasonal Success Focus." Review the specific goals and images of achievements you want to accomplish in the next ninety days in order to fulfill your mission. As you write these goals on paper, remember the methods of stating your goals positively and in the present tense that I discussed in a previous chapter. Also, ask yourself *why* you want to achieve each goal. Once you have done this review, determine what the present reality is. Where are you right now in relationship to the accomplishment of these goals.

And finally, list all the action steps that will be required to make your goal a reality! I suggest that you break your goals down into the smallest possible increments. This makes your goals seem more achievable and less formidable.

The process of going through these exercises will assist you in developing a seasonal focus that will precede your personal and financial success. Make the next ninety days your season of success!

Overcoming Self-Imposed Limitations

Most human limitations are self-imposed. We literally hold ourselves back from realizing our own dreams. We become inflexible and despondent rather than adaptable and motivated. In my studies of human behavior, I've become familiar with three basic categories of people whose self-sabotaging emotional lives prevent themselves from achieving success. I refer to the three categories as "victims," "failure avoiders," and "dreamers."

Victims are preoccupied with the past and are excessively concerned about things they can't control. As time passes, they develop a loser's mind-set, and their conversations are peppered with phrases like "could have," "might have," "should have," and "if only." They fix the blame for failure on others. They see themselves controlled by external circumstances rather than as having control over their own destiny. Victims believe they are always in the wrong place at the wrong time. They trust their horoscopes more than their inner dreams. Since they believe the cards are always stacked against them, they eventually conclude nothing is even worth trying. "If I don't risk anything, I won't lose anything"—that is how their thinking runs.

Failure avoiders are similar to victims, but instead of doing nothing, they just keep doing the same thing over and over. They are perfectly willing to settle for the way their lives are right now, even if their lives are very far from what they had once hoped for. Above all, failure avoiders don't want to rock the boat. They are happy to make it through the work week, and they frequently make remarks like "Thank God it's Friday." They hold down their jobs so they can relax and do nothing on the weekends, and they look forward to retirement, when they can do nothing all the time.

The last of the emotionally self-sabotaging categories is the dreamers. They believe they've already done everything necessary for success, and now it's just a matter of waiting for the rewards to start rolling in. A dreamer may think of an engineering breakthrough in the shower, but somehow he never gets the concept out of the shower and into the real world.

Do you recognize anything of yourself in these categories? To become a highly motivated achiever, you must take control of your life and make sure you stay out of the victim, failure-avoider, or dreamer syndrome. To make sure you are not in any of these thinking ruts, take some time to ask yourself the following questions:

Am I using someone or something as a scapegoat? Am I blaming something for my lack of success? What keeps me from greater achievement? Why do I avoid developing in new directions? Am I wandering around in a field of dreams rather than planting real seeds for the future? Am I deliberately hiding myself and, at the same time, expecting success to somehow find me? Am I loading myself down with all sorts of emotional baggage and then trying to climb to the pinnacle of success?

Getting Rid of Emotional Baggage

That last question about being loaded down with emotional baggage is one that has a tremendous impact on your ability to remain motivated in the face of challenges. Let me illustrate this with an anecdote from history.

Alexander the Great was one of the most powerful and charismatic men who ever lived. Although he died in his early thirties, Alexander unified Ancient Greece and created an empire that stretched from Egypt to India. Over a period of about ten years, Alexander's army marched more than seven thousand miles and fought innumerable battles. The army also accumulated a great deal of wealth that was plundered from defeated enemies. Even the common soldiers became rich, and after a number of years of combat, most of them were ready to go home.

At one point, the soldiers announced to Alexander that they simply wouldn't fight anymore—wouldn't battle any more chariots and elephants, wouldn't risk their lives for military glory, even though that's what men were expected to do in those days. To the soldiers' surprise, Alexander seemed to accept their ultimatum and even agreed with them. At dawn the next day, the army was lined up to begin the march back to Greece. Each man had his personal supply of plunder to take back home, and Alexander of course had most of all.

Before the march began, Alexander announced that he wanted to say a few words to the army. He began by asking if all the soldiers had their winnings carefully packed, since he was sure no one would want to drop anything on the way home. He then asked the men to take notice of the fact that he, as king, had far more treasure than anyone else—a whole wagon train of gold and silver, in fact.

Then he did an extraordinary thing, and it demonstrates why Alexander has come to be recognized as one of history's most compelling leaders. Instead of ordering the march to begin, Alexander announced that he would be taking nothing home from his conquests; that what he really wanted was more adventures, not memoirs of what had already been done. Rather than wanting to be weighed down by the past, he desired the possibility of an unencumbered future. Then he ordered kerosene poured over his wagons full of gold, and he personally set them all on fire. The sight of this had a dramatic effect on all of Alexander's soldiers. Incredibly, they too immediately set fire to their valuable baggage, and instead of marching home, the army headed off toward new conquests.

I'm not suggesting that you should destroy everything you've earned in order to travel lightly. Rather than a prescription for physical action, I think this anecdote is most useful as a metaphor of a certain very common state of mind. All of us accumulate a lot of mental stuff over the years that we think is important in some way but that we would really be a lot better off without. Without it, we'd be freer to do what we really want to do instead of weighed down by what we've done—or, what we believe someone else has done to us.

My studies of great achievers, as well as my personal experience with them, has taught me that these people do whatever it takes to succeed, and because they know they've done what it takes, they confidently expect success to occur. High achievers have the ability to vividly picture exactly where they want to go and to quickly get rid of anything that might hold them back.

Partly because they expect to succeed, achievers always have their eyes open for new opportunities. "Also-rans" and other unhappy individuals never seem to see anything except fear and danger. Emotionally stiff people, people who carry a great deal of useless baggage with them through the years, have a certain way of looking at the world. It's as if they're saying, "I've been disappointed before, and since I'm still servicing that disappointment, I don't have room for any more. Therefore I'll just keep doing all the same things."

The highly motivated achiever, however, looks at life and says, "I expect the best of others and of myself. I've come to understand that I may not always get what I want, but in the long run, I'll get what I expect."

Becoming a Master of Change

Are you skilled in the art of change? Being a master of change involves, first, recognizing unpredictable change as a basic fact of life, and, second, adapting to change so well and so naturally that the process is virtually effortless.

Above all, we must not assume that what happened yesterday in any way implies that something similar can be expected tomorrow. The world doesn't work that way, and when we start looking for security and stability rather than celebrating transformation and transition, we are making a big mistake.

Let me suggest some quick questions you can ask yourself to determine your level of change skillfulness.

First question: *Are you optimistic about the future?* If you're not, you must be frightened of change, because the future is going to include transformations in all areas of life at greater and greater speed. If you see this more as a threat than an opportunity, you're going to be very uncomfortable in the twenty-first century.

Second question: *Are you highly curious and observant?* If you are, this is probably the most exciting time in history to be alive, with massive restructuring of power and populations taking place before our very eyes. But if you're not naturally inquisitive about what's going on around you, you're going to be surprised again and again by developments that seem to come out of nowhere.

Third question: *Are you able to take control by recognizing and breaking self-destructive habits?* This may not be as simple as it sounds. Knowing that you drive too fast or eat too much is a relatively straightforward process of thinking—if you're not aware of it, the police or the numbers on the bathroom scale will soon clue you in. But it's not always so easy to tell when you've slipped into a rut in your ability to communicate with your spouse or your children. It's not always obvious when you've begun to take a subordinate's hard work for granted or when your own productivity has perhaps lost a bit of its edge. A high achiever has the ability to accurately asses his or her behavior, just as a ship's navigator can plot the position of his vessel. If he or she sees that his or her course is heading in the wrong direction, that course gets changed forthwith.

Let me illustrate that last point with one of the most remarkable stories of achievement motivation I've ever come across. To say that the subject of this story was able to recognize and break a self-destructive habit is putting it much too mildly. He was literally able to change the course of his whole life despite many apparent disadvantages, and he did it when he was only twelve years old.

You see, Benjamin Carson was a twelve-year-old African-American boy living in Michigan when he got into a dispute with a classmate at school. Suddenly, Benjamin found himself in a blind rage, and he also had a knife in his pocket. Benjamin took out the knife, opened it, and plunged it into the center of his adversary . . . but incredibly, nothing happened! The other boy just stood there. The knife blade had hit the metal of his belt buckle, and with the force of Benjamin's thrust, the blade had broken off.

Was this the first attempted assassination in the life of a career criminal? Hardly. Benjamin went home and locked himself in the bathroom. He sat down on the edge of the bathtub and began to think about who he was, what he had done, what he was going to do, where he was heading. He sat there thinking for three hours, and at the end of that time, the boy who walked out of the bathroom was not the same one who had walked in.

What became of Benjamin Carson? Well, he never went to jail. Instead, he earned scholarships to Yale and University of Michigan's medical school. He became a neurosurgeon at The Johns Hopkins University. In fact, today he is one of the foremost brain surgeons in the United States, and his patients come from all over the world.

How can we understand this redirection by an inner-city youngster away from the well-worn path to oblivion and toward a unique contribution to humanity? Was it a miracle? Perhaps, but it was a miracle he brought about by sheer force of taking responsibility and control. In any case, this transformation was most certainly an example of intense motivation: emotional, intellectual, and spiritual. Benjamin

Carson had the power to see the direction he was heading and to decide to go a different way.

What about you? Is it time to make some changes in your life's direction? I urge you to take a moment and think about it. If this self-scrutiny reveals that a change is warranted, make it at all costs.

The True Nature of Success

To create your destiny, you must embrace the realization that success is neither a particular level of achievement nor a status. The success process is an ongoing one leading to wholeness.

One of the best interpretations of success recounts the running of a marathon in a small town in Brown County, Somewhere USA. Over one hundred runners are entered in the race, but this story focuses on only three of them. There is a young woman whose goal for the day is to better her time by at least a few seconds. She knows that many of the marathoners can beat her former best time of three hours, fifty-three minutes. But she's hoping today she can do at least 3:50 or 3:51.

Next, we meet a young man who looks hopeful but not completely confident. His idea of success is simply finishing the marathon, something he has never done before. He isn't interested in running a 3:53 or even a 4:53. For him, success will be crossing the finish line and knowing that he has what it takes to complete the twenty-six grueling miles.

Our third runner is a young man who has come to "go for broke." He's not sure he can win, but he's intrigued by reaching down deep inside to see how good he really is.

The gun sounds, and all three runners break from the starting point with dozens of others in the race. Soon, they spread out along the highways of Brown County and settle in to run at their own pace.

Who wins the race? None of our three runners. A stranger, new to the area, crosses the line first. But does that mean all the others have lost? It depends on how you want to look at it.

Externally, there can be only one official winner who breaks the tape. But internally, the other runners know they win, too. The finish line that really matters is not the one drawn across the road back in town. Each runner has a different finish line: the goal each person has set. All three of the runners on whom we focused have won, as well as many others who participated.

The woman did beat her best time by a few seconds; the man who wanted to finish did so; and the man who wanted to see how good he was pushed himself to a new level.

For all three, the race was a process of personal growth, of reaching an objective and creating the potential to move on to an ever-greater goal. No runner is a loser. They all know the real prize in the race is not first place, but the race itself. They feel that special exhilaration, that refreshing high that comes from knowing they have done the very best they can do.

Instead of achieving or performing to impress the world or your peers, seek to do something that is beautiful, excellent, and heartwarming. Suppose you planted a rose garden, cultivated and watered it, and were rewarded by the fragrance and the blooms of the most beautiful roses you have ever seen. No one else saw them. You didn't win a ribbon at the flower show. But you nurtured their growth and enjoyed them. You need no one else to measure your gardening skills. Your gallery is your inner applause, your self-respect, and your spiritual connection to your own creation.

Real success comes in small portions, day by day: a smile, a hug, a sunrise or sunset, beach sand between the toes, a satisfied customer, a child's happy squeal, a hand extended, a phone call from a loved one, a tree, a tasty meal eaten without haste. The list is endless, but our minutes to enjoy and appreciate life's small successes are not. If there's one thing I want my children to learn from me, it is to take pleasure in life's daily little treasures. It's the most important thing I have discovered about remaining resilient and motivated for a lifetime. Life's daily treasures become a reservoir of strength in the face of adversity.

What is the measure of winning a race? It depends on how you look at it. Competitors spurred on by intrinsic motivation will always win just by competing.

A LIFE IN BALANCE

eleven

Juggling Your Priorities • The Assets of Time and Health • Controlling Your Lifestyle • The Importance of Being Flexible • Separating Personal from Professional • A Commitment to Excellence • Evaluating Your Life Balance • DevelopingHope • Living Positively • Focusing on Positive Motivations

"Of all the wisdom I have gained in my life, the most important is the knowledge that time and health are two precious assets that we rarely recognize or appreciate until they have been depleted. As with health, time is the raw material of life. You can use it wisely, waste it, or even kill it. But by killing time, we also mortally wound our own hopes, dreams, and opportunities."

"Each day, we will continue to encounter deadlines we must meet and 'fires,' not necessarily of our own making, we must put out. Endless urgent details will always beg for attention, time, and energy. What we seldom realize is that the really important things in our life don't make such strict demands on us, and therefore we usually assign them a lower priority."

"Think about the expression that's usually on your face. When you catch a glimpse of yourself in the mirror during the day, are you usually smiling, or do you look preoccupied or even hostile? Studies have shown that a three-year-old child laughs as often as six hundred times a day, but with age, this figure then begins to decline until, unfortunately, some elderly people find it difficult to laugh or smile at all."

Juggling Your Priorities

When was the last time you went to a circus? Hopefully, it wasn't as long ago as when you were a child. That's the purpose of grandchildren: to give us a reason, before we rust out, to become childlike again. When I gather my grandchildren and take them to the circus in San Diego, I always try to get front-row seats so we can get a close look at the performers. I guess it's because the performers remind me of myself sometimes. They have devoted their lives to developing certain skills, and they travel from city to city performing for the benefit of others. As I travel nearly every day, lecturing to corporations about individual and team achievement, I feel a certain kinship to the performers under the big top.

Jugglers have always fascinated me. I am spellbound by their dexterity and agility. I always wonder if they practiced juggling as kids while the rest of us were learning to throw and catch just one ball. One night at the circus, while the juggler was throwing eight balls up in the air at once, I pulled out my notepad and started writing. My wife, Susan, stuck her cotton candy in my face and frowned at me, thinking I was working while she and our grandkids were enjoying the show. I wasn't working; I was thinking about the analogy between my own life and the life of a juggler, and I scribbled these notes, which still have pink cotton candy stains on them:

"In a sense, we are all jugglers. Each day of our lives, we juggle our career, home life, family, friends, creditors, health, hobbies, and peace of mind . . . some of us are better at it than others. But we all have about eight to ten 'balls' up in the air at any given time. When the circus juggler drops a ball, he lets it bounce and picks it up on the next bounce without losing his rhythm or concentration. He keeps right on juggling. Many times, we do the same thing. We lose our jobs, but get another one on the first or second bounce. We may drop the ball on a sale, an opportunity to move ahead, or in a relationship, and we either pick it up on the rebound or get a new one thrown in to replace what we just dropped."

However, it also occurred to me that night that some of the balls or priorities we juggle don't bounce. They are as fragile as fine crystal, and if we drop them, they break. What are the glass spheres and delicate priorities that you are juggling in your life? Are any of them labeled "loved ones" or "health" or "moral character?" My problem was that many of the priorities I was most attentive to and careful with were "rubber balls" associated with self-imposed deadlines and workloads that had more elasticity than my precious, irreplaceable spheres like family, health, integrity, and life-long relationships.

The reason I always ask people to list the benefits of reaching their goals is so they can arrange them in the true order of importance to them and give them a sufficient amount of attention as they juggle them within their time constraints. Handle your priorities with care. Some of them just don't bounce!

The Assets of Time and Health

Of all the wisdom I have gained in my life, the most important is the knowledge that time and health are two precious assets that we rarely recognize or appreciate until they have been depleted. As with health, time is the raw material of life. You can use it wisely, waste it, or even kill it. But by killing time, we also mortally wound our own hopes, dreams, and opportunities.

To accomplish all we are capable of, we would need a hundred lifetimes. If we had forever, there would be no need to set goals, plan effectively, or set priorities. We could squander our time and perhaps still manage to accomplish something, if only by chance. Yet in reality, we're given only this one life span on earth to do our best.

Each human being has exactly 168 hours per week. Scientists can't invent new minutes, and even the super rich can't buy more hours. Queen Elizabeth the First of England, the richest, most powerful woman on earth of her era, whispered these final words on her deathbed: "All my possessions for a moment of time!"

We worry about things we *want* to do—but can't—instead of doing the things we *can* do—but don't. How often have you said to yourself, "Where did the day go? I accomplished nothing," or "I can't even remember what I did yesterday." That time is gone, and you never get it back.

Staring at the compelling distractions on a television screen is one of the major consumers of time. You can enjoy and benefit from the very best it has to offer in about seven total hours of viewing per week. But the average person spends more than thirty hours per week in a semi-stupor, escaping from the priorities and goals he or she never gets around to setting. The irony is that the people we are watching on the screen are achieving their own goal, which is to have us look at them.

Even so, time is amazingly fair and forgiving. No matter how much time you've wasted in the past, you still have an entire today. If you've just frittered away an hour procrastinating, you will still be given the next hour to start on priorities. Time management contains one great paradox: No one has enough time, and yet everyone has all there is. This paradox confirms the point that time is not the problem; the problem is how we utilize time.

Social scientists stress that every decision we make has what they call an opportunity cost. Every decision forfeits all other opportunities we had before we made it. If I take my vacation this year by a lake in the mountains, I'm not only going to have to pay the proprietor for the use of his cabin,

I also have to give up the opportunity to vacation on an island with a sandy beach. Having allotted only one week for the trip, I have neither the time nor the resources to go both places. This is the cost of choosing one opportunity over the other. I can't be two places at the same time.

In their excellent management book *Tradeoffs,* Drs. Greiff and Munter discuss the difficult and often conflicting options that face us in all areas of our lives. One case in point illustrates a common opportunity cost. It's a true anecdote they call, "Bicycle vs. Mother:"

"John is a precocious eight-year-old boy. Both his parents work. His mother is a management consultant and travels frequently. After being away for several days, she arrived home late one night and hugged her son.

"He said, 'Mom, I missed you. Why were you away so long?'

"She smiled and replied, 'One of the reasons I was away was to make enough money to buy the bicycle you wanted.'

"Young John looked at her reflectively and stated, 'Mom, I really did want the bicycle. But mothers are more important than bicycles. So please stay home.' "

Even though we all are aware of the tradeoff of "quality time vs. quantity time" in our relationships, we are not used to thinking specifically about how our decisions cost us other opportunities. Without this understanding, our decisions will often be unfocused and unrelated to helping us achieve our most important goals.

Would you rather have the bicycle or the mother? Even though we are all aware of the tradeoff between quality time and quantity time, we are not used to thinking specifically about how our decisions cost us opportunities.

Controlling Your Lifestyle

For highly motivated achievers, controlling their lifestyles is the number one goal. They have a regular exercise routine. They pay attention to nutrition, with lean source proteins and fiber-based carbohydrates as their basic food choices. They relax through musical, cultural, artistic, and family activities. They get sufficient sleep and rest to meet the day renewed and invigorated.

In addition to blocking periods of time for recreation and vacations, they also schedule large, uninterrupted periods of work on their most important projects. Contrary to popular notions, most books, works of art, inventions, and musical compositions are created during uninterrupted time frames, not by a few lines, strokes, or notes every so often. Every book or audio program I have written has been done with the discipline of twelve to fifteen hours per day during a specific block of time.

True enough, I may have sacrificed a ski trip or week or two at the beach. But by trying to focus on prime projects in prime time, the opportunity costs have been outweighed by the return on invested resources.

With your material, time, and energy resources allocated well, you should be able to use your cognitive powers to focus on goal achievement. Effective time management creates freedom. Freedom provides opportunity to make decisions. We make our decisions and our decisions, over time, make us.

Freedom from urgency . . . that's what will allow us to succeed and live a rich and rewarding life. You may have thought your problem was "time starvation," when in truth, it was in the way you assigned priorities in your decision-making process. Have you allowed the urgent to crowd out the important?

Each day, we will continue to encounter deadlines we must meet and "fires," not necessarily of our own making, we must put out. Endless urgent details will always beg for attention, time, and energy. What we seldom realize is that the really important things in our life don't make such strict demands on us, and therefore we usually assign them a lower priority.

Our loved ones understand when we are preoccupied with our urgent business, but it's hard for us to understand, many years later, why they appear preoccupied when we finally find some time for them. Harry Chapin's classic song "Cat's in the Cradle" is still a mirror reflecting our priorities.

All the important arenas in our life are there awaiting our decisions. But they don't beg us to give them our time.

The local university doesn't call us to advance our education and improve our life skills.

I've never received a letter from a health spa ordering me to show up and work out for thirty minutes each day. My bathroom scale has never insisted that I lose thirty pounds. The grocery clerks have never made me put back all the junk food I put in the cart. A fast-food restaurant has never refused me a double cheeseburger with large fries because of my high cholesterol. Nor have I ever been subpoenaed by the National Park Service for failing to appear for relaxation and solitude, exploring the beauty and grandeur of nature. Yet when we drive by our local sports car dealership, we hear that car calling us by name.

You see, it's the easiest thing in the world to neglect the important and give in to the urgent. One of the greatest skills you can ever develop in your life is not only to tell the two apart, but also to assign the correct amount of time to each.

The Importance of Being Flexible

Flexibility is a key building block for continued motivation and a balanced life. This refers to the speed and the ease with which you're able to adjust to changing conditions. To a great extent, flexibility depends less on physical circumstances than on imagination and a special kind of intelligence. Let me explain exactly what I mean by this.

There are a great many people who assume that things are never going to change. They may be rich or poor, hard-working or lazy, strong or weak, healthy or unwell—but they are convinced that permanence is a fundamental characteristic of the world around them.

Of course, nothing could be further from the truth. There was a time when it was assumed that the sun revolved around the earth . . . this was the permanent condition of the universe, and there was no way to imagine that it could ever possibly change. And during the postwar years, as we all know, America came to assume that it would permanently be the world's leading manufacturer of automobiles. This was "proven" by the very appearance of the cars themselves. They were so big and powerful, just like . . . well, just like dinosaurs.

This assumption of permanence can set the stage for big problems long before anything changes on the physical or practical level—and let me say again, things are *always* going to change. In contrast to the permanence-based thinkers, people who exhibit great flexibility are always aware that just because something happened yesterday doesn't mean it's going to happen tomorrow. Flexible thinkers see the many facets of any situation. They're mentally and emotionally prepared for change—even for sudden change.

I think it was F. Scott Fitzgerald who defined an intelligent person as someone who is to able to see the validity of two seemingly contradictory ideas, but I consider this flexibility more than intelligence. Are you able to believe that a situation is going to turn out for the best while at the same time mentally preparing yourself for the possibility that many things may go wrong? Are you able to see the future opportunities that are present even in a serious problem that you may be facing today? Could you be described as an optimistic pessimist or an idealistic realist? If so, you've got the kind of internal flexibility that makes long-term, continued motivation possible, come what may.

Separating Personal from Professional

One of the most challenging aspects of personal relationships is in making the transition from your professional role to that of spouse, parent, or friend. Sometimes, success at work can make this even more complicated. I knew a very ambitious young attorney who was assigned to an important anti-trust case in his firm. He was told that the case would demand all his time and energy for more than a year—and that he should prepare his family for the stress that would result—but that if he performed well, he would be rewarded with a partnership when the case was closed.

As it turned out, the year he spent actually working on the case was the easy part. Everyone pulled together. But afterward, when the young attorney received his partnership and all the status in his office that went with it, coming home and just being "Dad" again became more and more difficult. When you're getting treated like royalty all day, the responsibilities of domestic life can seem pretty mundane.

Some of the most successful people I know have an almost magical ability to prevent their work lives from intruding on their relationships with their loved ones. This takes real self-discipline and emotional resiliency at a very basic level. It can be so tempting to blame domestic tensions on the pressures of work, but that kind of cop out is seldom, if ever, justified. When someone says, "You don't know the pressure I'm under, I'm working myself to the bone all day long," what they're really saying is they want to be excused from any responsibility in the most important areas of their lives. Don't fall victim to this cop out. Learn to separate your professional role, which is secondary, from the personal relationships that are the basis of who you really are. Your job may come and go, but your family will always be there—or that should at least be your very strong desire and intention.

One way I accomplish this transition is to not talk about my work day, business problems, or finances when I first arrive home or throughout dinner. I focus completely on unwinding and making casual conversation with other members of the family. The music is turned on instead of the evening news. The wine or soft drinks are poured. I get into relaxing clothes and ask general questions, keeping the conversation light and upbeat.

I also sign off each day with a positive, caring thought to my wife, and I begin the next day day with an optimistic idea or compliment. My rule, just like brushing my teeth, is to begin and end each day with inspiration.

A Commitment to Excellence

In 1644, a child was born. He lived to be ninety-three at a time in history when the average life span was but thirty-five to forty. He taught himself his trade and began his career. He often worked alone with primitive tools, but his focus every day was to put the best he had into his work. The man made violins. He labored over each and every process and step to ensure that he had "autographed" each with excellence and the best that was in him. He created his own personal standard of excellence for his craft, and he actually signed his name on each instrument that passed the test.

Today, some three hundred years later, the name of this craftsmen who was committed to excellence is the benchmark for the best in musical instruments. His name? Antonio Stradivari! His Stradivarius violins sell for hundreds of thousands of dollars because they are the best.

When Stradivari labored, he did not know of the legacy

he was creating. He was doing his best, day in and day out, to reach his standard of excellence. He didn't spend the extra time and care to get the accolades of upper management or to be the top producer in the company. He did it because excellence was part of his focus, mission, and obsession.

It is easy to do world-class work when a boss is looking or a supervisor is around. But the test is in what you do when no one is looking. High achievers have developed the ability to stay focused when no else is around. Does your quality of performance fluctuate based on who is in the office or which customer you are servicing? Excellence is not something that you can just turn on and off whenever you feel you need it. It is a habit rooted in your attitude about your life and career.

Are you just going through the motions day to day, or are you creating a masterpiece? Autographs are valuable because they are rare and are tied to excellent performance. In today's world, superior effort and service are becoming endangered species. Is the autograph you place on your work and service each day a Stradivarius or a Michael Jordan? Or is it an unknown with little value? Autograph your career and your life with excellence.

Having a firm commitment to excellence, like Stradivari, has an amazing effect on your achievement motivation. In my studies, I have found that when people who are simply going through the motions or who are just working for a paycheck hit a challenge or obstacle, they usually do one of three things: They either give up, they run to their boss and get him or her to do it, or they procrastinate by getting a cup of coffee or shuffling the papers on their desk. On the other hand, when individuals who are committed to excellence hit

Are you just going through the motions day to day, or are you creating a masterpiece? Having a firm commitment to excellence, like Stradivari, is a strong motivation for lasting achievement.

a similar challenge, they immediately bounce back with energy, and they are actually exhilarated by the chance to stretch themselves to overcome the problem. A commitment to excellence will create focus, and focus will assist you in maintaining your positive motivation and in creating a balanced life.

Evaluating Your Life Balance

I firmly believe that if your life is out of balance, your continued positive motivation to achieve your long-term will be greatly diminished. There are eight different areas of your life that you must keep in balance. The eight areas are: personal development, professional, family, financial, physical, social, spiritual, and community or service.

How do these eight areas effect your motivation? Let's say, for instance, that you are out of balance in your physical area. You aren't getting enough rest, you aren't eating properly, and so forth. Then you are suddenly faced with a challenging situation that requires you to work late and use a lot of physical energy. Would you be able to find the motivation to do what you need to do? Probably not. A lack of balance in one area of life can inhibit your motivation in another.

Here is an exercise to help you evaluate your life balance.

Let's look at all the different areas of your life: As you read about each area, answer the questions provided and give yourself a mental score as to whether or not you are satisfied with this part of your life.

Personal development: What are you doing to develop yourself? Are you developing new skills? Are you overcoming weaknesses? Are you maximizing your strengths? When was the last time you read a nonfiction book, attended a class, or learned something new?

Professional: How are you doing? Do you love what you do? Is it satisfying? Are you growing and developing? What does the future look like for you as the president of "You, Inc."?

Family: How is your relationship with your spouse, children, parents, siblings, grandparents, et cetera? Do you feel like you are growing closer to people or are you growing apart? When was the last time that you spent quality and quantity time with those that mean the most to you?

Financial: Are you where you want to be? Are you earning the most that you can at this moment? Do you have the best that you can have? Are you living the dream? Where are you in relationship to your financial goals? Are you building assets? Are you strengthening savings? What are you doing right now to accomplish financial freedom?

Physical: What is the shape of your shape? Are you getting stronger and more healthy? Are you treating your body like a Mercedes or an old jalopy? What do you put in your body for fuel? Do you consider yourself active, or are you a couch potato?

Spiritual: When was the last time you thought deeply about your spiritual self? Do you take the time to read spiritual things? How often do you ponder, meditate, or pray? Do you share your thoughts with others in a religious setting? How would you rate your spiritual strength as opposed to your physical strength.

Social: Do you have a circle of people you consider good friends? How often do you get together with them? How often do you call friends on the phone or, even better, when was the last time you wrote a personal letter? Do you get out on the weekends and interact with others?

Community or service: When was the last time you went out of your way to help another? Are you involved with any volunteer organizations? Do you know the needs of people or causes in your local community? Have you shared your talents and abilities with others?

This reflection can be a little painful, but remember that unless you know the condition of your life balance, you cannot make any positive changes.

After you have evaluated what present reality of your life balance is, you may want to consider this question: If you were functioning at your best in each of these areas, what would you be doing each day? In other words, what would you be as a professional? What actions would you be taking every day as a father or mother? What would your spending, saving, and asset-building habits be? You get the idea. What would the best you look like and be doing in each of these eight areas? Developing life balance is essential to your ability to develop and maintain the motivation that will see you through to achieving your goals.

Developing Hope

One of the most meaningful relationships of my life was my friendship with the late Dr. Hans Selye. Dr. Selye, who died in 1982, really originated the modern concept of stress, and his life's work was devoted to understanding the effects of stress on the human mind and body. He believed that each of us has a kind of reservoir in our bodies that exists to put out the fires of stress. The reservoir is really our life force, the power that keeps us from being overwhelmed by circumstances.

The task before us, in Dr. Selye's terms, is to use the contents of this reservoir wisely and over the longest possible time. This is critically important because the fire-fighting contents of the inner reservoir only flow outward. Once they've been used, they can never be replenished. The reason that people age at different rates, according to Dr. Selye's theory, is that they utilize their life force at varying speeds. If you squander the contents of your internal reservoir, in other words, you will age more quickly.

What does it mean to waste your inner resources? To a great extent, it means overreacting to petty circumstances as if they were life-and-death matters. We frequently see that kind of waste in progress on our freeways, in our airports, in our offices, in restaurants, and at home with our children.

By developing hope in your life, you may not be able to directly alter your external circumstances, but you can certainly moderate the demands that are made on your coping resources. If I had to pick the one single quality that most characterizes a highly motivated person, it would be the constant and undying presence of hope.

Hope might be defined as "optimism infused with a spiritual dimension," and since ancient times, the supreme importance of hope has been recognized in art and literature. In fact, when Dante composed his poem known as "The Inferno" during the Middle Ages, he quite simply described hell as a place without hope. Even earlier, the Ancient Greeks referred to hope as the most important gift of the gods that remains in the possession of mankind.

It's a shame that so many individuals are ready to throw away this gift in their own lives. Every day, we hear people say things like "I'm so exhausted by the daily grind that I haven't got any energy left for thoughts of the future. How can I constantly be struggling to survive and feel hopeful, optimistic, and motivated on top of it all?"

This kind of thinking is based on an assumption that hope requires energy, the way a car needs gasoline or a television set demands electric power. But that's a mechanical interpretation of an essentially internal human experience. In fact, the opposite explanation would be more true. Hope doesn't require energy, it yields energy.

Documentation of this can be found in a study devised by researchers from Carnegie-Mellon University and the University of Miami. They developed a scale for measuring levels of pessimism and hopefulness. The scale was then used to evaluate the relationship between a person's attitudes and his ability to cope with difficulties and remain motivated. The researchers discovered that people who were generally hopeful handled stress better, recovered faster from surgery, and were more successful in overcoming self-destructive behaviors, such as alcoholism or addiction to drugs.

In a study of college students, the same researchers found that hopeful students reported fewer stress-related symptoms during final exams than did pessimistic students. And a Dartmouth college professor who monitored students while they were actually taking a test found that optimists had a significantly lower heart rate and blood pressure than pessimists.

Hope may not erase stress entirely or reverse the aging process, but it can mitigate their harmful effects on your body. I believe that hope can not only help you to live a longer life, but it can make the time you have a richer and more positive tapestry of experience.

Living Positively

If the presence of hope can make you feel better inside and improve your performance in the external world at the same time, it would seem very worthwhile to maximize that presence. But are there really techniques that can influence such a basic element of your personality? The answer is an emphatic yes, but the way to change these deep-rooted feelings is really to begin acting as if they were already changed.

For example, think about the expression that's usually on your face. When you catch a glimpse of yourself in the mirror during the day, are you usually smiling, or do you look preoccupied or even hostile? Studies have shown that a three-year-old child laughs as often as six hundred times a day, but with age, this figure then begins to decline until, unfortunately, some elderly people find it difficult to laugh or smile at all.

But there are important reasons to keep smiling. Scientists have discovered that the physical act of having a smile on your face relaxes facial tension while also producing subtle chemical changes throughout the body. I urge you to make conscious effort about this. Have a good laugh at yourself!

I am glad that I love to laugh, not at the misfortunes of others, but at my own talent for unintentional comedy. There was, for example, the time that I was the keynote speaker for a United States Congressional luncheon. I felt very distinguished, and I must have looked it too, because a senator thought I was the waiter and asked me for two rolls, some butter, and a napkin! Then there was the occasion that my skis won the ski-jump competition at a large resort, but I wasn't wearing them. I was upside down in a snowdrift right in front of the lodge, in full view of an appreciative audience! They laughed, and I'm glad to say that I laughed with them.

Another tip is for you to maintain good posture. Having good physical posture throughout the day is important for the same reasons as smiling. Standing up straight gives a lift to your spirit as well as your spine. Hopeful, positively motivated people stand tall, sit tall, and walk tall. This sends a message to yourself, as well as to others, that you're capable of striding strongly and confidently into tomorrow. And it actually takes no more energy to walk tall than it does to slouch.

Also, make it a habit to speak in a clear, easily understood tone of voice. Mumbling doesn't generate enthusiasm in anyone, including the mumbler.

Don't approach your daily tasks as interruptions of something else you'd rather be doing. Train yourself to see each activity as a new and exciting activity. Even if you can't really feel pumped up about giving the dog a bath, try to act that way. If the phone rings while you're making dinner or typing a memo, don't sigh in disgust that you've been interrupted. Think of the ringing phone as a separate task that deserves a quality response. Even if it's someone selling something that you have no interest in buying, take the opportunity to give that person an encouraging word that will keep him hopeful and motivated on his own quest for success. By doing so, you'll give yourself new energy and motivation at the same time.

As the day progresses, discipline yourself to keep your eyes off the clock. Even if you're working under the pressure of a deadline, don't check the time every few minutes. Clock watching will only add to the tension and waste your energy. For the same reason, avoid looking at the clock if you're feeling bored because time will literally seem to stand still. The fact is, of course, that the time is passing at the same speed no matter how you feel. It's your *response* to time that causes stress. So focus on whatever you're doing, give your full attention to the task at hand, and let time take care of itself.

Try to give a creative twist to all your activities. According to Phil Jackson, the most difficult part of coaching the Chicago Bulls is not the moments of extreme tension during close playoffs games. What's really hard are the hundreds of repetitive practices that must take place over the long season. To deal with this, Jackson tries to inject a note of surprise or unpredictability into every practice. Sometimes, he'll ask a player to beat a drum to create an upbeat tempo during the workout; other times, he'll direct the team to sit quietly for a period of time and pay attention to the rhythm of their breathing and the beating of their hearts. If you're facing a task that's dull and repetitious, think of a way to make it more interesting. Make your work into a game. Try to surpass a self-imposed quota. Take a new route to work. Alter your morning routine. Imagine that some vital outcome depends on how well and how quickly you do your job. By using your imagination, you can replace tedium with energy and enthusiasm.

Finally, end each day with consciously created hopefulness and joy. Concentrate on something that makes you happy before you go to sleep. Don't drift off imaging worst-case scenarios, dwelling on the frustrations of the day, listening to negative news reports, or worrying about what may happen a year from now. Make your last conscious thought of the day a hopeful, happy, and positively charged one. Your dreams will be more pleasant, and you'll awaken fully refreshed and renewed in the morning.

These are practical suggestions for changing your behavior, and they will make it easier for you to be open to the hope that is a vitally important source of your continued achievement motivation.

Focusing on Positive Motivations

There's nothing wrong with competition when it's employed in a friendly manner to push one another to greater heights. But too often, people today associate rivalry with aggression and find it difficult to conceive of competition that doesn't escalate into a free-for-all, with benches in opposing dugouts pouring onto the mound as they do in major league baseball every week or so. There will always be a place for competition, in athletics, business, and life. But what must change is the spirit that turns the mere acquisition of points into the number one goal.

When the extrinsic motivation of competition becomes the basis for our motivation, it drives us away from self-knowledge and self-discovery. This is what over-competitiveness shares with fear of failure. Both are misplaced motivations, distracting our attention from the big dreams and goals of self-actualization. When we are worried about beating other people, we can't focus on developing our own potential. We become outer-directed, instead of inner-inspired.

Remember that all motivations arise from the same source: the desire to be satisfied with yourself. Even fear of failure, in its most basic form, masks a desire to feel good about oneself, and competitiveness also derives from the need for self-esteem.

So the roots of even these motivations are quite sound. They are present in all of us to some degree. How we frame our desires and how we define the benefits we expect to receive will determine what drives us forward and how far it will take us.

By focusing on positive, healthy motivations and letting the more negative ones pass, you can purify the source of your imaginative power. The longer you work on it, the easier it will be to frame your motivation toward intrinsic and positive achievement.

QUALITIES OF SUCCESS

twelve

What Is Success? • What Makes a Person Successful? • Having High Aspirations • Becoming Worthy of Your Own Approval • Successful Self-Expectation • What is Courage? • Cultivating Courage • Practicing Courage • Persistence: The Essence of Motivation • Becoming a Persistent Person

"If you measure your success only by what you purchase or produce, you are doomed to eternal dissatisfaction. There is always someone who can purchase or produce faster or better than you can. There is always someone younger, prettier, more popular, quicker, smarter, and stronger than you are."

"Compared to our other resources—time and energy—money is the least important in our lives. Our time and energy have a much greater value than any material resource . . . that is, as long as we have the minimum amount of money needed to live with dignity."

"Most of us have settled in on a level of aspiration much lower than our potential and our innermost desires. It's as if we were waiting for someone to come along and confirm that we're worthy of greater challenges, when, in fact, no one can do that except ourselves."

"In a way, you and I are astronauts. We are launching ourselves into new personal and professional orbits, levels of achievement we would not have dared to attempt a few years ago. What we might have feared to attempt, we now have the courage to accomplish."

What Is Success?

Success is not something to be possessed. Rather, it is the continuing process of becoming all we can and should be. We must remember that success has little to do with money, although there is nothing wrong with being a rich success. Some rich people are extremely successful; others are not.

Success has little to do with your personal "score" in life, although there is nothing wrong with putting plenty of points on the board when you can do it fair and square. Beware, however, of the idea that to be a real success you must outscore everyone else.

If you measure your success only by what you purchase or produce, you are doomed to eternal dissatisfaction. There is always someone who can purchase or produce faster or better than you can. There is always someone younger, prettier, more popular, quicker, smarter, and stronger than you are. Whatever you could use as your material measuring stick, success is always just beyond your fingertips.

To say "I am a success" is to attach some kind of permanence to the word, as if nothing will ever change, as if things will always be the way they are now. But things don't stay the same. Time and energy are in motion. The global market shifts on a daily basis. Interest rates fluctuate. We are physically vulnerable to our actions upon it. Everything changes.

In an interview in *Parade* magazine, Normal Lear, the creator of some of America's most popular television series, reflected on his own concepts of success and fulfillment. He said, "Throughout the American scene—television, sports, government, and business—the message seems to be that life is made up of winners and losers. If you are not number one or in the top five, you have failed. There doesn't seem to be any reward for living up to your own potential and meeting or exceeding your own, personal expectations."

"To me," Lear continued, "success is how you collect your minutes. You spend millions of minutes to reach one triumph, one goal; then you spend a few thousand minutes, or a few hundred minutes, or just a few minutes enjoying it. If you are unhappy through those millions of minutes of achieving, what good are those fewer minutes of triumph? It doesn't equate. Happiness is to take pleasure in life's daily small successes. It's the most important thing I've learned in all my life."

And it's the most important thing *anyone* can learn.

What Makes a Person Successful?

At every stage in life, successful individuals look back and reflect, "I've enjoyed every mile and every day of the journey to this point in some way." Unsuccessful individuals bitterly complain, "I've worked myself to the bone, and now I'm too tired and don't have enough time or money to enjoy the fruits of my labors. Is this all there is? I hope the 'Great Beyond' is better than life here on Earth!"

Perhaps the greatest mistake humans have made in history—a mistake that we continue to make to this day—is to equate achievement solely with material possessions. Too often, we spend our time and energy and invest our resources in an attempt to gain the outward trappings of what we believe others will regard as success: the vehicles, mansions, adornments, memberships, and travel stickers. Why try so hard to prove something to someone else—or even try to prove something to ourselves—with a display of toys, gadgets, bay windows, and other "luxuries"?

The so-called "me" generation often glorifies and encourages a display of worldly goodies to a great extent because it views these accoutrements as saying to the world, "I've arrived!" Actually, a concentration of status symbols is more likely to say to others that the owner is void of inner purpose and at least slightly lacking in self-esteem. With the "Three-Trillion-Dollar-Federal-Deficit Mentality," almost anyone with a steady job can display a foreign sports car, a power boat, or a camper in the driveway . . . whether or not it will ever actually be paid for.

Please don't misunderstand this message. I am all for purchasing items of quality and fine workmanship because they endure and function properly and safely. But I see little point in purchasing items with high price tags simply because they are expensive or I might impress someone by wearing or displaying them. That's not how I define success.

Many of the most successful people in the world project a modest image. If they have a great deal of money, you wouldn't notice it by what they wear or drive. In fact, you will likely discover their wealth only when a worthy cause needs a sponsor. The largest gifts ever made to sponsor New York's Lincoln Center, The Metropolitan Opera, and many of our finest universities and medical schools have been from anonymous donors. They gave for the cause, not the recognition.

Truly successful people project, by the unassuming way they live, work, and interact with others, that they have dreamed great dreams, set worthy goals, made plans . . . and achieved all of them. The real examples of genuine success don't brag. They are neither blowhards or showboats.

Value is something quite apart from a price tag. The toys and trappings of affluence tell nothing about how important a person truly is. The true value of a person is measured by other scales: the integrity, generosity, contributions, and work of that person. The truly successful person inspires others to do more than they have thought possible of themselves.

Compared to our other resources—time and energy—money is the least important in our lives. Our time and energy have a much greater value than any material resource . . . that is, as long as we have the minimum amount of money needed to live with dignity. Beyond the ability to function with dignity and educate ourselves and our children with the knowledge and skills to shape our potential, money should be viewed as a plane ticket to global understanding. A ticket does no good unless we employ it as a way of traveling. Money and knowledge are very much alike. They mean nothing when we simply gain them and keep them to ourselves. They mean everything when we employ them, share them, and put them to work.

Having High Aspirations

Just as motivator Zig Ziglar is known by his favorite quote: "I'll see you at the top," so was Earl Nightingale identified with what he used to refer to as "The Strangest Secret": "We become what we think of most of the time."

When he greeted someone, Earl had another favorite saying. He would say, "How's your A.Q., Waitley?" Once, I said, "What's my A.Q., Earl?" He chuckled in that deep, resonant voice of his and replied, "A.Q. stands for 'Aspiration Quotient.' How are your aspirations these days, Denis?"

Earl Nightingale said that an ulcer is a jilted imagination taking its revenge. Suppose you find yourself with a perfectly wonderful daydream that keeps coming back to inspire your idle moments, but instead of going after that daydream, you keep pushing it back until it turns into an ulcer or some other form of internal stress to punish you. Hell hath no fury like a scorned aspiration!

It's a good habit to pull out your want list and see how many aspirations you can check off since the last time you looked at it. Decide if you still want the same things—or if you still think they're worth wanting. In short, test your Aspiration Quotient.

We have to exercise and lubricate our aspirations often. Years tend to do the same things to our habits as they do to a piece of exposed machinery, which is to rust and fuse them until the moving parts don't move anymore. We tend to settle for minimums. Except for occasional flashes of bigger and better aspirations, which don't last and therefore go unrealized, we tend to play it ridiculously safe. Sometimes, you get the feeling that people think they're going to live forever.

Most of us have settled in on a level of aspiration much lower than our potential and our innermost desires. It's as if we were waiting for someone to come along and confirm that we're worthy of greater challenges, when, in fact, no one can do that except ourselves.

There is a true story that illustrates this point nicely. It was a stormy night many years ago when an elderly couple entered the hotel lobby and asked for a room. "I'm very sorry," responded the night clerk. "We are completely full with a convention group. Normally, I would send you to another hotel that we use for our overflow in situations like this, but I couldn't imagine sending you out into the storm again. Why don't you stay in my room?" The young man offered this with a smile. "It may not be a luxury suite, but it's clean. I can finish up some bookkeeping here in the office since the night auditor won't be coming in."

The distinguished-looking man and woman seemed

uncomfortable at inconveniencing the clerk, but they graciously accepted his offer.

When the gentleman arrived to pay the bill in the morning, the clerk was still at the desk and said, "Oh, I live here full time so there's no charge for the room. The room is already taken care of."

The older man nodded and said to the clerk, "You're the kind of person that every hotel owner dreams about having as an employee. Maybe someday I'll build a hotel for you."

The hotel clerk was flattered, but the idea sounded so outrageous that he was sure the old man was joking.

A few years passed, and the hotel clerk was still at the same job. One day, he received a registered letter from the elderly man. The letter expressed his vivid recollections of that stormy night, along with an invitation and a round-trip ticket for the hotel clerk to visit him in New York.

Arriving a few days later in Manhattan, the clerk was met by his friend at the corner of Fifth Avenue and Thirty-Fourth Street, where a magnificent new building stood. "That," exclaimed the old man, "is the hotel I have built for you to run! I told you at the time it might happen, and today you can see that I was serious."

The clerk was stunned. "What's the catch? Why me? Who are you anyway?" He stammered.

"My name is William Waldorf-Astor, and there is no catch. You are the person I want." The hotel was the original Waldorf-Astoria, and the name of young clerk who accepted the first managerial position was George C. Boldt.

There's a personal message in this true story for you and me. It's not that, if we're good people, a millionaire is going to come along and make all of our dreams come true,

Why wait for someone to come along and make your dreams come true? Some opportunities, like the Waldorf-Astoria, wait for a specific person, but people with high aspirations can create their own success without relying on others.

although that would certainly be very nice.

The message is in the form of a question: Why *should* a benefactor to come along to make us believe in our dreams? How is it that an outsider can see more potential in us than we can sometimes see in ourselves? By keeping a realistic eye on our aspirations and where we are currently in relation to their achievement, we can succeed on our own without prompting from anyone else.

Becoming Worthy of Your Own Approval

We are not all cut of the fabric to become world leaders like Abraham Lincoln and Golda Meir, or best-selling authors like Stephen King, or NBA stars, or ballerinas, or CEOs. But we are designed to make the most of what abilities, talents, and intelligence we do possess. Why do we seldom think of what we have but always of what we lack? The happiest people in the world have decided to live happily in the present, not yearning for something that they don't have that they think will fully satisfy them.

For each of us, meaningful success needs a very personal definition. It's built from inside out. It's an intrinsic force than compels behavior. Success is not a pie, with only so many slices to go around. The success of others has nothing to do with your success.

Nor is your success measured by what others say or what others accomplish. We all have the tendency to compare ourselves with others, but the highly motivated achievers know it's not against others that we compete.

Most of us believe success, once earned, should be permanent. But you and I know it must be constantly renewed. Perhaps the most splendid achievements of all is the constant striving to surpass yourself and being worthy of your own approval.

The happiest people of all are those who look in the mirror and see the person they have dreamed they could be.

Successful Self-Expectation

Psychologist Robert Kriegel conducted a program for sales executives in a management-training business that had been suffering from the effects of a tight economy. In his book *The C Zone,* which he coauthored with his wife and which deals with performance under pressure, he describes two different people dealing with the same problem.

Louis was in the biggest slump of his career. "Everybody's cut their budget for training," he complained. "And a lot of the programs I sold are being canceled. There's just no money around. The way I'm being avoided, I feel like I'm peddling a communicable disease. It's gotten to the point that I'm not even making calls."

Charlene, on the other hand, had sold twenty-five percent over quota for the previous quarter. She said, "I know the economy is tight and budgets for our programs are being cut. But some people are still buying. I've just got to work harder to find them. Actually, the economy has helped me in one way. There's less competition because a lot of companies in the field have laid people off. So when I do find someone who is interested, I usually get the order. I've actually opened quite a few new accounts."

The difference between the two responses is like night and day. The economy didn't cause Louis to fail and Charlene to succeed. Self-expectation did! And with Charlene's attitude of self-expectation comes the flexibility to look at setbacks not as obstacles to overcome, but as opportunities to expand. This is truly the successful mind-set of a motivated twenty-first century goal setter!

What is Courage?

Ralph Waldo Emerson said, "What a new face courage puts on everything. It is by having the courage to make the decisions that represent our real gut choices . . . to take responsibility for our decisions . . . that we will find our true powers."

As a former Navy pilot, my own favorite quote about courage is from the most famous woman aviator of our times: Amelia Earhart. Before her fateful transoceanic flight in 1937, she wrote, "Courage is the price that life exacts for granting peace. The soul that knows it not, knows no release from little things. Knows not the livid loneliness of fear, nor mountain heights where bitter joy can hear the sound of wings."

S.J. Rachman, the Canadian psychologist who has devoted his career to studying fear and courage, notes that many people think of courage as fearlessness. There are, of course, people who just do not react to fear-provoking situations like the rest of us. This has been confirmed by physiological tests.

But psychologists don't define *courage* simply as "fearlessness." In fact, the inability to feel fear can be cognitive deficit rather than as asset.

Instead, Rachman defines courage as "perseverance in the face of fear and stress." He also notes a study that illustrates how people change their views on fear as they grow older. While younger individuals tend to view courage as not being afraid, older people look at courage as the capacity to act effectively in spite of fear. When I talk about courage in this book, I mean "perseverance in the face of stress or danger."

Courage is one of the most interesting qualities of human motivation. It actually encompasses two strong, conflicting impulses. Part of us wants to run away as quickly as possible. Part of us wants to stand our ground. Fear is one of the strongest motivating emotions we can experience, yet we do have the power to choose an even stronger motivation that can override fear and cause us to act courageously.

When fear leads us to run from a threatening situation, this does not necessarily mean the danger of bodily harm. We can also become frightened and run away from personal or professional challenges, as do failure avoiders. We can run from relationships, we can run from opportunities, and we can even run from success.

Courage means to keep working on a relationship, to continue seeking solutions to difficult problems, and to stay focused during a stressful periods. I think of courage as holding your ground when you'd rather run away, counting to ten when you'd rather lash out, keeping a smile on your face when you'd rather cave in, and working hard when you'd rather give up.

Courage means refusing to quit when quitting would be the easiest and safest thing to do.

Cultivating Courage

S. J. Rachman discovered that people can cultivate a great capacity for courage in themselves, even if they initially lack a high degree of self-confidence or a natural ability to persist under pressure.

One study he conducted involved military bomb-disposal officers serving in the British Army in Northern Ireland. I can't think of a more fear-inspiring assignment. Obviously, all of these officers face extreme personal danger every time they respond to the call to defuse a terrorist's bomb, and they certainly received many such calls. In a ten-year period, the bomb-disposal squad dealt with 31,273 incidents, which computes into almost ten incidents per day. And you and I complain about the traffic during our commute back and forth to the office . . . think of the pressure and constant stress these officers endured every day!

To Rachman, this group of subjects was especially interesting because they were not volunteers, nor had they undergone any special selection process to demonstrate suitability for working with explosives. In fact, when they joined the service, a majority of those who ended up in the unit didn't know that there was even a remote possibility of being assigned to bomb disposal.

These officers represented a better cross-section of various levels of innate courage than did a group of carefully tested volunteers. Rachman's study of them revealed important information on how a broad spectrum of individuals can learn to develop courage.

The most impressive finding in the study was that self-perception of courage did not have much bearing on how the subjects performed in dangerous situations. Each officer in the study kept a confidential diary that would be seen by no one except the members of the research team. In the diary, the officers recorded how fearful they felt from incident to incident and from day to day. They also noted their perceptions of mood and physical condition—whether they felt fresh and alert, for instance, or lethargic and bored.

When Rachman and his associates correlated the contents of these diaries with the performances of the officers, they found that individuals with a high degree of fear and frequent unstable moods performed just as well as officers who reported calm and self-confidence. For example, one officer became increasingly unhappy and listless as his tour with the bomb disposal unit continued. He also had episodes of uncharacteristic anger and irritability throughout his assignment. However, he was very successful in dealing with forty-six bomb incidents, an unusually high number during his four months of bomb-squad duty.

Rachman also found little difference in the performance of those officers who had been evaluated by their superiors as above average and in the performance of those whose superiors had evaluated them as average or below average. Instead, he found the superiors were basing their differing evaluations of calmness and steadiness of manner rather than on actual effectiveness in disposing of the bombs in a safe and responsible way.

The interesting difference in the more-confident and less-confident men was not in their performance, but in their eagerness to perform. Highly self-assured officers didn't like long periods of inactivity. Boredom bothered them much more than danger. Rachman also concluded that many of the officers were intrinsically motivated to want to prove themselves by successfully carrying out a highly skilled, delicate, and extremely dangerous mission. Once again, you see the immense power of intrinsic motivation.

Though some of these officers admitted significant feelings of stress and fear, they were in fact molded into a highly effective team. Rachman wanted to know how this was done. He found that the ability to persist and function well in the face of great danger was largely a function of intense and specialized training for their job. And not only were the men well prepared to deal with bombs, they also *knew* they were well prepared. Rachman surveys administered to the group after their specialized training but before actual bomb disposal assignments indicated that they already were at an eighty-percent confidence level compared to what they would have been after significant and uniformly successful experience with live explosives.

Remember, these officers were not specifically selected

for hazardous duty. They were not necessarily fearless or innately courageous. The key to dealing effectively with unusually stressful or especially dangerous situations was careful, diligent advance preparation.

You may never be called upon to defuse a bomb, but there are many everyday challenges that can be very frightening. Most people, for example, find that public speaking generates a high degree of anxiety. Fortunately, it's an activity that lends itself well to adequate planning and preparation. Research, writing, rewriting, and rehearsal may not eliminate the fear associated with speaking in front of an audience, but they will give the anxious speaker the confidence to persist, to go ahead and present the speech successfully.

But what if you're about to give an oral presentation, or participate in some other stress-producing activity, and you still feel debilitatingly fearful, even though you've carefully prepared yourself? In this situation, you should review the nature of your preparation. Perhaps you've concentrated on the mechanics of what you're about to do but have neglected some of the psychological and emotional factors that we've covered in this book, such as positive framing and attributional analysis.

In pursing success or in facing challenging situations, concentrate on the factors over which you have the most direct control. That means high-quality advance preparation for both what you're going to *do* and how you're going to *feel*.

Practicing Courage

Courage can be contagious, but so can fear. If a soldier panics in battle, for example, there is a strong possibility that others will follow his example unless a leader is present to take control of the situation. If their leaders set a courageous example, the soldiers respond accordingly.

I was at a football game when someone got sick after eating a hot dog from a vending stand. This person underwent a global catastrophic attributional reaction. She yelled that she had food poisoning from salmonella in the mustard.

Actually, she'd merely had too many beers, but that didn't stop group hysteria from setting in. At least ninety-seven failure avoiders suffering from acute nausea were taken to Sharp Memorial Hospital by ambulances and paramedics!

Troops in battle are well aware of the contagious nature of fear and courage. S.J. Rachman found that one of the prime reasons for a soldier's courage is the desire not to let his buddies down. He referred to this as a "situational demand."

In our own lives, if we heard a burglar in a downstairs area of our home, the best course of action would be to call the police quietly, secure our bedroom door if it was unlocked, and prepare to defend ourselves or escape if the burglar attempted to enter the room before the police arrived.

It would not be worth risking our lives to see if the burglar was armed. That is, unless our daughter was sleeping downstairs. Fearing for her safety, the situational demand would motivate us to act in a courageous manner. We would go downstairs and protect her at the risk of our own lives.

Situational demands represent extrinsic motivation to act courageously. We act out of external need, not to increase our self-esteem. If we did not find the courage to actually act, we would experience a good deal of cognitive dissonance in this situation.

In reviewing our discoveries about the development of courage, we can learn from the Ruff and Korchin study of the Project Mercury astronauts. As you may recall, Mercury was the first space program involving orbital flight and was followed by Gemini and Apollo. The astronauts were thrust into a completely new and foreign environment involving an inordinate amount of stress. They were well aware that they had to assume full responsibility for their own actions and that if they made one error in judgement in space, there would be no one to cover for them. The consequences would be critically dangerous, perhaps fatal.

In spite of the tremendous pressure, they reported little experience of fear during their flights. They attributed their confidence to the fact that their training had prepared them to deal with any realistic problems they might encounter.

It's important to note that they made no mention of unrealistic problems. Highly motivated achievers like astronauts don't give any thoughts to remote threats for which there can be no preparation. They concentrated their efforts on what they themselves could control and what they themselves could do to prepare.

Each of the astronauts had admitted to a greater level of fear associated with their former combat flying experiences than with space travel, although both situations had a high level of associated stress. By putting themselves in stressful situations repeatedly over time, they gradually moved from a type of courageous behavior in the face of fear toward a higher level of courage known as "fearless behavior."

These findings about the development of courage reinforce what we talked about in the chapter on self-efficacy. Just as your total self-efficacy grows with any achievement, so courage also grows and spreads as we exercise it.

From flying combat missions in the face of fear, the astronauts learned they could operate successfully under pressure, regardless of the situation. The repeated experience of self-efficacy, with success breeding more success combined with the knowledge that they were expertly and adequately trained, gave the astronauts increased confidence that their mission would succeed.

Alan Shepard was the first American to be launched via rocket and retrieved from the sea at Cape Canaveral, Florida

The long experience and lengthy training of pioneer astronauts Alan Shepard, John Glenn, Neil Armstrong, gave them the courage to operate successfully under pressure, regardless of the situation.

on May 5, 1961. John Glenn became our first astronaut to succeed in orbital flight in his spacecraft "Friendship 7" on February 20, 1962.

And in the subsequent Apollo XI launch, Neal Armstrong made history July 24, 1969 when he landed on the moon and reported back: "Okay, I'm going to step off the ramp now. That's one small step for man and one giant leap for mankind."

But for our purposes here, another message he radioed back was even more significant. Armstrong also said, "It was just like drill. It was just like we planned it."

In a way, you and I are astronauts. We are launching ourselves into new personal and professional orbits, levels of achievement we would not have dared to attempt a few years ago. What we might have feared to attempt, we now have the courage to accomplish.

It's so exhilarating to feel in control while operating at the higher limits of your potential. You can have that feeling now. With preparation and reinforcement day by day, it will be your internal pilot light to keep the spark ignited.

Persistence: The Essence of Motivation

The science of psychology is barely a hundred years old. Certainly thinkers throughout history had been wondering about the human mind long before this—probably since the dawn of civilization. Yet it was only in the last decades of the nineteenth century, in the time of Sigmund Freud, that scientific method was first seriously applied to human behavior.

Even Freud, the founder of modern psychology, overstated his discoveries, and theories were advanced without the support of hard, empirical data. Over the years, psychology branched out into separate schools of thought, some of which fostered a rigor and precision unprecedented in the study of human behavior. These included such famous doctrines as behaviorism and cognitive psychology.

Psychology doesn't have the equations of physics or the repeatable classroom experiments of chemistry. The human mind is too complex for formulas. And as I've pointed out, our quest for understanding has just begun.

We are, however, at a point where we have a unified field of inquiry, in which studies and findings corroborate and illuminate one another. In a similar way, Isaac Newton was able to discover a set of laws that seemed accurate for all physical transactions in our universe. Newton's laws were reinforced by what Galileo learned, and more recently there have been the revolutionary discoveries of twentieth-century physicists like Einstein and Bohr. Working from different perspectives, all these investigators shed light on one another's contributions. They made sense together, as well as independently.

There is a non-scientific essence of motivation, as well, that needs to be woven into the pattern. It is the quality of persistence. Since persistence can only be tested over a long period of time, it is difficult for both the researchers and their subjects to monitor. Certainly some of the experiments we talked about have tested persistence over several days, even years in the case of creative imagination at it applied to high achievers.

But the really meaningful, important persistence is the persistence of a lifetime. Like that of the Roebling family who built the Brooklyn Bridge.

Near the beginning of his great novel *The Brothers Karamozov,* Dostoevsky has his narrator observe that many a young man who would give up his life in a second for someone he loved or to advance some great ideal would be completely incapable of settling down to study hard for five or six years in order to have a life worth giving up. Dostoevsky was talking about the difficulty of persistence, a subject he knew a great deal about, since he spent years in a prison camp, never losing hope that he would return to society and to his writing.

Lifelong persistence isn't impossible to muster. It only requires the setting of worthwhile goals and the courage, self-confidence, and continuing motivation to achieve them.

Becoming a Persistent Person

Sometimes, it almost seems that a truly persistent person needs the capacity to suspend his or her intellectual faculties in a given situation. Worrying too much about the outcome can interfere with the process. A persistent salesperson says, "I'm going to call on ten prospects today, and tomorrow I'm going to call on ten more, and I'm just going to keep calling on ten prospects every day from here on out, no matter what."

Success takes time, and it demands the ability to persistently stay with the program. Ray Kroc and his team didn't build McDonald's into a billion-dollar company overnight. It took twenty-two years of persistence—and remember, Mr. Kroc was already in his fifties before he even got started in the business that would make him an legend.

Overnight success is a myth. Only the lottery or a fairy godmother can grant you instant results. Every human being who has tried to accomplish something worthwhile has failed numerous times before the objective was achieved. This is true in raising a family, learning a technical skill, operating a piece of heavy machinery, mastering a sport, or any other truly challenging undertaking.

Any time you decide to stretch yourself or your lifestyle—any time you really make an effort to implement the kind of change I'm discussing in this book—you can count on a temporary drop in your productivity and efficiency.

I have a friend who had always been a moderately successful tennis player, and who might have continued being moderately successful if he hadn't encountered a coach who finally showed him how to serve a tennis ball. Until then, my friend had always been able to get the ball into the service court with enough accuracy to win the majority of games against opponents on his level. But the coach showed him that his form was all wrong, and then he offered my friend a choice. It was the same choice that we all face whenever we contemplate real change: We can stay where we are and be satisfied with mediocrity, or we can risk a period of painful transition in order to achieve real excellence.

My tennis-playing friend decided to adjust his serve as the coach suggested, and of the first hundred serves he tried, only two cleared the net. But gradually, with practice, he began to become more accurate and powerful with the new technique. Before long, he was winning ninety percent of his matches, including a regional tournament. A change meant temporary failure, but persistence brought an even higher level of success.

In many organizations, change is aborted after only a

few weeks or months because of the temporary reduction in productivity. When the dip in productivity comes, everyone throws up their hands and says, "I knew this wouldn't work, lets just go back to the old way of doing things." Only those companies with motivation and persistence work through the tough learning curve of change and enjoy the benefits of improvement and long-term success.

Make no mistake, however: Persistence takes guts. There are going to be setbacks and failures on the way to reaching your goals. In fact, there had better be! Unless you are failing at least fifty percent of the time in things you are trying to improve, you are not trying hard enough and probably won't succeed in the long run. You simply must be willing to lose some battles in order to win the war.

About the Author

Denis Waitley is an internationally sought-after keynote speaker, consultant, and former chairman of psychology for the U.S. Olympic Comittee's Sports Medicine Council. He is a graduate of the U.S. Naval Academy at Anapolis and a former Naval Aviator. His best selling audio programs and books include *The Psychology of Winning, Seeds of Greatness, Being the Best, The New Dynamics of Winning, The Winner's Edge, Empires of the Mind,* and *The Power of Resiliency.*